Strategy, Structure, and Economic Performance

Strategy, Structure, and Economic Performance

RICHARD P. RUMELT

Assistant Professor
Iran Center for Management Studies
Tehran, Iran

DIVISION OF RESEARCH
GRADUATE SCHOOL OF BUSINESS ADMINISTRATION
HARVARD UNIVERSITY
BOSTON · 1974

Library of Congress Catalog Card No. 73-93776
ISBN 0-87584-109-0

*This book won the Richard D. Irwin Prize for the
Best Doctoral Dissertation 1972–1973 at the
Harvard Business School*

Distributed by
Harvard University Press
Cambridge, Massachusetts

Printed in the United States of America

Foreword

S*trategy, Structure, and Economic Performance* is a study of the evolution of large-scale industrial enterprise in the United States in the period 1949–1969. Basing its analysis on more than 200 companies drawn from the *Fortune* 500, this investigation breaks new ground in relating the economic performance of the firm to the type of strategy and structure adopted. For the first time, so far as we are aware, the author has demonstrated an analytical relationship between economic performance and two of the key variables which the manager can influence.

Richard P. Rumelt's research, leading to his receipt of the doctoral degree, was carried on under the auspices of the Business Policy Area, long one of the central teaching and research areas at the Harvard Business School. Given the complexity of the modern firm, much of this research has consisted of individual company studies or "cases," which were aimed at achieving a better understanding of the role and functions of top management. Many of the Faculty members engaged in this research were sufficiently impressed with the complexities of the phenomena they were observing that they were reluctant to generalize, particularly with respect to the broad trends shaping the "population" of large enterprises from which the case studies were drawn.

In the 1960's, however, there was a shift in research emphasis, which led to intensive work on developmental models of the firm and to the study of larger populations of firms. Following the lead of Alfred D. Chandler's *Strategy and Structure*,[1] the new thrust included the study of developmental trends in the United States and in Western Europe, and, on occasion, it also considered the implications of these trends for public policy.[2]

New ground was broken by Leonard Wrigley who helped to reconceptualize

---

[1] Alfred D. Chandler, *Strategy and Structure* (Garden City, N.Y.: Doubleday & Company, 1966).

[2] John H. McArthur and Bruce R. Scott, *Industrial Planning in France* (Boston: Division of Research, Harvard Business School, 1969).

the developmental model and to classify the strategies and structures of 100 companies drawn from the *Fortune* 500 as of 1967. Wrigley's thesis, "Divisional Autonomy and Diversification," set the pattern for five subsequent doctoral dissertations covering five countries.

Using Wrigley's classification scheme, four researchers (in addition to Rumelt) made parallel studies of the *evolution* of the top 100 firms in the United Kingdom, France, Germany, and Italy,[3] for the years 1950–1970. These four studies were planned together and followed closely similar methodologies. Each found broadly similar trends affecting the respective national populations.[4] The researchers' major problems were those of developing adequate data to trace the evolution of the firms; none found economic data which would permit a serious attempt to relate economic performance to strategy or structure.

Fortunately such data were available for the United States, and were available in a form that was readily usable for analytical purposes. Rumelt has traced the evolution of strategy and structure in some 200 firms for the period 1949–1969, and then has analyzed the relationship between that evolution and their economic performance. Rumelt's findings point to relatively strong performance for firms combining a strategy of diversification into related areas with a structure of divisional organization on a product-line rather than a functional basis. Significantly, these findings are quite in line with the growing number and importance of such firms in the business population of all five countries studied. Thus, it would seem that the leading businessmen had discovered this important set of relationships before the academicians did, and that we as researchers were truly learning from the leading businessmen.

The implications of the trend toward large, diversified, divisionalized companies for public policy are obviously of interest. It is in this direction that our research at the Harvard Business School has now turned: Recent investigations have included empirical case studies on the Canada Development Corporation and the Plan Calcul in France, as well as two more loosely related works on government efforts to promote the export of manufactured goods from developing countries.

The results of this research effort are now finding their way into the classrooms as our required curriculum takes more and more account of trends among populations of firms, comparisons among leading industrial nations, and the impact of public policy in shaping the business environment. In this respect, this strand of the ongoing research is supportive of the broadly stated

---

[3] Derek F. Channon, *The Strategy and Structure of British Enterprise* (Boston: Division of Research, Harvard Business School, 1973). Gareth Pooley Dyas, "The Strategy and Structure of French Industrial Enterprise"; Robert J. Pavan, "The Strategy and Structure of Italian Enterprise"; Heinz T. Thanheiser, "Strategy and Structure of German Industrial Enterprise"; all unpublished doctoral dissertations, Harvard Business School, 1972.

[4] Bruce R. Scott, "The Industrial State: Old Myths and New Realities," *Harvard Business Review,* March–April 1973.

purpose of the Harvard Business School to increase its understanding of the management problems and processes associated with the multiproduct, multidivisional, multinational enterprise. It is in light of this broad sense of purpose that I should like to acknowledge the continuing support of our Dean, Lawrence E. Fouraker.

Financial support for this project was administered by the Division of Research at the Harvard Business School by an allocation of funds from gifts to the School by The Associates of the Harvard Business School. Under the guidance of Professor Richard E. Walton, Director of the Division of Research, the School has been generous in its support both of the European field work and the computer costs for this study. In addition, two European companies encouraged the research in both psychological and financial terms, and it is with warm thanks that, on behalf of the School, I acknowledge this support from Industrie Buitoni Perugina of Perugia, Italy, and Granges A.B. of Stockholm, Sweden.

Bruce R. Scott
Professor of Business Administration

Soldiers Field
Boston, Massachusetts
May 1974

Acknowledgments

Associating with the Faculty of the Harvard Business School for an extended period leaves one with a great many intellectual debts. I deeply appreciate the knowledge, advice, support, and encouragement that have been given me by individuals too numerous to mention here.

Professor Bruce R. Scott, chairman of my thesis committee, provided the original stimulus for this work and was a constant source of ideas and encouragement. During the many lengthy sessions that his unstinting gifts of time and energy made possible, he aided in the interpretation of data and often reawakened my sense of priorities when the thicket of details seemed about to become impenetrable. Professor Kenneth R. Andrews, who has always believed that systems of classification frequently obscure more than they reveal, nevertheless agreed to serve on my thesis committee, and his probing questions have been invaluable in helping me draw the line between the data and what they may imply. Professor Jesse W. Markham brought to my committee the wealth of his experience as an economist. His knowledge of large sample methodology and the interpretation of statistical results was patiently made available to me and is deeply appreciated.

Professor Alfred D. Chandler, Jr., kindly agreed to comment on the classification system I developed and was an unusually useful source of feedback. Professor John Pratt contributed extremely helpful and practical advice on questions of statistical estimation. To Dr. Leonard Wrigley I owe special thanks for the pioneering insights I have tried to build upon.

Financial support for the data-processing costs of this study was provided by an allocation of funds administered by the Division of Research of the Harvard Business School and is gratefully acknowledged. Publication of the study by the Division of Research was made possible by virtue of its having won the Richard D. Irwin Prize for the Best Doctoral Dissertation 1972–1973 at the Harvard Business School.

I should especially like to thank my wife, Elizabeth, who was not content to merely encourage me in my work, but took an active role in the research. Her careful notes on the contents of hundreds of company annual reports greatly shortened what would have otherwise seemed an interminable task.

For whatever merits this study may have, I owe much to those who have helped and guided me. However, the responsibility for its failings is mine alone.

RICHARD P. RUMELT

Tehran, Iran
September 1973

Table of Contents

List of Tables

List of Figures

Strategy, Structure, and Economic Performance

Introduction

WHEN AN INDUSTRIAL CORPORATION decides to diversify its product line, it is making a strategic decision whose consequences may alter the fundamental nature of the firm and may involve as well a substantial redeployment of resources and a redirection of human energy. Diversification, however, is neither a goal nor a plan; each firm that diversifies must choose the types of businesses it will enter, the degree to which it will build on past strengths and competences or require the development of new ones, and the total amount of diversity that is appropriate. There is no single strategy of diversification.

The interrelationship of diversification strategy, organizational structure, and economic performance in large American industrial corporations is the subject of this study. In addition to investigating the relative prevalence of various types of strategy and structure, the relationship between strategy and structure, and the association between these two variables and economic performance, this study will be concerned with the validation of a research method that combines the managerially meaningful but essentially descriptive concept of diversification strategy with the analytic power of statistical techniques applied to large samples.

Although product line diversification is an increasingly common attribute of large industrial corporations, it does not fit neatly into any of the current theories of economic and business behavior. As Gort has noted,

> There has been so much discussion of diversification that the phenomenon seems perfectly natural and something to be taken for granted. But in fact it runs against a pervasive trend in our society toward greater specialization in most channels of economic life. The broader the market for a given product and the more complex the production process, the more *specialized* one would normally expect producers to be. And yet, notwithstanding the growth in markets and the increasing complexity of

technology, the trend for companies seems to be toward greater diversification rather than toward specialization.[1]

Economists who have studied diversification have been concerned chiefly with developing ways to measure the diversity of a firm's product-market posture and to relate such measures to pricing behavior, research decisions, and overall concentration. They have been intent, as well, on studying the public policy implications of an economy that is increasingly composed of diversified firms. Economists have used statistical methods to show that diversification has been increasing continuously since the 1920s, and that it has been greatest in industries based on the newer, more sophisticated technologies. They have found its impetus to have come from internal growth rather than from merger, and that the degree of diversification correlates with a number of other quantitative attributes of companies and industries.[2]

While such studies have been valuable in describing the extent and locus of diversification activity, it was a historian, Alfred D. Chandler, using the traditional techniques of historical data gathering and analysis, who made one of the most important contributions to our understanding the role of diversification in the development of the modern firm. By tracing the patterns of development of seventy large corporations from 1909 to 1959, Chandler found that diversification had given rise to the need for a new administrative system that would insure the efficient utilization of diverse resources, and that the multidivisional structure came into use as an adaptive response to this need.[3]

In turn, the multidivisional structure has served to institutionalize diversification. It has permitted the insulation of a set of business managers from the vicissitudes of the capital markets, and has created a type of managerial environment that encourages rapid redeployment of resources and places a premium on economic performance and the skills of the generalist. As a consequence of this new understanding, diversification can no longer be viewed as a simple quantitative increase in the number of products produced and sold by a firm. Instead, Chandler has demonstrated that diversification has been causally related to, and eventually dependent upon, the rise of new types of business enterprises that are qualitatively different from the more traditional form of corporation.

The insight that the diversified multidivisional firm is fundamentally different from the more primitive type of enterprise has sparked a number of

---

[1] Michael Gort, "Diversification, Mergers, and Profits," in William W. Alberts and Joel E. Segall, eds., *The Corporate Merger* (Chicago: University of Chicago Press, 1966), p. 32.

[2] See Chandler's report of Livesay and Porter's data in Alfred D. Chandler, Jr., "The Structure of American Industry in the Twentieth Century: A Historical Overview," *Business History Review,* Autumn 1969, pp. 255–298; and Gort, "Diversification, Mergers, and Profits," p. 31.

[3] Alfred D. Chandler, Jr., *Strategy and Structure* (Garden City, N.Y.: Doubleday & Co., 1942).

further insights and research efforts. Scott, taking a cue from Rostow, has developed a "stages" model [4] of corporate growth and development that views the corporation as moving through several archetypal forms as its product-market complexity increases. He sees the firm as developing from a small "one man show" to a functionally organized (e.g., sales, production, research) single-business company as management seeks to gain control over all the factors important to the production and sale of a particular product. Then, as the firm begins to diversify and develop multiple product lines, it adopts the multidivisional structure. Scott's central thesis is that these three stages are not only different in outward form, but that they impose different "ways of life" on management and require quite different styles and systems of reward, control, resource allocation, review, and new business development.

Bower has studied the process of capital investment decision making in a large diversified multidivisional company and reports that the managerial climate created for the division general managers by the headquarters office is of crucial importance; traditional theories of capital budgeting are neither descriptive of the actual process nor normatively useful.[5] Stopford, investigating the relationship between structure and behavior in direct investment abroad, has stated that the relatively large number of generalist roles created within the multidivisional organization is an important factor in explaining the increased ease with which such firms formulate and implement multinational strategies.[6] Vernon has generalized these findings with the conjecture that the multidivisional structure is the critical factor in permitting firms to grow through diversification and to make use of a large spectrum of skills without experiencing gross diseconomies of scale. "Once the basic change in structure is achieved," he says, "the diseconomies of scale which threaten any large organization are pushed off to a new, more distant level or, perhaps more accurately, . . . new economies appear sufficiently important to offset for an added period the diseconomies associated with large organizations." [7]

Wrigley's recent survey of the 1967 *Fortune* 500 was built on Chandler's pioneering study by recognizing that there are significant differences in the ways in which firms have elected to diversify.[8] He stratified his random sample of 100 firms into four categories: firms that were not diversified (Single Product Firms); firms primarily committed to a single business but that had diversified

---

[4] Bruce R. Scott, "Stages of Corporate Development" (unpublished paper, Harvard Business School, 1970).

[5] Joseph L. Bower, *Managing the Resource Allocation Process* (Boston: Division of Research, Harvard Business School, 1970).

[6] John M. Stopford, "Growth and Change in the Multinational Firm" (unpublished doctoral dissertation, Harvard Business School, 1968).

[7] Raymond Vernon, "Organization as a Scale Factor in the Growth of Firms," in J. W. Markham and G. F. Papanek, eds., *Industrial Organization and Economic Development* (Boston: Houghton Mifflin Company, 1970), p. 64.

[8] Leonard Wrigley, "Divisional Autonomy and Diversification" (unpublished doctoral dissertation, Harvard Business School, 1970).

TABLE A. Wrigley's Sample of the 1967 *"Fortune 500."*

Category	Percentage of Firms in Sample Falling in this Category	Percentage of Firms in Category Having Multi-divisional Organizations
Single Product	6	0
Dominant Product	14	64
Related Product	60	95
Unrelated Product	20	100

to a small degree (Dominant Product); firms that expanded into new areas bearing either a technological or market relation to current activities (Related Product); and firms that diversified without regard to such relationships (Unrelated Product). In particular, the Dominant Product group, defined to consist of firms that obtained more than 70 percent of their sales from a single product area, represents a new and important distinction. His results are shown in Table A.

Wrigley discarded the time-honored "product count" measure of diversification and employed instead a system of categories based on a qualitative evaluation of the firm's product-market scope and diversification rationale. Although other researchers have admitted that measuring diversification according to the number of products the firm sells or the number of industries in which it participates gives no weight to the "differentness" of the various areas of activity or to their relative importance, most have been reluctant to abandon what seemed to be the only available "objective" measure. Wrigley's categories, although not totally objective, at least distinguish among firms that have diversified in different ways (such as Litton Industries and General Electric), and among firms that are fully diversified and those that remain wedded to a single major product line (such as Dow Chemical and Ford Motor).

The data show the strategy of diversification and the multidivisional structure to be widely accepted in 1967, and Scott has commented that this represents a dramatic shift from the immediate postwar era. In addition, Scott has observed that the Wrigley data call into question theories of corporate growth and development that emphasize the importance of technology and integration rather than diversification and decentralization.[9] Galbraith, as a proponent of the former view, sees the corporation becoming ever more dedicated to a particular product-market area and increasingly immune to top management direction.[10] Chandler's model, Scott suggests, which links technology to diversification and diversification to administrative structures, more accurately describes the bulk of large modern corporations.

Considering both the special properties that theorists and practitioners at-

---

[9] Scott, "Stages of Corporate Development," pp. 39, 42.

[10] John K. Galbraith, *The New Industrial State* (Boston: Houghton Mifflin Company, 1967).

tribute to the diversified firm and its increasing prevalence, there are a number of intriguing questions that deserve investigation:

1. How has the shift to diversification come about? Do firms generally move from the Single Product category to the Dominant, then to the Related, or do they jump past the Dominant (or perhaps the Related) stages?

2. How much of the change in the composition of the largest 500 has been due to changes by firms themselves and how much has been due to new firms entering the top 500 to replace those that have been acquired or dropped from the list because of insufficient growth?

3. Is the Dominant Product group stable, or does it consist of firms that are on their way to full diversification? If it is stable, do these firms face any special barriers to diversification or have they purposefully elected to limit their product-market scopes?

4. What is the relation between strategic change and structural change over time? Can changes in structure be directly correlated with changes in diversification strategy or are they parallel but independent trends?

The present study seeks answers to these and similar questions and presents, as a result, an enriched model of the pattern of development of the large industrial corporation.

In addition to extending the Wrigley census and investigating the usefulness of alternative categories, this study also compares the economic performance of firms belonging to different strategic and organizational categories. In a sense, this portion of the research repeats past efforts, since several investigators have sought a relationship between diversification and profitability or growth. In no case, however, was a definite relationship found between economic performance and product-count measures of diversification.[11] If the strategic category method can reveal significant performance differences among the various strategies of diversification, it will not only be a finding of high intrinsic interest, it would also lend support to our approach to the study of diversification.

In looking at economic performance and diversification, I have tried to compare groups of firms with different strategies of diversification—rates of growth in sales and earnings, returns on investment, price-earnings ratios, and debt-to-capital ratios. In addition, marginal relationships between growth and profitability and, for the case of acquisitive conglomerates, between earnings growth and the price-earnings ratio, were investigated.

The group under investigation was composed of the 500 largest industrial firms in the United States, as listed annually by *Fortune* magazine. The time period selected was the 20 years between 1949 and 1969. While a longer time span might have been more revealing, data on the product lines, economic performance, and the organizational structure of firms prior to 1950 were sparse

---

[11] For example, see Michael Gort, *Diversification and Integration in American Industry* (Princeton, N.J.: Princeton University Press, 1962), pp. 75–77.

and difficult to locate. Given the choice between studying only those firms for which data were available and studying an unbiased random sample of large firms over a period for which more data were available, the second choice seemed a better one.

The sample was constructed by selecting 100 firms randomly from the largest 500 in 1949, another 100 from the largest 500 in 1959, and another 100 from the same category for 1969. Since a number of firms were selected in more than one of the three samples, the total sample size was 246 rather than 300.

This sampling procedure made it possible to (1) investigate the composition of the largest 500 in 1949, 1959, and 1969; (2) study the changing composition of the largest 500; and (3) obtain groups of firms that were members of the 500 throughout a decade in order to have a sample representative of large firms during that time period.

Once the sample was obtained, each firm was placed in one of the categories of diversification strategy and in one of the categories of organizational structure. The data used in making these classifications came from published sources, and included company annual reports, prospectuses, books, articles, *Moody's Industrials,* and, less often, from a variety of other sources. Financial data on most of the companies in the sample were obtained from a computer tape originally created by Standard and Poor's and maintained by The Boston Company.

The information obtained from these sources was then placed on a computer file that contained for each firm in the sample a record of its strategic categorization, structural history, and a continuous record of its financial performance during the period 1950–1969. A number of computer programs were then written to manipulate this file so that analyses could be made of the composition of the largest 500, changes in the composition, the relationship between changes in strategy and changes in structure, and the financial performance of firms falling into various categories of strategy and structure. As in any project of this type, the range of analyses performed greatly exceeded the scope of those presented in the final report.

In addition to the classifying and financial data for each firm, a large amount of descriptive data was gathered from published sources. Although not used in the quantitative analyses, this information played an invaluable role in the interpretation of statistical and census results.

OUTLINE OF THE STUDY

Chapter 1 describes the classification scheme and the research methodology. It begins with a detailed description of Wrigley's classification scheme and then turns to the development of an improved system of discrete categories of diversification strategy. Wrigley's four basic categories are maintained, although with slightly different definitions. Subcategories of the Dominant, Related, and Unrelated groups are defined. In defining these subcategories, the concept of "constrained" versus "linked" diversification is introduced in order to capture the difference between firms that built their diversification strategies on some central skill or strength and firms that continually branch out in new directions. In addition, a distinction is made between Unrelated class firms that are acquisitive conglomerates and those that operate unrelated businesses without engaging in rapid diversification through acquisition. Finally, a special subclass of the Dominant category is defined for vertically integrated firms.

The system of structural classification is then presented, and its five categories are defined: functional, functional with subsidiaries, product division, geographic division, and holding company. Of these, the functional-with-subsidiaries category is new to the literature and corresponds to a functional organization that has created a few semi-autonomous product divisions in order to manage activities not directly connected to the major business. The research methodology is then described. Sources of data are given, the type of data processing used is discussed, and an evaluation of the replicability of the classification system is made by comparing the results obtained in this study with Wrigley's.

Chapter 2 presents and analyzes the census data on the composition of the largest 500 firms in terms of the categories of diversification strategy and structure. It compares the breakdown of the top 500 by strategic category with a simpler measure of corporate diversity, and suggests that the simpler measure is not sufficiently rich to serve as a proxy for diversification strategy. Turning to the changing composition of the top firms, this chapter investigates the degree to which internal change and the effects of entry to and exit from the top 500 are responsible for the overall observed change. Both factors seem to have had similar effects, and have been of about equal magnitude. The net result has been a marked decrease in the number of Single Business firms and a substantial increase in the number of Related Business and Unrelated Business firms.

A closer inspection of the patterns of strategic change shows that transition rates between major strategic categories have been fairly stable over the past 20 years, with the only important exception being a recent increase in the transition rate into the Acquisitive Conglomerate class. An investigation of the patterns of structural change shows that during the period 1949–1969 the product-division structure moved from a position of minor importance to the major organizational form employed by large corporations. Again, the sources of change are investigated and it is shown that while increasing diversification explains about one-half of the increase in divisionalization, the remainder of the increase must be attributed to a trend toward the adoption of the product division structure among almost all types of firms.

Chapter 3 deals with the relative financial performance of firms following different strategies of diversification and having different organizational structures. After a brief look at the major differences, the possibility of obtaining industry-corrected results is discussed, but diversification strategy is so intimately mixed with industry that it is impossible to separate the two effects.

A number of hypotheses regarding financial performance are explained and tested. The most important results are: (1) firms that have diversified to some extent but have restricted their range of activities to a central skill or competence have shown substantially higher rates of profitability and growth than other types of firms; (2) business firms in the Unrelated category that participate in science-based industries, while having rates of profit that are average in an overall sense, are less profitable than other types of science-based firms; (3) of the structure categories, the product-division performs best; (4) the poorest performing firms are the vertically integrated and Unrelated Business (but not conglomerate) companies; and (5) firms with product-division structures are faster growing and at least as profitable as other types of firms and also seem to rely less on high profits to power growth than other types of firms.

Chapter 4 looks closely at the two strategic categories that showed the poorest financial performances: the vertically integrated group and the Unrelated-Passive (unrelated but not conglomerate) category. It is suggested that the vertically integrated firms face special barriers to diversification so that, unlike many other less diversified companies, they find it very difficult to remedy low performance through diversification. In examining the properties of the Unrelated-Passive group we find that most consist of a few unrelated clusters of businesses, diversified but internally related. This type of structure presents particularly difficult administrative problems and the histories of most of these firms indicate that they have not had either the opportunity or the willingness to solve them.

Chapter 5 summarizes the findings of the study and points out the implications for managers and public policy makers. The Appendixes present the estimation techniques (Appendix A), statistical procedures (Appendix B), and information in tabular form on each of the firms in the sample (Appendix C). Included are data on each company's product line, its rank in the *Fortune* 500, and strategic and structural classifications for 1949, 1959, and 1969.

CHAPTER 1

Definitions, Concepts, and Methodology

THERE IS NO GENERALLY ACCEPTED DEFINITION or measure of diversification. An annual report to stockholders may call attention to a refrigerator manufacturer's diversification into home freezers, while a statistical study on the extent of diversification in large firms may ignore any product addition that does not take a company into a new industrial sector. Some describe an oil company's move into petrochemicals as diversification while others refer to it as vertical integration. Further complicating the issue is the recent upsurge of interest in conglomerate corporations. Among the firms that have been called "highly diversified conglomerates" are Ford Motor, Crown Cork & Seal, General Electric, and Pittsburgh Plate Glass, as well as Textron, LTV, and Gulf & Western.

The lack of a clear-cut definition of diversification stands as both a problem and an opportunity for the researcher; he shoulders the burden of developing his own concept of diversification, but enjoys the freedom of tailoring a concept to suit his interests. For example, economists who have attempted to relate diversification activity to industry structure, or to relate product additions to mergers, have generally used a simple count of the number of products produced and sold by the firm as both the measure and the implicit definition of diversification. Berg, on the other hand, has studied extensively the nature of the headquarters office of large diversified firms and has found that a classification system based on the method of growth—internal or acquisition—best suits his needs.[1]

---

[1] Norman A. Berg, "What's Different About Conglomerate Management?" *Harvard Business Review*, May–June 1965, p. 112.

A goal for this study was the formulation of a set of concepts and measurement techniques that would be managerially meaningful, and which would capture the essence of top management's view of diversification. At the same time, these concepts and techniques would have to be simple enough to permit the examination of a large number of firms. In developing this framework, the concept of corporate strategy will be used, along with the notion of categories of diversification strategy derived from the work of Wrigley. For the study, interest in diversification grew out of questions about its interaction with the tasks of general management. Diversification may be seen as both the result of general management decisions that are of great importance to the future of the firm and as the cause of problems in coordination, planning, and control at the highest levels—in other words, as strategy.

In conceptualizing diversification as a strategy we are following Chandler's usage of the term. He defined strategy as "the determination of the basic long-term goals and objectives of an enterprise, and the adoption of courses of action and the allocation of resources necessary for carrying out these goals." [2] Then, by distinguishing among the strategies of "expansion of volume," "geographical dispersion," "vertical integration," and "product diversification," Chandler showed how each poses a different type of administrative difficulty and therefore tends to lead to a different form of organizational structure.

More recently, the Business Policy group at the Harvard Business School developed a more elaborate concept of corporate strategy. [3] In the Harvard framework, strategy is the result of a balanced consideration of a firm's skills and resources, the opportunities extant in the economic environment, and the personal desires of management, presumably tempered by its sense of social responsibility. Although this concept was not developed to deal specifically with diversification, it does suggest that the task of matching opportunity with corporate skills and strengths is the most important of top management's responsibilities and may be taken as the primary component of diversification strategy.

Using as a point of departure the range of skills possessed corporately by a firm, a *diversification move* is taken to be any entry into a new *product-market* activity that requires or implies an appreciable increase in the available managerial competence within the firm. Thus, the essence of diversification is taken to be a "reaching out" into new areas, requiring the development of new competences or the augmentation of existing ones. A new business activity may be related in several ways to a current activity but may still require the understanding of a different production technology, of different marketing concepts and methods, or of new approaches to investment decisions, planning, and control. This definition identifies diversification in terms of the degree to

---

[2] Chandler, *Strategy and Structure*, p. 16.

[3] See, for example, Kenneth Andrews, *The Concept of Corporate Strategy* (Homewood, Ill.: Dow Jones-Irwin, 1971).

which a new product-market activity taxes the ability of the firm's *management,* particularly its general management, together with the administrative structure it has created. The fact that companies with operating skills in a given area can usually be purchased outright underlines the importance of management ability as one of the primary nonfinancial restrictions on entry into new businesses.

The concept of a diversification move applies only to a particular product-market addition. In order to compare the diversification postures of different firms, some way of expressing the cumulative total of a firm's diversification moves is needed. The concept of "diversification strategy," which combines Chandler's concept of diversification as a strategy and the Harvard view of strategy as the relation between competence and opportunity, is defined here as (1) the firm's commitment to diversity per se; together with (2) the strengths, skills or purposes that span this diversity, demonstrated by the way new activities are related to old activities.

DEVELOPING CATEGORIES OF DIVERSIFICATION STRATEGY

The measurement technique that has been used to test these definitions is a modified version of the classification system developed by Wrigley. Taking the term *specialization ratio* (*SR*) to characterize the proportion of a firm's annual revenues attributable to its largest discrete product-market activity, Wrigley's original categories may be described as follows: [4]

> Single Product: Firms with *SR* between 0.95 and 1.0. Such firms grow only through expansion in the scale of their operations.

> Dominant Product: Firms with *SR* between 0.7 and 0.95. Such firms have diversified to a small degree but are still quite dependent upon and characterized by their major product-market activity.

> Related Product: Firms with *SR* less than 0.7 which have diversified by adding new activities that are tangibly related to the collective skills and strengths possessed originally by the firm.

> Unrelated Product: Firms that diversify (usually by acquisition) into areas that are not related to the original skills and strengths, other than financial, of the firm.

By identifying the specialization ratio as a measure of the "firm's commitment to diversity per se" it becomes clear that these categories represent one

---

[4] Wrigley, "Divisional Autonomy and Diversification," Ch. 3, p. 9.

possible way of implementing our concept of strategic posture. In the early stages of research these categories were used without modification, so that the results would be directly comparable with Wrigley's. It soon became apparent, however, that (1) the terms "single product" and "dominant product" tended to be interpreted too narrowly by those not familiar with the methodology; (2) for the classifications to be replicable by other researchers more precise definitions were needed; (3) it would be useful to have some subcategories to describe certain observable and persistent differences in kind among the firms falling in several of the categories; and (4) vertically integrated firms posed special problems in classification. Because of these problems, using Wrigley's categories was less important than incorporating the knowledge gained from a larger sample into an improved set of categories. The new categories were similar in spirit and broad outline to Wrigley's, but differed in a number of important respects.

Discrete Businesses

Wrigley's placement of firms like Texaco and Deere in the Dominant Product class indicates that he employed a broader concept of a "product" than is usually meant by the term. In order to minimize any confusion over this point, a revised set of category titles was adopted: Single Business, Dominant Business, Related Business, and Unrelated Business.

Underlying these categories and central to the scheme is the idea that a corporation's activities can be conceptually divided into a number of discrete businesses. A discrete business means one that could be managed independently of the firm's other activities. Since interdependencies are difficult to observe or judge in a static situation, the separability of a particular business is assessed by evaluating the degree to which its basic nature and scope could be altered without meeting constraints imposed by the firm's other businesses, and without materially affecting the operation and strategic direction of other activities.

The difficulty of breaking a firm's operations into discrete business activities is greatly reduced by stipulating that the classification depends only upon the relative size of the company's largest distinct business, so that only one line of demarcation need be drawn among each firm's activities. Even in making this one judgment, however, the standard lists of businesses, such as the Standard Industrial Classification categories, were not helpful. Each company had a unique history and had developed its own pattern of relationships among technologies, products, and markets. *What was a discrete business for one firm was often an integral and nonseparable part of a larger business in another firm.*

Because the factors that influenced interdependency among business activities varied from firm to firm, it was not feasible to develop an exhaustive description of the properties of a discrete business. Instead, the approach taken was (1) to tentatively identify a firm's largest discrete business; (2) to assess the results of applying a number of different types of strategic change to this or another of the firm's businesses; and (3) to evaluate the degree to which any of these changes would involve strong interdependency effects among the firm's businesses. Three types of strategic change were helpful in assessing strategic interdependencies:

(1) *A decision to drop the product-market activity entirely or, conversely, to greatly increase its relative size.* Consideration of this very basic type of strategic change highlights the degree to which a business activity is functionally related to other activities. Ford, for example, could leave the truck business without material repercussions on its automobile business. On the other hand, if Ford were to drop one of its automobile model lines, the price, quality, and volume of its other lines of automobiles would be affected. Thus, the automobile business, taken as a whole, is a discrete business separate from the truck business.

When this type of strategic change is applied to a vertically integrated firm, product-flow interdependencies are almost invariably present. Alcoa, for example, could not drop any of its fabrication businesses without affecting its basic aluminum production activities. A paper company could not change its product mix from one emphasizing boxboard to one emphasizing white paper without making compensating changes in the types of trees used for pulp and in its pulp-processing technology and capacity.

(2) *A decision to employ a different production technology or process or to use a different type of raw material.* Evaluating the effects of this type of strategic change can aid in assessing the degree to which a business activity is bound to others by production technology. A company, for example, that produces a wide variety of die castings for automobiles, aircraft, and industrial machinery, might find that a change to plastics in a few high volume items would not leave enough casting business to support the overhead costs of the facility. By contrast, an "auto parts" producer that makes springs, batteries, valves, and spark plugs, and necessarily employs a variety of production technologies, and the decision to produce any of these products by a different method, would not strongly affect the other activities. Thus the "diversified" casting company consists of a single discrete business while the auto parts company may be divided into several distinct businesses (barring inseparability on the marketing end).

(3) *A decision to significantly alter the price, quality, or services associated with the product.* Evaluating this type of strategic change aids in identifying products that are part of "product lines" rather than of discrete businesses. Xerox's paper business, for example, cannot be strategically separated from its copying machine business, nor can Crown Cork & Seal alter the nature of its custom packaging-design services without considering the effect on its con-

tainer production business. Similarly, a firm that produces large electronic computers and also designs special purpose systems cannot lower the price of its general purpose machines without producing problems for the other part of the business.

These criteria should make it clear that while our method of identifying discrete businesses does require judgment, it is consistent with the "top down" approach to the study of diversification. While it necessarily introduces problems associated with the lack of totally objective standards, it is doubtful whether such standards are attainable in business research of this type. Many researchers have commented on the failings of the SIC categories as definitions of "businesses," but argue that such an approach is at least objective. We would argue, in turn, that even more "objective" measures can be found, but they bear even less relation to the real issues under investigation. In this research we have sought to balance the measurable aspects of the problem with the most relevant ones. When in doubt, we have tended to favor relevancy over exactness.

The Specialization Ratio

In keeping with the formulation of a discrete business, the specialization ratio was redefined as the proportion of a firm's revenues that can be attributed to its largest single business in a given year.

Wrigley's choice of a specialization ratio of 0.7 as the dividing line between the Dominant, and the Related and Unrelated groups was based on his empirical evidence:

> At one stage in the research, a serious attempt was made to discover whether the basis of a diversification system could be the proportion of the "main" product in the total output. If this were successful it would have led to an ordered series of magnitudes of the kind (in per cent): 100; 90; 80; 70; 60; 50; 40; 30. However, the attempt met with a particular phenomenon among firms in the sample. While there were some 14 firms in the category 80–100 per cent, few firms were in the category 60–80 per cent. It seemed that in designing a strategy for expansion, businessmen did not adopt what might be called "half diversification"; they tended either to diversify by a small amount in relation to total output or to go the whole way.[5]

Figure 1.1 shows the distributions of specialization ratios for 1949, 1959, and 1969, which were obtained from the sample used in the present study. Because data were unavailable for certain points, and the specialization ratio

---

[5] Wrigley, "Divisional Autonomy and Diversification," Chap. III, p. 6.

FIGURE 1.1. Frequency Distributions of Specialization Ratios for 1949, 1959, and 1969.

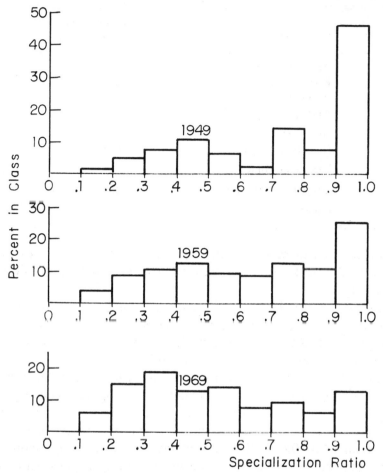

for many highly diversified firms was difficult to identify, these distributions must be considered suggestive rather than definitive. Still, their general shape tends to confirm Wrigley's findings. Since no technical argument can be advanced for choosing any other figure in the range of 0.6–0.85, the 0.7 line of demarcation was retained.

The Related Ratio

A detailed inspection of the firms that Wrigley classed as Unrelated revealed some that we decided to place in the Related class, and vice versa. The judgments of several other individuals engaged in parallel research were obtained, but the results revealed no consistent pattern of assessment. Although there was general agreement about which businesses were unrelated to any other

TABLE 1-1. DISTRIBUTION OF REVENUES, NORTH AMERICAN ROCKWELL, 1969.

Business Area	Percentage of Total Revenues
Aircraft and missiles	14.3 ⎫
Rocket engines	6.7 ⎬ 61.2
Aerospace systems	19.5 ⎪
Aerospace electronics	20.7 ⎭
Auto parts	20.8 ⎫ 25.4
Industrial machine parts	4.6 ⎭
Textile machinery	3.8
Graphic arts equipment	4.6
Other	5.0

activity of the firm, there was no clear-cut agreement about what constituted, *in toto,* an Unrelated Business. Consequently, a more precise definition of this class was sought.

A new ratio was introduced—the *related ratio,* or *RR,* defined as the proportion of a firm's revenues attributable to its largest group of related businesses. For example, North American Rockwell's distribution of revenues by business area in 1969 was approximately as shown in Table 1-1.[6]

The two major groups of related businesses within North American Rockwell were (1) the set of businesses related by aerospace technology and the NASA-government market; and (2) auto and industrial parts. The former was the larger, in terms of revenues, so that North American's related ratio for 1969 is taken to be 0.612. The related ratio is particularly helpful, as this example demonstrates, in dealing with firms that are active in several unrelated areas, each of which is a diversified business in its own right. The related ratio also minimizes the number of judgments that must be made: in this case, the questions of whether or not the textile machinery business and the graphic arts equipment business were related, or whether either, or both, was related to the parts manufacturing business, need not be answered, since the related ratio would remain 0.612.

The dividing line between Related and Unrelated firms was taken to be a related ratio of 0.7. North American would be classified as an Unrelated Business in 1969. The 70 percent cut-off was chosen because it seemed to match fairly well the judgments expressed by informed observers. Also, setting the critical *RR* equal to the critical *SR* insures that a company cannot qualify for the Dominant category on the basis of its *SR* and, at the same time, qualify for the Unrelated category on the basis of its *RR.*

---

[6] This information and similar information about other companies presented elsewhere in this chapter were obtained from annual reports.

Constrained and Linked Relatedness

Before the work of classifying the firms was begun, it seemed useful to subdivide the Related Business category into three subclasses. These subclasses would serve to differentiate among those firms that had diversified by relying chiefly on (1) relationships among markets served and distribution systems; (2) relationships based on similar production technologies; or (3) the exploitation of science-based research. It was found, however, that while individual moves to diversify were easily placed in one of these subclasses, few firms had used one type of relationship with enough consistency to warrant its use as characterizing the firm's strategic posture as a whole. Consequently, the attempt was abandoned.

A search through the Related group for other types of patterns revealed a further distinction. On one side could be placed the firms that had stayed relatively "close to home." On the other were those that had added new activities to old in such a way that they were eventually active in businesses which, considered by themselves, were virtually unrelated. The first type of strategic posture was termed *Related-Constrained,* and the second *Related-Linked.*

The change in the strategic posture of Carborundum, Inc., between 1949 and 1969 is illustrative of this distinction (see Figures 1.2, 1.3). In 1949 all of Carborundum's businesses were closely related to the firm's basic strengths: the efficient production of high quality grains of silicon carbide and aluminum oxide, and the competence in the materials sciences necessary to engineer these materials to various uses. These materials were sold in bulk, fabricated into bricks and tiles for high temperature applications, bonded or coated to produce abrasives, or made into electrical resistors and heating elements. The firm was categorized as Related-Constrained because, although it was diversi-

FIGURE 1.2. Businesses of Carborundum, Inc., in 1949.

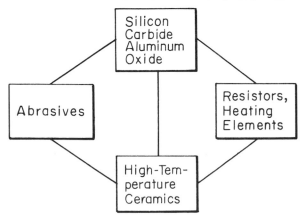

SOURCE: Company annual report.

FIGURE 1.3. Businesses of Carborundum, Inc., in 1969.

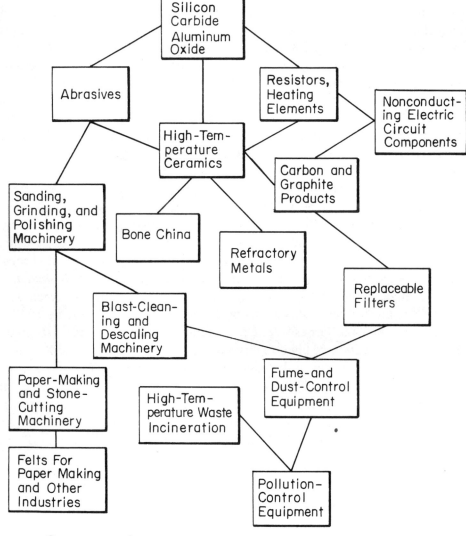

SOURCE: Company annual report.

fied, each business was related to each other business and all could be seen as radiating from a common core.

During the 1950s, however, Carborundum began to produce a line of grinding, cutting, and polishing machines to complement its line of abrasives. Then, beginning in 1962, a Related-Linked strategy was inaugurated. The skills acquired in manufacturing abrasive machines were applied to other types of industrial machinery, and nonabrasive cleaning and descaling equipment was added. Ceramics technology led to ceramic electrical components and carbon and graphite materials, which in turn provided a base for expansion into filtering media. High temperature technology led to the refractory metals business. Recently, the company's activities in filtering media, cleaning machinery, general industrial machinery, and high temperature technology have been brought together through a position in the solid waste disposal and pollution control fields. Carborundum's 1969 posture was thus Related-Linked; by adding new businesses in such a way that each was related to at least one—but often no more than one—of its current activities, the firm gradually became involved in a linked network of widely disparate businesses. Examples of other Related-Linked firms in 1969 were General Electric, Borden, and Monsanto.

In deciding whether a firm was Related-Linked or Related-Constrained, these questions were found to be useful: (1) "Is each of the firm's businesses related to virtually all of its other businesses, taken one at a time?" and (2) "If not, did logical relationships exist between each business and some other business of the firm at the time it was added?" In cases involving a mix between the two postures, the firm was classified according to the group of businesses (constrained or linked) that, in terms of revenues, was the larger.

The Dominant Business category can also be subdivided along these lines. The Dominant-Constrained and Dominant-Linked categories represent the same type of diversification pattern as the Related-Constrained and Related-Linked categories, except that total diversity is less, since the largest single business contributes between 70 and 95 percent of total revenues.

The Dominant-Unrelated subclass was created to deal with Dominant Business firms whose minor business or businesses was unrelated to its major business. An example is Ford Motor—while basically an automobile company, its electronics business (Philco) places it in the Dominant-Unrelated category. The quantitative criteria for a company to be in the Dominant-Unrelated class were $SR \geqq 0.7$ and that revenues received from activities unrelated to the largest group of related businesses be larger than revenues due to businesses related, but not including, the largest single business. The latter requirement is equivalent to: $RR < \frac{1}{2} (SR + 1)$.

Vertically Integrated Firms

Often growing by absorbing their suppliers and industrial customers, vertically integrated firms possess what Thompson calls "long-linked technologies."[7] The major activities of these companies consist of stages in the sequential processing of a particular material from its raw form to a finished product, or a variety of products. These firms are mainly found in the oil, rubber, basic metals, and forest products industries.

Before the research began no special provisions were made for dealing with

---

[7] James D. Thompson, *Organizations in Action* (New York: McGraw-Hill Book Company, 1967), p. 15.

vertically integrated firms apart from the stipulation that diversification was to be considered in terms of products *sold*. It was found, however, that vertically integrated firms often did not seem to belong in any of the categories defined. Attempts to classify these firms as either Single, Dominant, or Related invariably required either too broad or too narrow a definition. Two difficult questions kept recurring: (1) Is a by-product a separate business or part of the business which produces it? and (2) Under what conditions should a firm that has integrated forward into a wide variety of manufacturing activities be considered diversified?

Examples of both these questions are provided by the Aluminum Company of America (Alcoa), whose materials flow and sales breakdown for 1969 are shown in Figure 1.4. Some descriptive statistics on Alcoa are:

> Largest single product area
>   (structural aluminum)   = 15.4% of sales
> All aluminum fabrication   = 68.8% of sales
> All aluminum and by-products = 93.4% of sales

Is Alcoa an aluminum company or a diversified producer of aluminum products? If the former, it should be classed as Dominant Business. However, applying this same broad view of a "business" to other firms results in Dow being a "chemical company," General Foods being a "food company," and so on. Such definitions would be absurd in a study of diversification, as they obscure the very differences with which we are concerned.

If, on the other hand, Alcoa is classed as a diversified producer of aluminum products, and therefore as a Related Business, another type of distortion has taken place: in terms of either assets or general management's tasks Alcoa is not really diversified. The preponderance of the company's assets are devoted to the extraction, transportation, and refining of ore, and the production of pig, sheet, bar, and tube aluminum, Alcoa's fabrication activities having historical roots in the need to increase primary demand by showing the variety of uses of aluminum. Much of the management task in this type of firm has to do with coordinating the elements in the processing chain; the emphasis is on balance, efficient through-put, and the adjustment of production capacity to demand. The interdependencies among the businesses of a vertically integrated firm mean that, no matter how many different forms the end products take, general management must view the firm as a whole when considering the effect of any change in operations or resource allocation.

United States Steel is another example of the vertically integrated firm. It is a fully integrated steel producer which appears on most lists of "highly diversified firms" when the measure is product count. Yet this recent description of United States Steel's business, approved by its own management, highlights

FIGURE 1.4. Product Flow and Revenue Breakdown for Alcoa in 1969.

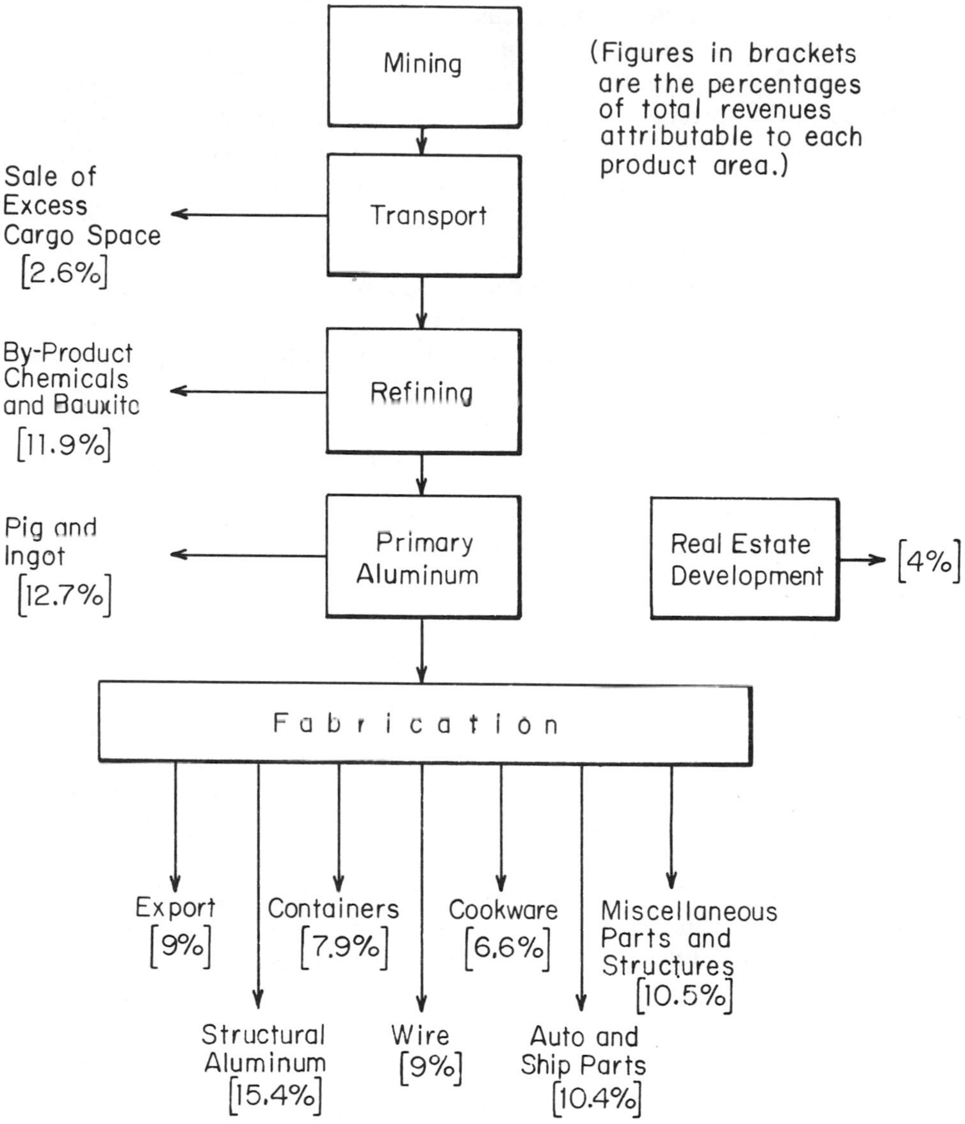

SOURCE: Annual report, 1969.

the interrelatedness of the product-market activities of the vertically integrated company:

> United States Steel Corporation is engaged in integrated steel operations, producing and selling iron, steel and related products in a variety of forms. The principal forms include: ingots, blooms, billets, slabs, tube rounds and skelp; structural shapes and piling; plates (and many other steel mill products). . . . also, certain raw materials, pig iron, ferro-

manganese, coal chemicals, and other items connected with, or closely related to, iron and steel making activities are produced and sold.

Integrated operations include the production of substantially all the iron ore and limestone, more than half the coal and part of the manganese ore used; the operation of coke ovens which supply the coke, coke oven gas and tar used; the generation of almost half the electric power required; and the operation of steamships, tugs, barges, and docks for the transportation of raw materials and steel.

The Corporation is engaged, through the American Bridge Division, in the fabrication and erection of bridges, buildings' and other steel structures and in the manufacture of large diameter steel pipe. Various other divisions manufacture steel drums, oil field drilling and pumping equipment, and other items made of steel. . . .

U.S. Steel produces and sells chemicals, a material amount of which is derived from the coal coking operations, through its divisions, USS Chemicals and USS Agri-Chemicals. These include agricultural chemicals, tar-based enamels for pipelines, other industrial chemicals and basic materials for the plastics fabrication operations.

Subsidiaries servicing the above operations include export distributors and a number of transportation companies including several common carrier railroads . . . Two transportation companies provide ocean transportation for the Corporation and others.

The products from the above operations are characterized by common raw material sources, interrelation of processed materials and substantial interplant, interdivision and intercompany transfers to such an extent that on a consolidated basis *such products and the services related to them are considered to be a single line of business* which accounted for approximately 95% of the Corporation's products and services sold, and in excess of 90% of its income before estimated United States and foreign taxes on income, in each of the years 1967 through 1970. [Emphasis added.] [8]

In principle, vertically integrated firms like Alcoa and United States Steel are sufficiently different from other firms to warrant an entirely separate set of categories to describe their diversification postures. However, it seemed unwise to complicate an already expanded classification system in order to deal with this numerically small subset of all large firms. A compromise approach was developed. Vertically integrated firms that had 95 percent or more of their sales in a single end-product business (such as sheet steel, petroleum refinery products, or white paper) were classed as Single Businesses. Those in which the sales of all intermediate and end products associated with the vertical chain comprised less than 70 percent of total revenues were treated as either Related or Unrelated Businesses, depending on the related ratio. The

---

[8] Prospectus for United States Steel Corp. $150 million 7¾ percent Sinking Fund Debenture due 2001 (New York, February 23, 1971), p. 6.

rest, which were the majority, were placed in a new subclass of Dominant Business firms, the Dominant-Vertical class.

The rationale for this procedure is that, regardless of the degree of variety of end-product firms, the company that has the preponderance of its output in areas linked to a vertical chain of processing steps is, viewed from the top down, more akin to a Dominant Business than to a truly diversified firm. When the output of the vertical chain is in only one product-market area (i.e., mill products or paper), there is, of course, no question about classifying the company as a Single Business firm.

To make these ideas more precise, the *vertical ratio* (*VR*) in any given year is defined as the proportion of the firm's revenues that arise from all by-products, intermediate products, and end products of a vertically integrated sequence of processing activities. The vertical ratio, specialization ratio, and related ratio are used in combination to classify the firm as follows:

> Vertical ratio greater than or equal to 0.7
> > Single Business if *SR* is 0.95 or greater
> > Dominant-Vertical if *SR* is less than 0.95
> Vertical ratio less than 0.7
> > Related Business if *RR* is 0.7 or greater
> > Unrelated Business if *RR* is less than 0.7

Conglomerates

Generally thought to be a fairly recent phenomenon, the conglomerate is a company that has rapidly diversified into several unrelated areas by means of a relatively large number of mergers and acquisitions. Although some writers have argued that firms like Westinghouse, selling products as unrelated as epoxy resin, television sets, and nuclear reactors, are conglomerates, such firms have been classified here as Related-Linked, because of the way in which they achieved diversification. Berg calls this type of firm a "diversified major" and has demonstrated that its approach to general management, particularly at the headquarters level, is quite different from that taken by conglomerates.[9] He found that conglomerates tend to be quite "thin" at the top, concentrating few headquarters personnel in the finance, legal, and planning functions. Their administrative structure is fashioned simply to watch over and allocate capital among a portfolio of businesses, there being no central research and development or central staff-coordinating offices.

In a thorough study of the financial strategies and performances of acquisitive conglomerates, Lynch offers evidence that their typically high rates of growth have been achieved by creating a positive feedback between their

---

[9] Norman A. Berg, "Corporate Organization in Diversified Companies" (unpublished working paper, Harvard Business School, HBS 71-2, BP 2, 1970), pp. 32–36.

growth in earnings per share and the market-determined price-earnings ratio; a high price-earnings ratio permits the acquisition of firms to be accomplished with little dilution, which in turn insures a high growth in earnings per share, thus justifying and maintaining the high price-earnings ratio.[10]

Although an Acquisitive Conglomerate is by definition an Unrelated Business firm, not all Unrelated Business firms are conglomerates. Companies such as Rockwell Manufacturing, Midland-Ross, and Pullman, while active in unrelated areas, have not experienced particularly high growth rates or price-earning ratios in the last twenty years, nor have they engaged in ambitious acquisition programs. This Unrelated-Passive group is, numerically, at least as important as the group of true conglomerates.

The distinction between these two types of Unrelated Business firms was incorporated in the classification scheme by defining two subclasses to the Unrelated Business category: the Acquisitive Conglomerate group and the Unrelated-Passive group. The criteria used to delineate the Acquisitive Conglomerate class were essentially those developed by Lynch. To qualify as a member of the Acquisitive Conglomerate subclass in any given year a firm had to fall in the Unrelated Business category ($RR < 0.7$) and, over the preceding five years (1) had to have experienced an average growth rate in earnings per share of at least 10 percent per year; (2) had to have made at least five acquisitions, three of which were diversification moves into new business areas unrelated to previous activities; and (3) had to have issued new equity shares whose cumulative market value (taken at the time of issue) was greater than the cumulative value of dividends paid during the same period. Taken together, these criteria identify firms that have been growing rapidly by acquisition of unrelated businesses, with the acquisition program chiefly financed through the issue of new equity shares.

USING THE DIVERSIFICATION CATEGORIES

The careful definition of concepts and the use of a number of quantitative criteria will increase the likelihood that separate researchers with access to the same data will classify a firm in a similar fashion. Nevertheless, the classification process is not logarithmic; it requires the exercise of a reasonable amount of judgment. Several examples illustrate the classification process, the kind of company each category represents, and the type of judgments that were made.

GAF. Known as General Aniline and Film before 1968, GAF's most widely

---

[10] Harry H. Lynch, *Financial Performance of Conglomerates* (Boston: Harvard Business School, Division of Research, 1971), pp. 67–68.

recognized brand name was Ansco, used to denote its line of photographic supplies and films. When the United States entered World War II, the federal government took 97 percent of General Aniline's stock, most of which had been held by German nationals. The company operated under government control until 1959, when the stock was sold in a public offering. As a consequence, few diversification moves were made in this period.

General Aniline's pattern of product-market activities in 1959 was not unlike its pattern in 1949. One half of its revenues derived from the sale of chemicals and dye stuffs, a third from its Ansco line, and the remaining sixth from sales of Ozalid equipment and paper for the reproduction of engineering drawings. The company's sales of chemicals and dye stuffs included (1) textile and paper dyes, (2) pigments for ink, paint, and plastics, (3) cleansing, wetting, and finishing agents for textiles, (4) surfactants—a proprietary name for surface active chemicals for detergents and emulsifiers, (5) a proprietary line of high pressure acetylene chemicals used in plastics, and (6) special iron powders used in electronic components.

The information available on its 1959 sales breakdown was limited to the following:

Area	Percentage of Total Revenues
Dyes and pigments	21
Other industrial chemicals	29
Cameras, Ansco film, chemical equipment	33
Ozalid machines and paper	17

The company was not vertically integrated and it was judged that all of its businesses were related in some way to some other of its businesses: thus, $RR = 1.0$. It is clear from the sales breakdown that the largest single business contributed no more than 33 percent of total revenues. Whether or not the Ansco business is a discrete business is quite irrelevant for classification purposes—SR is obviously less than 0.7. Therefore, GAF falls in the Related Business class. The various chemical activities constitute a "constrained" type of diversification, while the Ansco and Ozalid businesses are "linked" to the chemical business. Since both groups provide 50 percent of revenues, the decision to classify GAF as Related-Constrained or Related-Linked in 1959 could go either way. It was classified as Related-Linked on the basis of its direction of movement.

Between 1959 and 1969 GAF moved into office copiers, agricultural and pharmaceutical chemicals, slide projectors and prepared slides, acquired a manufacturer of a variety of business forms, and in 1967 it acquired Ruberoid. The latter firm was itself a diversified producer of asphalt roofing and siding, tile and sheet floor coverings, and asbestos belts and insulatory materials. GAF's 1969 sales breakdown was:

Chemicals	27
Ansco	24
Business forms, copiers, duplicators, microfilm	13
Builders' roofing, siding, flooring	29
Asbestos belts, filler, insulation	8

The Ruberoid acquisition was judged to be an unrelated move. Any relations between Ruberoid's business and GAF's were tenuous at best and there was no evidence that management had sought to build relationships. Hence, by 1969 GAF's related ratio had dropped to 0.64, placing it in the Unrelated Business class. However, since GAF did not follow up its one unrelated move with others—in fact making only one other acquisition between 1967 and 1969 (which was horizontal), it was judged not to be a conglomerate. Hence, it was classified as Unrelated-Passive in 1969.

Litton Industries. Incorporated in 1953, by 1959 Litton had rapidly diversified by acquisition into these major areas:

Business calculators & accounting machines (Monroe)	38
Electronic communications, movie & sound recording	9
Military electronics and systems	38
Electronic components	14

In this case the classification rests on whether or not the business machines business is related to other of Litton's activities. We judged that it was, given Litton's experience in electronics and its strategy of modernizing Monroe's line of calculators. For 1959 Litton was placed in the Related-Linked category.

By 1969 Litton had made an astounding number of acquisitions, many of them unrelated to past businesses. The largest single business (inertial guidance, navigation, and control systems) contributed only 10 percent of revenues. The largest group of related businesses (calculators, computers, data systems, and electronic components) contributed 30 percent of all revenues. With a ten-year average growth in earnings per share of 23 percent, a price-earnings ratio of 36, and a growth in equity three times as large as retained earnings, Litton was clearly an Acquisitive Conglomerate.

Philip Morris. The manufacture and sale of cigarettes, regardless of the number of brands, is, by our definition, a single business. In 1949 Philip Morris derived 98 percent of its revenue from cigarettes and the remainder from pipe tobacco. Thus, for 1949 Philip Morris fell in the Single Business category even if pipe tobacco were to be judged a different business.

By 1959, sales of the company's tobacco products had dropped to 86 percent of total revenues. The remaining 14 percent were generated by two acquired firms, which specialized in glassine paper, packaging adhesives, textile-processing chemicals, and printing on difficult-to-print substances (i.e., slick transparent papers). While some of these activities had slight connections with Philip Morris' tobacco products packaging activity, the company's original competence in this area did not go beyond the minimum required and there was no evidence that potential relations were exploited. Hence, Philip Morris, for the year 1959, had $SR = 0.86$ and was classified as Dominant-Unrelated.

By 1969 Philip Morris had acquired the Miller Brewing Company, and a number of other firms, which produced gum, razor blades, labels, toiletries, and surgical blades and hospital supplies. Tobacco products accounted for 75 percent of revenues, and beer was the largest nontobacco business, accounting for 15 percent of total revenues. Thus, the company still fell in the Dominant Unrelated class. Note that categorization did not depend on whether gum, razor blades, medical products, and packaging were related to one another or any other business. The company was Dominant because of tobacco and Dominant-Unrelated because beer (unrelated to tobacco or any of the other activities) constituted more than one half of nontobacco activities.

AMAX. In 1949 AMAX (previously American Metal Climax) was an integrated producer of refined copper, lead, zinc, silver, and gold. Ores were obtained both competitively and through mining subsidiaries and joint ventures. Fifty-four percent of AMAX's sales were of copper, giving it an SR of 0.54. However, the company's mining, transportation, and refining activities for copper, lead, and zinc were not separate; the similarities in ores and refining processes among these metals having been exploited by vertically integrated operations encompassing all three. Sales of copper, lead, and zinc were 74 percent of total sales; thus $VR = 0.74$. AMAX was placed in the Dominant-Vertical category for 1949.

During the next decade AMAX moved into potash mining, oil and gas exploration and production, and light metals, and merged with Climax Molybdenum. By 1959 the company's sales breakdown was:

Copper	59
Lead, zinc	6
Tin, silver, and gold	14
Molybdenum	9
Uranium and vanadium	1
Potash	2
Oil and gas	9

Since $VR = 0.65$, less than 0.7, AMAX no longer fell in the Dominant-Vertical class. An $SR = 0.59$ placed it out of the Dominant category and since the only candidates for unrelated activities (potash and oil and gas) had sales less than 30 percent of total sales, AMAX was placed in the Related class. Since AMAX had obviously applied the constraints of "primary metals" and/or "mining and mineral extraction" to its diversification strategy, it was placed in the Related-Constrained subcategory.

In the 1960s AMAX moved into the aluminum business, first by acquiring smelting fabrication facilities and then by integrating back into mining. It also entered the concrete, general building products, and mobile homes businesses, but sold these operations and most of its oil and gas interests in 1966–67. In 1969 it merged with Ayrshire Collieries Corporation, a coal company. Its 1969 sales breakdown was:

Coal, potash, oil	6
Copper, lead and zinc	36
Aluminum	37
Molybdenum and other refractory metals	21

The specialization ratio is difficult to estimate but is certainly less than 21 percent. Since the constraints on the company's diversification did not seem to have changed, it was again placed in the Related-Constrained group.

Cincinnati Milacron (formerly the Cincinnati Milling Machine Corporation). In 1949 Milacron's basic business was the manufacture and sale of machine tools, machine tool parts, and cutting fluid. The company also produced several chemicals used in cutting fluids and sold these and related chemicals to industrial customers for use in lubricating oils, food, soap, and other products. In addition, Milacron marketed a limited line of tools for home use and engaged in contract construction of machines designed and sold by others. While no sales breakdown was available, an examination of Milacron's sales over time, its sales breakdown in later years, and total United States machine tool sales indicated that machine tools and cutting fluid accounted for substantially more than 70 percent of total sales in 1949. Hence, Milacron was classified as Dominant-Constrained for that year.

During the 1950s Milacron introduced a line of grinding wheels, extended its chemical business into the area of "organo-metallic" compounds for use in paints and plastics, and developed a line of heat-treating and metal-forming equipment. In 1959, sales of machine tools, cutting fluid, and grinding wheels constituted 83 percent of total sales, so that it still fell in the Dominant-Constrained class.

Between 1959 and 1969 Milacron introduced a line of plastic-processing machinery and a laminator for printed circuits. The machine tool business was radically altered by the new technology of numerical control, and Milacron developed a competence in special purpose computers, software, and the design and development of automated systems for metal forming, machining, and industrial process control. In 1969 Milacron began to market a special purpose digital computer; its sales of machine tools had dropped to 73 percent of total sales. It was categorized as Dominant-Linked for 1969.

SUMMARY OF DIVERSIFICATION CATEGORIES

Four major categories of diversification strategy have been defined, and all but the Single Business category have been further divided into subcategories, giving a total of nine different classifications. Figure 1.5 presents a flow diagram that describes the process of categorizing a firm and Figure 1.6 provides a graphic clarification of the relationships between the ratio criteria and the categories. To facilitate further reference to the diversification categories the following condensed descriptions are provided:

• A firm's *diversification strategy* is defined as its commitment to diversity per se, together with the strengths, skills or purposes that span this diversity, shown by the way in which business activities are related one to another.

• The primary measure of diversity is taken to be the *specialization ratio,* defined as the proportion of a firm's revenues that is attributable to its largest discrete product-market activity. A *discrete business* (or product-market activity) is one that is strategically independent of the firm's other businesses in that basic changes in its nature and scope can be made without meeting constraints imposed by other of the firm's businesses and without materially affecting the operation and strategic direction of other of the firm's businesses.

• Businesses are related to one another when a common skill, resource, market, or purpose applies to each. A firm's *related ratio* is defined as the proportion of its revenues that are attributable to the largest group of businesses that are related in some way to one another. Each member of this group need only be related to one other business in the group (linked relatedness), though it may be related to all and all may be directly related to one another (constrained relatedness).

• The *vertical ratio* is defined as the proportion of a firm's revenues attributable to all of the by-products, intermediate products, and final products of a vertically integrated sequence of manufacturing operations.

In any given year a firm's diversification strategy may be described as corresponding to one of the following categories:

(1) *Single Business:* firms that are basically committed to a single business. Among nonvertically integrated firms ($VR < 0.7$), Single Business companies are those with specialization ratios of 0.95 or more. Among vertically integrated firms ($VR \geqq 0.7$), those that have an end-product business that con-

FIGURE 1.5. Assigning Diversification Categories.

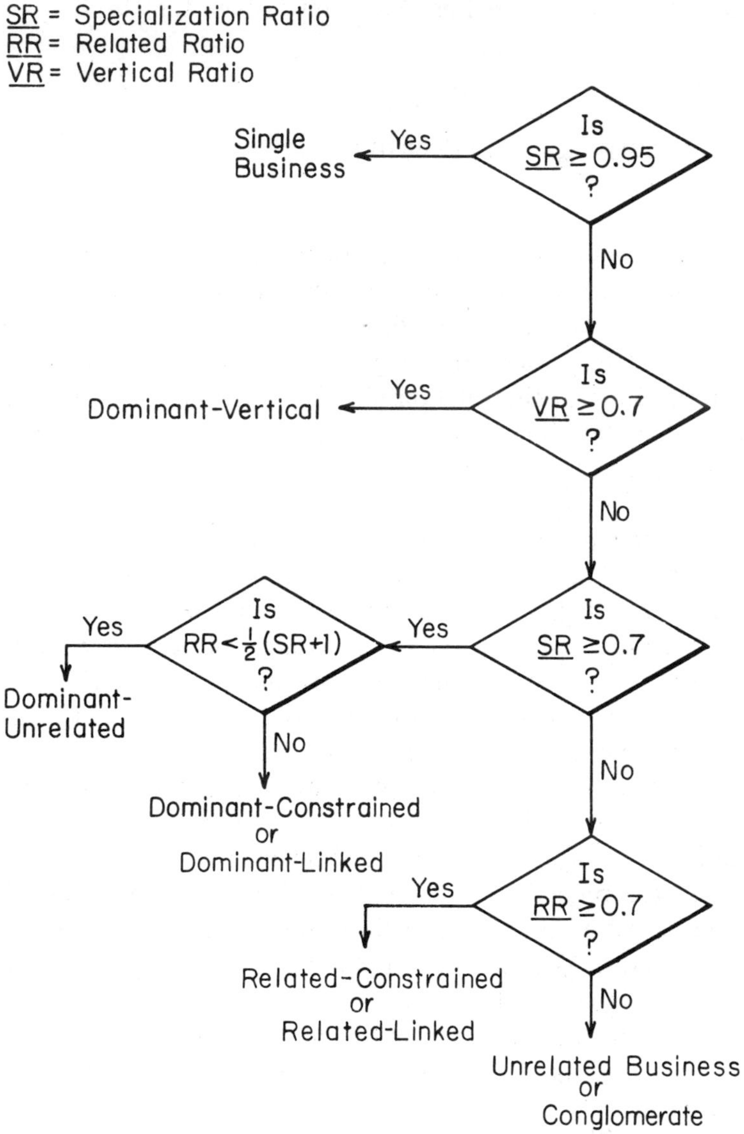

$\underline{SR}$ = Specialization Ratio
$\underline{RR}$ = Related Ratio
$\underline{VR}$ = Vertical Ratio

tributes 95 percent or more of total revenues are classified as Single Business firms.

(2) *Dominant Business:* firms that have diversified to some extent but still obtain the preponderance of their revenues from a single business. Among nonvertically integrated firms ($VR < 0.7$), those with specialization ratios greater than or equal to 0.7 but less than 0.95 are Dominant Business firms. Among vertically integrated firms ($VR \geqq 0.7$), those that do not qualify as Single Business companies fall into the Dominant category.

(a) *Dominant-Vertical:* vertically integrated firms (having vertical ratios

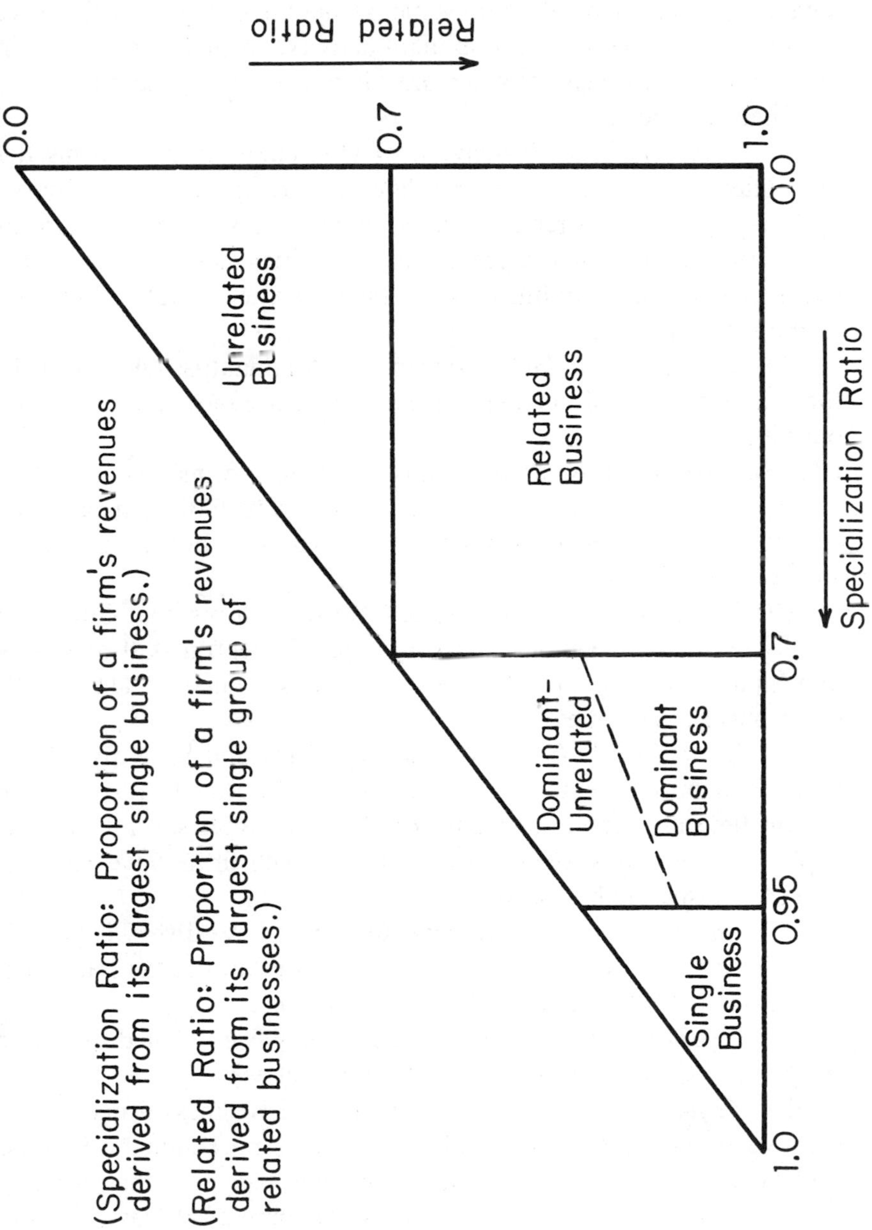
(Specialization Ratio: Proportion of a firm's revenues derived from its largest single business.)
(Related Ratio: Proportion of a firm's revenues derived from its largest single group of related businesses.)
Related Ratio
0.0
0.7
1.0
Unrelated Business
Related Business
Dominant-Unrelated
Dominant Business
Single Business
1.0
0.95
0.7
0.0
Specialization Ratio

FIGURE 1.6. Strategic Classes Defined in Terms of the Specialization Ratio and the Related Ratio.

of 0.7 or more) that produce and sell a variety of end products, no one of which contributes more than 95 percent of total revenues.

(b) *Dominant-Constrained:* nonvertical Dominant Business firms that have diversified by building on some particular strength, skills, or resource associated with the original dominant activity. In such firms the preponderance of the diversified activities are all related one to another and to the dominant business.

(c) *Dominant-Linked:* nonvertical Dominant Business firms that have diversified by building on several different strengths, skills, or resources or by building on new strengths, skills, or resources as they are acquired. In such firms the preponderance of the diversified activities are not directly related to the dominant business but each is somehow related to some other of the firm's activities.

(d) *Dominant-Unrelated:* nonvertical Dominant Business firms in which the preponderance of the diversified activities are unrelated to the dominant business.

(3) *Related Business:* nonvertically integrated firms that are diversified, having specialization ratios less than 0.7, and in which diversification has been primarily accomplished by relating new activities to old, so that the related ratio is 0.7 or more.

(a) *Related-Constrained:* Related Business firms that have diversified chiefly by relating new businesses to a specific central skill or resource and in which, therefore, each business activity is related to almost all of the other business activities.

(b) *Related-Linked:* Related Business firms that have diversified by relating new businesses to some strength or skill already possessed, but not always the same strength or skill. By diversifying in several directions and exploiting new skills as they are acquired, such firms have become active in widely disparate businesses.

(4) *Unrelated Business:* nonvertical firms that have diversified chiefly without regard to relationships between new businesses and current activities. Such firms are defined by a related ratio of less than 0.7.

(a) *Unrelated-Passive:* Unrelated Business firms that do not qualify as Acquisitive Conglomerates (see definition below).

(b) *Acquisitive Conglomerates:* Unrelated Business firms that have aggressive programs for the acquisition of new unrelated businesses. More specifically, such firms are defined as having had, over the past five years, (1) an average growth rate in earnings per share of at least 10 percent per year; (2) made at least five acquisitions, at least three of which took the firm into businesses unrelated to past activities; and (3) issued new equity shares whose total value (using market prices at the time of issue) was at least as great as the total amount of common dividends paid during the same period.

CATEGORIES OF ORGANIZATIONAL STRUCTURE

No two firms possess the same organizational structure and the number of possible structures is virtually unlimited. As in the case of diversification, the enormous complexity of reality will be simplified by looking at the firm from the "top down," focusing on the major organizational options open to top management and their potential impact on the general management task.

General management entails the management of a complete economic unit: a firm or a subunit of a firm that has sufficient resources and autonomy to act on its own behalf in the market place. A manager whose responsibilities include the design, development, manufacture, and sale of any particular product or set of products is a general manager, since he commands a complete economic unit. On the other hand, a manager whose task is, for example, the efficient production of automobiles, trucks, and tractors, perhaps on a worldwide scale, is not a general manager; his responsibilities are functional and must be coordinated with the engineering, research, marketing, and finance functions on a routine basis.

Consideration of the commonly employed variations in the organizational locus of general management activity and the rationale for specialization of major organizational subunits leads directly to three basic categories of organization. In the *functional* structure the major subunits deal with business functions, such as sales, engineering, and production, rather than complete businesses. General management occurs solely at the topmost level and the coordination of the functional subunits is one of its important responsibilities. In *product-division* organizations the organization is split into a number of quasi-autonomous divisions, each headed by a general manager and supplied with the resources necessary for it to operate as an independent economic entity. The product-division structure implies the existence of at least two levels of general management and an increase in the number of general management roles over that of the functional structure. Figure 1.7 shows the organization chart of a typical functional organization and Figure 1.8 that of a product-division organization. Both charts are suggestive rather than definitive.

Organizational structure, however, consists of a great deal more than the differences that can be shown by charts. Systems of control, planning and information flow, methods of reward and punishment, the degree of delegation and techniques of coordination are among the important determinants of the way of life within the enterprise. The usefulness of the distinction between functional and multidivision organizations depends upon the degree to which these structures are associated with consistent differences among many other

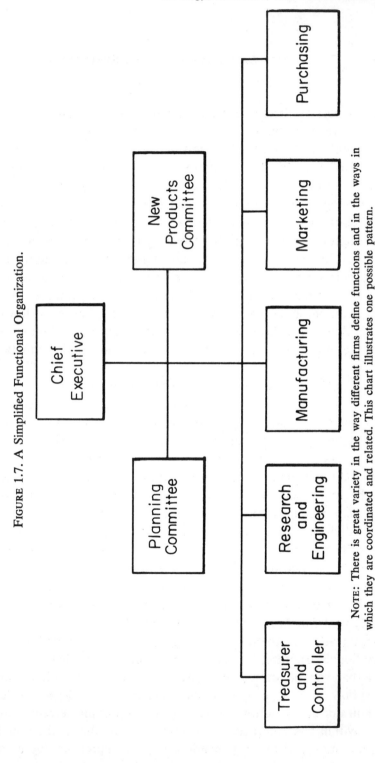

FIGURE 1.7. A Simplified Functional Organization.

NOTE: There is great variety in the way different firms define functions and in the ways in which they are coordinated and related. This chart illustrates one possible pattern.

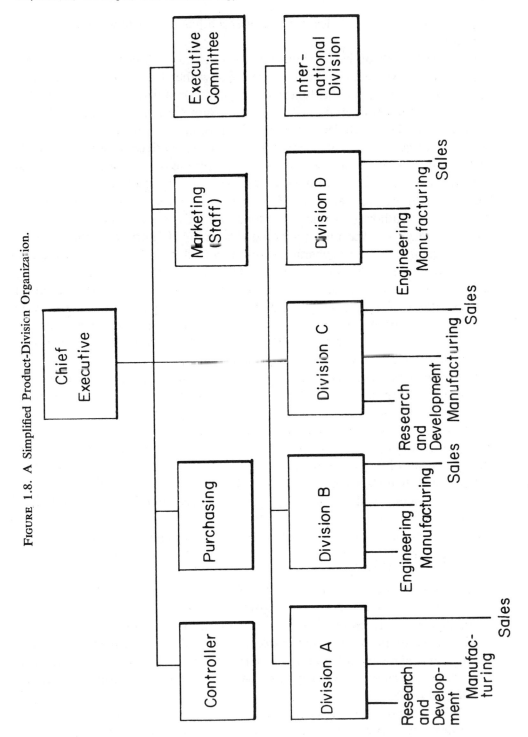

FIGURE 1.8. A Simplified Product-Division Organization.

organizational characteristics. Recent research has shown that such uniformities do exist.

Chandler's study of the development of seventy large American corporations was, in part, devoted to an examination of how the strategy of diversification placed great strains on the functional type of organization and led to the adoption of the product-division structure. Summarizing the impact of this change, Chandler concluded that the multidivisional organization, by creating two levels of general management "removed the executives responsible for the destiny of the entire enterprise from the more routine operational activities and so gave them the time, information, and even psychological commitment for long-term planning and appraisal. Conversely, it placed the responsibility and the necessary authority for the operational administration in the hands of the general managers of the multifunction divisions." [11] He also noted that in addition to freeing a group of generalists from day to day problems, the headquarters office of a multidivisional structure, because it is not associated with any particular business area, can develop staffs to supply objective information on the operations of each business, thus providing the framework for relatively unbiased evaluations of performance. These evaluations can then offer the division managers a more comprehensive view of their businesses than might be supplied by their own staff.

Following Chandler, Scott developed a paradigm of corporate development that views the firm as moving through successive stages as its product-market relationships become more elaborate.[12] In this "stages model," the firm is seen as growing from a "one-man show" to a functionally organized structure and then, as it develops multiple product lines, to a product-division structure. Since the firms of interest in the present research have all grown past the point of being one-man shows, that portion of the model will not be discussed here. The stages model predicts these differences between functional and multidivisional organizations:

(1) Research and development in functional organizations tend to focus on product and process improvement while in multidivisional firms R & D also stresses the search for new products.

(2) Performance criteria in functional firms tend to be based on technical and/or cost measures while product-division firms tend to employ market-based measures such as return on investment and market share.

(3) Rewards in multidivisional organizations tend to be based on formal systems that relate rewards to market performance while functional firms tend to have less systematic reward systems and base them on functional efficiency and stability.

(4) The major strategic choices considered by top management in functional firms tend to center on the desired degree of integration, market share

---

[11] Chandler, *Strategy and Structure,* p. 382.
[12] Scott, "Stages of Corporate Development."

and the breadth of the product line. In multidivisional firms top level strategy is concerned with entry and exit from businesses, allocation of resources among businesses, the overall rate of growth, and the balance between internal expansion and growth by acquisition.

In addition, Scott has pointed out that multidivisional organizations act as "a built-in 'school of management,' training middle-level general managers in the problems and opportunities associated with economic responsibility. As a result, this form of organization provides a pool of trained talent from which to draw, a pool from which a new group may be formed in a few days or weeks to take over and manage a new activity." [13]

In addition to the support provided by Chandler's data, Salter's research has tended to confirm those portions of the stages model that deal with reward and control systems. Ackerman has provided some additional support for the hypothesized resource allocation differences.[14] Salter has also suggested that a fourth type of structure, the geographic-division organization, corresponds to a definite stage in corporate development. Somewhat similar to the product division structure, the geographic-division structure is characterized by semi-autonomous divisions each of which operates in a different geographical area, though frequently all deal with the same range of products. Although few firms among the largest 500 possess this type of structure, it is included in the classification scheme for the sake of completeness.

Many of the differences noted above seem to favor the multidivisional structure, perhaps giving the impression that the functional structure is an outmoded holdover from the past. Such a conclusion is unwarranted. While the multidivisional structure is generally thought to be superior in situations in which the firm has many diverse products and the economic and technological environments are subject to rapid change, research by Lawrence and Lorsch and others has indicated that functional organizations tend to perform well or better than divisionalized organizations when environmental change is slow and the product line is not too broad.[15]

All of these arguments offer assurance that these organizational categories do not just reflect superficial differences in how activities are grouped, but represent substantial differences in kind among a wide range of organizational properties. In addition to these, two other categories were used in this research: the *holding company* and the *functional-with-subsidiaries* organizations. Although there is no empirical evidence on the subject, it is expected that these categories also represent organizational patterns that are significantly different in kind.

---

[13] Ibid., p. 14.

[14] Malcolm S. Salter, "Stages of Corporate Development," *Journal of Business Policy,* Vol 1, No. 1 (1970), pp. 40–51; and Robert W. Ackerman, "The Impact of Integration and Diversity on the Investment Process" (unpublished paper, Harvard Business School, 1969).

[15] Paul R. Lawrence and Jay W. Lorsch, *Organization and Environment* (Boston: Harvard Business School, Division of Research, 1967).

The holding company consists of a set of virtually independent firms that are owned and, at least legally, controlled by a parent corporation. Its distinguishing characteristic is the almost complete lack of management at the top. Each unit (or division) operates autonomously, with quarterly dividend payments to the parent often being the only visible connection between it and the rest of the company. The headquarters office is quite small, usually composed of only a few individuals who carry out financial, legal and other activities that must be performed by the parent.

It is important to note that *holding company* is also a legal term that refers to a particular type of corporation. While the *legal* holding company may have a structure similar to the one described here, there are holding companies that engage in much more thorough supervision of their constituent corporations. On the other hand, firms that are not *legal* holding companies may have organizations like the one described here. Thus, the holding company organization is not necessarily associated with firms that in legal terms are holding companies.

The *functional-with-subsidiaries* organization is a hybrid form that does not seem to have received prior attention in the literature. It is often employed by vertically integrated firms with some side activities and by firms that are moving from functional to product-division structures. Figure 1.9 shows a typical organization of this type. It is clear from the diagram that the functional-with-subsidiaries organization consists of a functional structure with one or more product divisions also reporting to top management (or in some instances to functional management). Usually, the functional part of the organization controls most of the firm's activities and the divisions exist to carry out side ventures, new experimental businesses, or have been added by diversification through acquisition. The critical feature of this structure is the lack of a true multidivisional type of headquarters office. General managers of the divisions are organizationally on a par with functional managers in the major area, and the central office must be active in day to day management of the major area and cannot gain a detached view of the firm as a whole. It is expected that the degree to which headquarters-division relationships in this type of firm approaches the product division pattern will be very sensitive to the detailed make-up of the headquarters office.

The five organizational categories can be summarized as follows:

(1) *Functional:* an organization in which the major subunits are defined in terms of the business functions of stages in the manufacturing process. Responsibility for coordination and product-market performance rests with the chief executive, his staff, and committees. Vertically integrated firms fall in this class despite the common practice of referring to their process-linked subunits as divisions.

(2) *Functional with Subsidiaries:* an organization that is basically functional but which also has one or more separate product divisions (not neces-

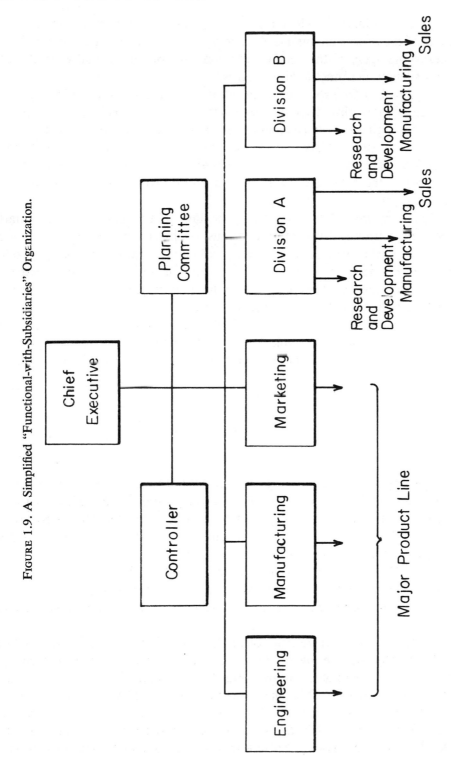

FIGURE 1.9. A Simplified "Functional-with-Subsidiaries" Organization.

sarily true subsidiaries) which report to top management or, in some instances, to one of the functional managers. The distinguishing characteristic is that the general managers of the product divisions are organizationally on the same level or below the functional managers.

(3) *Product Division:* an organization that consists of a central office and a group of operating divisions, each having the responsibility and resources needed to engineer, produce, and market a product or set of products. In some instances the product divisions are clustered into groups and a third line of general management is placed between the division and headquarters. At some point below the division level, the organization reverts to a functional or geographic form.

(4) *Geographic Division:* an organization that consists of a headquarters office and a group of operating divisions, each having the responsibility and resources needed to engineer, produce, and market a product or set of products in a different geographic area. The areas may be portions of the United States or multinational. At some point below the division level the form of organization reverts to a functional or product form.

(5) *Holding Company:* an association of firms (or divisions) commonly owned by a parent corporation. Each firm is virtually autonomous and formal organization above the level of the individual firm is virtually nonexistent.

METHODOLOGY AND SOURCES

The group studied was taken to be the 500 largest United States industrial companies, as listed annually by *Fortune* magazine. To qualify as a member of the *Fortune* 500 a company must be (1) based in the United States; (2) derive at least 50 percent of its revenues from manufacturing or mining; (3) provide public reports on its financial status; and (4) be among the largest 500 such companies in terms of consolidated revenues. Excise taxes collected by the firm for the federal government are not included in revenues, a fact of some importance in the case of companies in the liquor and beer industry.

A study of the characteristics of the largest 500 firms cannot be based on a single sample, because the set of corporations changes over time as firms grow in relation to one another or are merged or acquired. It was decided that the data requirements could be met with three independent random samples of the largest 500 firms in 1949, 1959, and 1969. The 1969 sample was constructed by taking the 100 firms that Wrigley had selected randomly from the 1967 *Fortune* 500, deleting those which were no longer among the largest 500 in 1969 and randomly selecting firms from the 1969 group to take their places. The 1959 sample was constructed by randomly selecting 100 firms from the *Fortune* 500 in that year. The 1949 sample, however, could not be obtained in this way, since *Fortune* first began publishing its list of the 500 largest industrials in 1953. The only document to come close to a list of the largest 500 firms in 1949 was a Federal Trade Commission report that gave (in alphabetical order) the 100, 200, 500, and 1,000 largest industrial firms, in terms of assets, in 1950.

A sample was constructed from this list of the 500 largest firms by arranging them in a random order and then selecting the first 100 firms from this new list that met certain criteria. To be selected a firm had to be a United States industrial in the sense used by *Fortune,* in existence in 1949, and not have had a sales-to-assets ratio that was substantially lower than that of other large firms. Unfortunately, this procedure could not avoid a bias against selecting companies with high sales and low assets in 1949, since they were not on the Federal Trade Commission list in the first place. This bias exists in the 1949 sample and its effect, although probably quite small, is difficult to estimate.

Some firms appeared in more than one of the samples, and the three independent random samples of 100 firms consisted in total of 249 industrial firms. Three firms were subsequently dropped because of insufficient data on their mix of products and organizations. This reduced the sample sizes for 1949, 1959, and 1969 to 100, 100, and 97 respectively and reduced the total number of individual firms under study to 246.

For each of the 246 firms a set of primary data was gathered and placed on a computer disk file. All subsequent analyses were carried out by manipulating the information in this file. Its contents included:

(1) An abbreviated form of the corporate name.

(2) The sample or samples (1949, 1959, or 1969) in which the firm appeared.

(3) The firm's rank among the 500 largest industrials in 1959 and 1969.

(4) If the firm was not in existence in 1949, the year it came into being and the way in which it was created: incorporated, resulting from a merger of two firms, with neither surviving, or previously part of a larger enterprise and divested.

(5) If the firm was not in existence or no longer qualified as a United States industrial by the end of 1969, the last year in which it was a valid member of the sample and the reason for its exit: acquired, merged with another firm with neither surviving, no longer based in the United States, no longer an industrial firm (more than 50 percent revenue from other than manufacturing or mining).

(6) The firm's specialization ratio in 1949, 1959, and 1969.

(7) The firm's related ratio in 1949, 1959, and 1969.

(8) The firm's vertical ratio in 1949, 1959, and 1969.

(9) The firm's diversification category in 1949, 1959, and 1969.

(10) The firm's organizational structure category in each year it was a valid member of the sample.

(11) The four-digit SIC code assigned to the firm by Standard & Poor's.

(12) A list of the identifiable businesses in which the firm had been active during the time it was a valid member of the sample. For each business a short description, the appropriate SIC code, and the year of exit, if any, was recorded. In addition, if the firm had entered the business after it became a valid member of the sample, the year of entry, and the method (internal development or acquisition) was recorded.

(13) Financial data for the years 1951–1970 for most of the firms still in existence in 1970. This data included annual consolidated figures for net sales, common dividends, earnings after tax and preferred dividends, interest expense, number of common shares outstanding adjusted for splits and stock dividends, the average of the high and low stock prices for the year, long-term debt, total equity, and total assets.

In addition to this formal data base, extensive files were kept, which contained a variety of descriptive and interpretive information on each company. Information on the history of the firms, their entries into and exits from businesses and their product mix at particular points in time was gathered chiefly from *Moody's Industrials, The Thomas Register of American Manufacturers,* corporate annual reports to stockholders, and prospectuses accompanying the issue of corporate securities. When necessary, books and articles about a particular firm were also consulted. The most constantly elusive information was the necessary breakdown of the firms' revenues by product-area in order to compute the specialization ratio, related ratio, and vertical ratio. The richest source of these data proved to be prospectuses. The legal requirement for the inclusion of all relevant information in these documents often produced quite a different view of the firm from that presented in annual reports. Still, in many instances the product mix had to be estimated from data that bracketed, but did not include, the year in question. In a few cases, no estimates could be made.

Specialization ratios, related ratios, and, if applicable, vertical ratios for each firm for 1949, 1959, and 1969 were estimated from the available data on revenue breakdowns by product. Whenever a ratio could be estimated to within an accuracy of ± 0.05 it was recorded. In over one third of the cases, this precision was unobtainable, either because the data were too sparse or because there was difficulty in identifying discrete businesses. However, since the ratios' major use was in determining diversification categories, the lack of accurate estimates was not a serious problem—for classification purposes it was only necessary to know if the specialization ratio lay in the range 0.7 to 0.95 or if it was above or below that range, and if the related and vertical ratios were above or below 0.7.

One of the nine strategic diversification categories was assigned to each firm for 1949, 1959, and 1969, except for those years in which a firm was not a valid member of the sample. The major category was determined by the estimated value (or range) of the various ratios and the subcategory was assigned by examining the firm's rationale for diversification, its product mix, the methods of entry into each business, and the degree to which potential relationships had been exploited. Most of this qualitative information was obtained by reading through twenty years of annual reports for each firm. In a few instances, the corporation's annual reports were so lacking in information or so abstract that books, newspapers and magazine articles and investors' surveys that dealt with the firm had to be consulted.

In two cases (Avco and Canada Dry in 1949) strategic categories were assigned that did not coincide with the values of the specialization and related ratios for that year. In both instances, the ratios were close to the critical value 0.7 and their values in nearby years indicated that the 1949 values were atypical. Hence, classification was based on the more normal values of the ratios.

Information on organizational structures was gathered from a wide variety of sources. Chandler's *Strategy and Structure* briefly discussed the organizational histories of seventy large industrials, and where his sample coincided with ours his observations on structure were used. A National Industrial Conference Board publication, *Corporate Organization Structure* by Stieglitz and Wilkenson, gave 1967 organizational charts for sixty-six firms, many of which were in the research samples. Other NICB books and pamphlets mentioned in passing or gave as examples the organizational structures of some of the firms in the sample. Two American Management Association publications were also useful; *Understanding the Company Organization Chart* by White and *Organizing the R & D Function* by Stanley and White provided charts and discussions of the organizational development that applied to several firms in the sample. Another useful source was *Corporate Diagrams and Administrative Personnel of the Chemical Industry* by Kern, which gave organization charts of chemical divisions and subsidiaries of oil companies and other diversified corporations.

Over half the information on structure, however, came from annual reports. Although any particular annual report, taken by itself, is a poor source of data on this subject, a twenty-year sequence of annual reports often reveals a great deal, especially when the structure at some point in time is known in advance. The titles assigned to key executives frequently provided important clues to structural change, as did discussions of how new acquisitions were

integrated into the firm and descriptions of the responsibilities of newly pro-
moted managers. Of course major reorganizations were almost always noted
in annual reports and perusal of the preceding and following reports usually
clarified the natures of the previous and new structures.

Although the original research plan only called for assigning organization
categories to the firms in the sample at three points in time, 1949, 1959, and
1969, because most structures were deduced by working forwards and back-
wards in time from evidence of a reorganization, data were available on structure on a year-by-year basis. Therefore, organization categories were assigned
to each firm for each year it was a valid member of the sample.

Data on individual diversification moves came from annual reports and
Moody's Industrials. The procedure followed was to first list every move that
might be considered a diversification move for each firm in the sample. Then,
given the benefit of this experience, moves were deleted that were judged to
be basically product line extensions, follow-up moves to previous diversification moves, or insignificant.[16]

The financial information was obtained from a computer data bank maintained by The Boston Company. These data had been originally obtained from
Standard and Poor's, providing twenty years (1951–1970) of annual observations on sixty financial variables for about 1,750 corporations. The financial
reporting was on a consolidated basis and had been adjusted by Standard and
Poor's to provide reasonable interfirm consistency in methods. One drawback
associated with this data base is that it includes only firms that existed in 1970.
Consequently, no financial data were available for the many companies in the
1949 and 1959 samples that were acquired in the late 1960s. Since the accepted practice in maintaining such data banks is to eliminate the information
on firms that become defunct, all other similar sources posed the same difficulty. The alternative of gathering the missing data from published sources
was deemed too time consuming and better left to experts. Consequently, the
financial data used in this research pertains only to firms still in existence in
1970 and is therefore biased in favor of surviving rather than acquired companies.

Since the 1969 sample used in the research was taken directly from Wrigley's
study, a comparison can be made between the classification of these firms by
Wrigley and the classifications assigned in this research. Such comparison can
point out those portions of the system that are most sensitive to the researcher's
subjective judgment. Wrigley's classification did not, however, influence the
classifications made for the current study; the comparison was not even attempted until the study was completed. The results are shown below:

---

[16] Appendix C has been prepared to provide a succinct summary of the nonfinancial data
used in the study. It contains a list of the 246 firms in the total sample and gives for each
(for 1949, 1959, and 1969) its important businesses, rank in the 500, specialization ratio,
related ratio, assigned diversification strategy, and assigned structure class.

	Percentage in Category	
Category	This Study 1969 Sample	Wrigley's 1967 Sample
Single Business	7.6	6.0
Dominant Business	31.0	14.0
Related Business	45.2	60.0
Unrelated Business	16.2	20.0

Of the 87 firms that were common to both studies, 28 were classified differently. Investigation of the source of discrepancies revealed that 14 percent were due to changes in the status of the firms between 1967 and 1969 (Wrigley used 1967 data), 7 percent were due to firms Wrigley classed as Related but which here fell into the Dominant-Vertical category, and 25 percent were due to the stricter conditions for placement in the Unrelated Business category used in this study. Fifty-four percent of the discrepancies were due to differences in judgment or data, the former being more important. The pronounced disagreement on the proportion of firms in the Dominant and Related Business categories was largely due to differences in judgment, the critical issue being the definition of a discrete business. The precise nature of the difference in the concept of a discrete business held in these two studies is difficult to determine, since the classification of firms was of secondary importance in Wrigley's study and he did not supply detailed operational definitions. Perhaps the definitions and examples provided in this study will insure a greater degree of comparability with future research.

SUMMARY AND COMMENTS

There is usually an underlying logic behind the development of a corporation over time—a logic we call "strategy," which includes, but need not be expressed in terms of, the microeconomics surrounding the production and sale of each of the firm's products. We chose to study diversification and structure by viewing the firm as a whole rather than as a host of separate pieces. Thus, instead of concentrating on individual diversification moves or on the total number of product-market activities, we have attempted to take the viewpoint of the top-level general manager and characterize the firm in terms of the total amount of diversity inherent in its strategic posture and the way in which business areas have been related to one another. This "top down" approach led to the definition of four major categories of diversification strategy, which were further subdivided to give a total of nine distinct classes of strategy.

The procedure used in classifying firms mixed quantitative measures and qualitative assessments. Of these, the most crucial were the decision as to what constitutes a firm's largest discrete business and the evaluation of the nature of the interrelationships among a firm's businesses. While the use of this type of classification system permits the consideration of nonquantifiable data, the apparent preciseness of definite category boundaries must not obscure the fact that the researcher's judgment plays an important role in the technique. In the present context this type of semisubjective technique has several strengths: (1) it permits the direct consideration of the most important, though nonquantifiable, aspects of the firm's strategy; (2) it is easy to understand and does not require the processing of complex multidimensional data; and (3) the constant need for judgment on the part of the researcher provides a continual check on the validity and usefulness of the conceptual framework. Of course, these advantages are only obtained by sacrificing a degree of objectivity and replicability. Since others have studied diversification by using "objective" measures, such as the product count and other indices, it was felt that creating another similar piece of research was not as important as exploring the possibility that a measurement scheme based on overall corporate strategy might yield different results.

CHAPTER 2

Changing Patterns
of Strategy and Structure

T HIS CHAPTER PRESENTS THE RESULTS of applying the strategic and organizational classification schemes to each of the 246 firms in the sample and begins the work of piecing together a composite picture of the changing patterns of strategy and structure among the largest 500 industrial corporations. As data are presented, several important problems will be discussed: the extent of diversification among large industrial corporations; the proportions of the largest 500 firms that fall into each of the diversification and structural categories and how these proportions have changed with time; the extent to which changes have been due to strategic and organizational change by firms rather than the changing composition of the 500; and whether there is evidence of a cause and effect relationship between strategic and structural change. All the estimates presented in this chapter were obtained by applying a weighting procedure to a stratification of the sample of 246 firms. The technique used to obtain these weighted estimates is described in Appendix A.

The use of strategic categories based on a mixture of quantitative and qualitative criteria breaks with the traditional techniques for measuring diversification. Although one of Gort's diversification indices and the measure used by Stopford were essentially equivalent to the specialization ratio used in this research, using this ratio together with information on the degree and nature of the relationships among business areas to define discrete categories was an innovation of Wrigley's, whose work was the immediate predecessor to and stimulus for this study.[1] Most prior research on diversification was based on

---

[1] See Gort, *Diversification and Integration in American Industry;* and Stopford, "Growth and Change in the Multinational Firm."

some type of product count, usually employing the product classes of the Standard Industrial Classification (SIC) system. Because of the wealth of data that has been accumulated on product-count measures of diversification, it is of interest to determine the extent to which such measures correspond to our diversification categories and thus the extent to which they might serve as surrogates for the categories.

In order to carry out a comparison, the number of 2-digit and 3-digit industries in which each firm in the sample participated was determined for 1949, 1959, and 1969. Neither the 2-digit nor the 3-digit measure is actually a "product count" as the degree of aggregation is quite high in 3-digit categories and the 2-digit categories correspond to entire industrial sectors such as food processing (SIC, 20), primary metals (SIC, 33), and so on. A true product count, however, would require the use of at least the 4-digit level of detail and probably should be based upon 5- or even 7-digit SIC categories. Nevertheless, a great many studies have used 3-digit and 2-digit categories as the measures of diversification both because of the difficulty of obtaining very detailed data and the observed high degree of correlation between measures at various levels of detail.

The data on 2-digit and 3-digit industry participation for each firm in the sample was obtained from annual reports, Moody's, and Standard and Poor's. In most cases, lists of the different SIC categories in which a firm was active were not used; they frequently conflicted with one another and with the actual data on products. If no mention of a product could be found in annual reports or standard references, it was assumed that it was either not produced or produced in inconsequential amounts.

Table 2-1 shows for each major strategic category the average number of 2-digit and 3-digit industries in which firms in that category were active and the standard deviations from these averages.

The pattern of average "industry count" was predictable; there was a trend in time toward increased diversification in all categories. The order of categories in terms of increasing numbers of industries participated in was Single, Dominant, Related, and Unrelated. The correspondence is far from precise, however. For example, several Single Business firms were, in 1969, active in more than one industry sector. Central Soya, in 1969, was basically a soybean processor, but it had products in SIC 204 (milling), SIC 281 (chemical by-products), SIC 130 (poultry production) and SIC 287 (agricultural chemicals). Nonetheless, the overwhelming preponderance of its revenues came from soy milling, so that it was classed as a Single Business firm in that year.

The undue weight given to minor activities is one of the major arguments against the product or industry count measure of diversification. Using a 4-digit level of detail, Gort noted that

It is rather surprising to find that for a majority of the 111 large enterprises, minor activities accounted for a substantial proportion of the total

TABLE 2-1. PARTICIPATION IN TWO- AND THREE-DIGIT INDUSTRIES
BY STRATEGIC CLASS.

	1949		1959		1969	
	Mean	Standard Deviation	Mean	Standard Deviation	Mean	Standard Deviation
			2-Digit Industries			
Single Business	1.33	0.88	1.23	0.50	1.39	0.77
Dominant Business	2.05	1.29	2.63	1.50	3.72	2.34
Related Business	2.50	1.72	3.37	2.08	4.63	2.52
Unrelated Business	4.29	2.87	5.14	2.57	7.90	3.03
			3-Digit Industries			
Single Business	1.46	1.00	1.42	0.85	1.77	1.17
Dominant Business	2.87	1.90	3.87	2.31	5.75	3.59
Related Business	4.03	2.89	5.57	3.83	8.12	4.38
Unrelated Business	6.86	3.81	8.71	4.63	12.21	5.35

NOTE: The Smirnov test was used to test the significance of the differences in industry participation among classes, each class being tested against each other class. For participation in 2-digit industries, these differences were *not* significant at the 0.1 level: between Dominant and Related firms in all years, between Related and Unrelated firms in 1949 and 1959, and between Dominant and Unrelated firms in 1949. For participation in 3-digit industries, the only differences not significant at the 0.1 level were between Related and Unrelated firms in 1949 and 1959. All other differences were significant at the 0.02 level. It appears that an increase in the number of Unrelated firms in the sample would have altered these results.

number of industrial activities in which the companies were engaged. In six of the thirteen groups (2-digit industries) at least one third of the manufacturing activities (4-digit product areas) individually contributed not more than 1 per cent to the manufacturing employment of their companies.[2]

The arbitrary nature of the SIC classifications is the other major source of inconsistency. A manufacturer of paper cups who adds a line of plastic cups is seen as entering a new industrial sector, according to the SIC system. The strategic category technique, while not having the degree of "objectivity" generally accorded to the SIC system, permits the researcher to choose to ignore the difference between paper and plastic in this case and call the firm a Single Business company.

A feeling for the degree of correspondence between the strategic categories and the industry count can be obtained by determining the industry count levels that provide the best possible discrimination among categories and measuring the resulting amount of overlap. In 1969, for example, the following scheme for assigning strategic classes using a 2-digit industry count would have produced the *least* number of misclassifications:

---

[2] Gort, *Diversification and Integration,* p. 35.

Category	Trial Criterion: Number of 2-Digit Industries Engaged In	Percentage of Firms in Categories Misclassified
Single Business	1	23
Dominant Business	2–3	62
Related Business	4–6	59
Unrelated Business	7 or more	41

The outcome of such a scheme would have been the placement of over half the firms in categories other than the ones assigned to them on the basis of specialization ratios, related ratios, and qualitative information. The major conflicts are caused by Dominant Business firms active in several sectors, and Unrelated firms active in few.

The conclusion is inescapable that the strategic categories reflect characteristics that are significantly different from those measured by a product or industry count, and, consequently, a product- or industry-count measure cannot serve as surrogate for the strategic categories.

STRATEGIES OF DIVERSIFICATION

Weighted estimates of the percentages of the 500 largest industrial corporations that fell within the four major and nine minor categories of diversification strategy are shown in Table 2-2. The same information is portrayed graphically in Figure 2.1. Both reveal a most dramatic pattern of change. Between 1949 and 1969 the number of truly diversified corporations more than doubled; the percentage of firms following Related or Unrelated Business strategies of expansion rose from 30 percent to 65 percent in this twenty-year period. Clearly, there has been a basic change in the product-market scope of the largest industrial corporations in the United States.

The most striking change in any individual group is the decline in the number of Single Business firms among the largest 500. Comprising more than one third of the 500 in 1949, by 1969 firms deriving 95 percent or more of their revenues from one business had dropped to 6.2 percent of the total. Equally noteworthy was the increase in large firms that follow Unrelated Business strategies. In 1949 this group accounted for only 3.4 percent of the 500 largest firms, but by 1969 one out of every five firms fell into the Unrelated category. Somewhat surprising is the evidence that this increase was *not* all due to growing numbers of Acquisitive Conglomerates; in 1969 fully 44 percent of Unrelated Business firms were Unrelated-Passive and 60 percent of these had appeared since 1949.

TABLE 2-2. Estimated Percentage of Firms in Each Strategic Category.

Strategic Category	1949	1959	1969
Major Classes			
Single Business	34.5	16.2	6.2
Dominant Business	35.4	37.3	29.2
Related Business	26.7	40.0	45.2
Unrelated Business	3.4	6.5	19.4
Minor Classes			
Single Business	34.5	16.2	6.2
Dominant-Vertical	15.7	14.8	15.6
Dominant-Constrained	18.0	16.0	7.1
Dominant-Linked	0.9	3.8	5.6
Dominant-Unrelated	0.9	2.6	0.9
Related-Constrained	18.8	29.1	21.6
Related-Linked	7.9	10.9	23.6
Unrelated-Passive	3.4	5.3	8.5
Acquisitive Conglomerate	0.0	1.2	10.9
Total number of firms used to derive the estimates	189	207	183

NOTE: Estimates were made using the weighting procedure described in the text.

The relative importance of the Dominant Business category, as a whole, decreased slightly during this twenty-year period, although it appears to have grown between 1949 and 1959 and then diminished by more than this amount in the second decade. The behavior of subclasses of the Dominant category shed some light on how this happened. The Dominant-Vertical group was extremely stable, accounting for about 75 of the top 500 firms throughout the period. As would be expected, most of the giant companies in oil, steel, aluminum, and forest products neither left the top 500 nor became truly diversified during these twenty years. The Dominant-Constrained group, on the other hand, became much smaller between 1959 and 1969, dropping from 16 percent to 7.1 percent of the top 500; this decrease is the chief reason for the overall drop in the size of the Dominant Business category. The Dominant-Linked and Dominant-Unrelated subclasses have both been small throughout the period, although displaying different patterns of change. The Dominant-Linked group steadily increased in size, from 0.9 to 5.6 percent between 1949 and 1969, while the Dominant-Unrelated group was at its largest in 1959, at 2.5 percent, and almost insignificant in size in 1949 and 1969, at 0.9 percent in both years.

The Related Business category became increasingly important between 1949 and 1969, not quite doubling in size. It is particularly interesting that almost all the increase in the Related category was in the Related-Linked subclass, which tripled in size between 1949 and 1969, increasing from 7.9 to 23.6

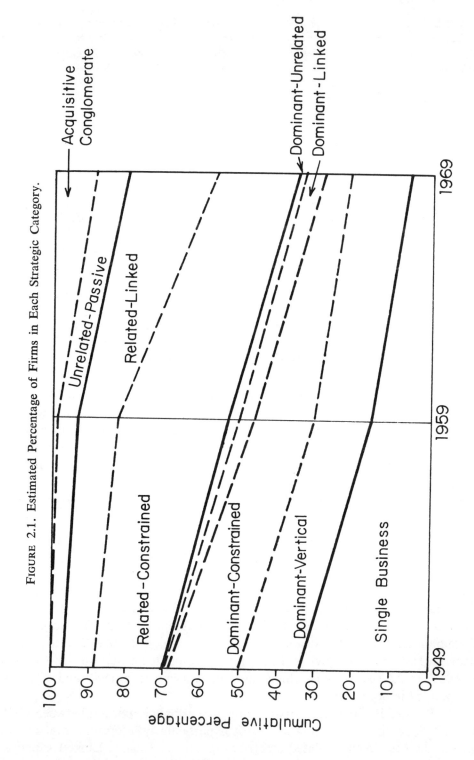

FIGURE 2.1. Estimated Percentage of Firms in Each Strategic Category.

percent of the top 500. The Related-Constrained subclass, by contrast, increased between 1949 and 1959 from 18.1 to 29.1 percent, but then dropped back to 21.6 percent by 1969.

Sources of Change

The basic pattern of change in the composition of the 500 between 1949 and 1969 was the increase in the Related and Unrelated categories at the expense of the Single Business category. But how did this and other redistributions come about? Did most of the Single Business firms of 1949 adopt strategies of diversification by 1969, or were they forced out of the 500, either by acquisition or displacement, to be replaced by firms in the Related and Unrelated categories?

In order to separate the effect of strategic change from that of entry and exit, it is useful to look at those firms that were among the largest 500 in both 1949 and 1969. An estimated 319 companies satisfied this condition, about 64 percent of the top 500 in either year. The distributions by category for these firms are shown in Table 2-3. Clearly, there was significant strategic change among these firms; 51.3 percent moved from one category to another between 1949 and 1969, and 95 percent of these moves were in the direction of increased diversification. The changes made by the firms that stayed in the 500 resulted in strategic-class populations very much like those of the full 500. The only significant differences were a higher proportion of firms in the Domi-

TABLE 2-3. FIRMS IN *"Fortune 500"* IN 1949 AND IN 1969.

	Percentage in Each Category		
Strategic Category	*1949*	*1959*	*1969*
Major Classes			
Single Business	29.2	16.1	7.3
Dominant Business	38.7	40.1	44.5
Related Business	29.2	38.0	44.5
Unrelated Business	2.9	5.8	12.4
Minor Classes			
Single Business	29.2	16.1	7.3
Dominant-Vertical	19.7	18.2	21.9
Dominant-Constrained	16.1	13.1	8.0
Dominant-Linked	1.5	4.4	4.4
Dominant-Unrelated	1.5	4.4	1.5
Related-Constrained	20.4	28.5	24.1
Related-Linked	8.8	9.5	20.4
Unrelated-Passive	2.9	5.8	10.2
Acquisitive Conglomerate	0.0	0.0	2.2

nant and a lower proportion in the Unrelated categories. These gaps were, of course, filled by the entry and exit effects.

Another way of looking at these phenomena is to determine for each category the amount of change caused by shifting (i.e., firms moving out of or into that category but staying in the top 500), and the amount caused by entry and exit. For example, between 1949 and 1969 the Single Business category dropped from 34.5 to 6.2 percent of the top 500, a total change of −28.3 percentage points. This change can be allocated as follows: −15.7 caused by exits; +1.8, entries—giving a net of −13.9 caused by entry and exit, −14.8, firms moving from Single to other categories, +0.4, firms moving from others into the Single Business category—giving a net of −14.4 caused by shifting. Thus the total change of −28.3 can be viewed as −14.4 from shifting and −13.9 from entry and exit. These results and those for the other three major categories are shown below in Table 2-4.

The effects of shifting and entry-exit were in the same directions in each category and about equally important in explaining the reductions in the number of firms in the Single and Dominant categories. In the Related and Unrelated categories shifting tended to be more important than entry-exit. Thus, from the data in Tables 2-2, 2-3, and 2-4 it is apparent that in the period 1949 to 1969 (1) the number of Single Business firms sharply decreased and the number of firms in the Related and Unrelated categories increased; (2) that this change was due to changes in strategy in about 164 firms and the displacement of about 181 firms and their replacement by an equal number; (3) that both strategic change and entry-exit had the effect of decreasing the size of the Single Business category and increasing the size of the Related and Unrelated Business categories; and (4) that both forces were of comparable importance in producing the changes in the number of firms in each category.

Entry and exit. Firms exited from the largest 500 firms either through acquisition or merger with another large firm, or through a drop in total revenues below the minimum required for inclusion. In the decade 1949–

TABLE 2-4. SOURCES OF CHANGE, 1949–1969.

	Category			
	Single	*Dominant*	*Related*	*Unrelated*
Percent of 500 in 1949	34.5	35.4	26.7	3.4
Percent of 500 in 1969	6.2	29.2	45.2	19.4
Change	−28.3	−6.2	+18.5	+16.0
Portion Due to Shifting	−14.4	−2.9	+11.6	+5.7
Portion Due to Entry-Exit	−13.9	−3.3	+6.9	+10.3
Percent Change Due to Shifting	50.9	46.8	62.7	64.4

1959 acquisition and displacement were of comparable importance; of the estimated 120 firms that left the leading 500 during the period, approximately 63 were acquired or merged and 57 displaced. In the period 1959–1969, acquisition and merger were of much greater relative importance, accounting for about 91 of the 127 firms that are estimated to have exited.

It was hypothesized that some strategic categories (namely the Single, Dominant-Constrained and Related-Constrained categories) would be more susceptible to acquisition and merger than the others. A statistical analysis of acquisition and merger rates, however, did not support this hypothesis. In fact, the data do not support any hypotheses of unequal acquisition rates among the categories in either decade. In other words, there is no evidence to suggest that Single Businesses, for example, were either more or less likely to be acquired than firms in any other category.

A statistical test did indicate that Single Business and Dominant-Constrained firms were more likely to be *displaced* than other categories of firms in the first decade.[3] However, this pattern was not repeated in the second decade. Furthermore, it is clear that a firm's size is the major determinant of its likelihood of being displaced, so that any relationship between displacement rate and category is most likely simply a result of a more basic difference in the average size of firms in each category.

The entry rates in the first decade seem to favor the Unrelated category at the expense of the Single category, but again the differences are not statistically significant. This pattern was repeated during 1959–1969 but this time the differences were quite significant. Of all firms that were among the 500 in both 1959 and 1969, only 4.8 percent had adopted acquisitive conglomerate strategies by 1969. By contrast, 28.7 percent of all firms that entered the 500 in this period were acquisitive conglomerates (this difference is statistically significant at the 0.1 percent level). All other entering firms were distributed among the categories in rough proportion to the number of firms already in them.

Strategic change. Tables 2-5 and 2-6 show the detailed pattern of change during 1949–1959 and 1959–1969 respectively. They give (1) estimates of the percentage of firms in each category that were acquired or merged during the next ten years (the acquisition and displacement rates); (2) of firms that stayed among the top 500, estimates of the percentage of companies in each category that had moved to or remained in each category ten years later (transition rates); and (3) estimates of the percentage of the firms that entered the 500 during the period that fell in each category and its end. For example, the first line of Table 2-4 indicates that among firms that were Single Business in 1949, 9.9 percent had been acquired or merged and 19.9 percent displaced from the 500 by 1959. Furthermore, of those that remained (70.2 percent of

---

[3] Binomial one-sided tests significant at the 10 percent level for Single Business acquisitions and at the 5 percent level for Dominant-Constrained acquisitions between 1949 and 1959.

TABLE 2-5. STRATEGIC CATEGORY TRANSITION RATES, 1949–1959.

1949 Category	Rate of Acquisition	Displacement	Percentage of Non-Exiting Firms Shifting to Each Category by 1959											
			Single	Dominant	Dominant-Vertical	Dominant-Constrained	Dominant-Linked	Dominant-Unrelated	Related	Related-Constrained	Related-Linked	Unrelated	Unrelated-Passive	Acquisitive Conglomerate
Single	9.9	19.9	57.0	33.9	6.0	15.1	7.3	5.5	9.1	7.3	1.8	0	0	0
Dominant	9.6	13.0	1.6	75.2	44.2	23.0	3.2	4.8	20.0	20.0	0	3.2	3.2	0
Dominant-Vertical	14.8	0	0	90.1	90.1	0	0	0	9.9	9.9	0	0	0	0
Dominant-Constrained	6.3	25.7	3.6	55.2	0	51.6	3.6	0	34.0	34.0	0	7.2	7.2	0
Dominant-Linked	0	0	0	100.0	0	0	50.0	50.0	0	0	0	0	0	0
Dominant-Unrelated	0	0	0	100.0	0	0	0	100.0	0	0	0	0	0	0
Related	17.0	0	0	0	0	0	0	0	96.0	65.3	30.7	4.0	4.0	0
Related-Constrained	18.2	0	0	0	0	0	0	0	94.3	94.3	0	5.7	5.7	0
Related-Linked	14.4	0	0	0	0	0	0	0	100.0	0	100.0	0	0	0
Unrelated	33.4	0	0	0	0	0	0	0	0	0	0	100.0	100.0	0
Unrelated-Passive	33.4	0	0	0	0	0	0	0	0	0	0	100.0	100.0	0
Acquisitive Conglomerate	—	—	—	—	—	—	—	—	—	—	—	—	—	—
New Entries			8.1	35.5	5.3	25.4	4.8	0	45.9	30.6	15.3	10.5	5.7	4.8

TABLE 2-6. STRATEGIC CATEGORY TRANSITION RATES, 1959–1969.

Percentage of Non-Exiting Firms Shifting to Each Category by 1969

1959 Category	Rate of Acquisition	Displacement	Single	Dominant	Dominant-Vertical	Dominant-Constrained	Dominant-Linked	Dominant-Unrelated	Related	Related-Constrained	Related-Linked	Unrelated	Unrelated-Passive	Acquisitive Conglomerate
Single	26.1	10.5	44.2	34.3	21.4	8.6	4.3	0	7.2	12.9	4.3	4.3	4.3	0
Dominant	17.7	1.8	1.5	70.3	36.7	17.6	13.1	2.9	20.0	9.3	10.7	8.2	4.9	3.4
Dominant-Vertical	17.1	4.6	0	95.1	95.1	0	0	0	0	0	0	4.9	4.9	0
Dominant-Constrained	25.5	0	0	57.2	0	43.9	9.6	3.7	35.4	23.2	12.2	7.4	7.4	0
Dominant-Linked	0	0	0	50.0	0	0	50.0	0	34.8	0	34.8	15.2	0	15.2
Dominant-Unrelated	0	0	16.7	50.0	0	0	33.3	16.7	16.7	0	16.7	16.7	0	16.7
Related	15.3	10.2	0	3.4	0	3.4	0	0	85.3	42.7	42.7	11.2	7.8	3.4
Related-Constrained	15.8	9.3	0	4.7	0	4.7	0	0	86.6	58.5	28.1	8.7	8.7	0
Related-Linked	13.9	12.6	0	0	0	0	0	0	81.9	0	81.9	18.1	5.5	12.6
Unrelated	18.2	10.5	0	0	0	0	0	0	0	0	0	100.0	66.0	34.0
Unrelated-Passive	22.1	12.7	0	0	0	0	0	0	0	0	0	100.0	87.5	12.5
Acquisitive Conglomerate	0	0	0	0	0	0	0	0	0	0	0	100.0	0	100.0
New Entries			4.8	14.2	9.4	0	4.8	0	47.6	19.0	28.6	33.4	4.8	28.6

the original 1949 group), 57 percent stayed in the Single Business category, 33.9 percent moved to one of the Dominant categories—6 percent to Dominant-Vertical, 15.1 percent to Dominant-Constrained, and so on. These "transition rates" refer only to firms that did not exit, and refer to the *proportion* of these that moved to another group, not to the absolute level of the flow.

These tables show a surprising degree of stability between decades in the pattern of transitions among the major categories. In the first decade, 43 percent of Single Business firms that stayed in the 500 moved to other categories; in the second decade, 56 percent moved. In both decades roughly one third of Single Business firms moved into the Dominant class. Similarly, 25 percent of Dominant Business firms moved to other categories in 1949–1959, and 30 percent in 1959–1969, and 20 percent of Dominant Business firms moved into the Related class in both decades. In both decades very few firms moved from more diversified to less diversified postures. The only major differences between the decades were that (1) the percentage of Single Business firms that moved into the Related category during 1959–1969 was almost twice as large as during 1949–1959, and (2) transition rates into the Unrelated category from all other categories were significantly larger in the second decade.

The detailed pattern of transitions among minor categories is more difficult to interpret directly. However, the effect of the changes in transition rates from the first to the second decade can be seen by determining what would have happened if the 1949–1959 transition rates had not changed, but had been repeated in 1959–1969. Keeping the 1959–1969 exit rates and entry pattern, but applying the 1949–1959 transition rates to the 1959 distribution of firms gives the results in Table 2-7.

The differences between these two distributions are purely due to the differences between the 1949–1959 and 1959–1969 patterns of strategic change. Clearly, the only *net* effects of this change that were of any significance were:

(1) All of the firms that were Dominant-Unrelated in 1959 dispersed to other categories by 1969, and the 1949–1959 pattern of movements into this class was not repeated.

(2) Unlike the first decade, the second decade saw a great many Related-Constrained firms move to the Related-Linked category; 26 percent of the 1969 Related-Linked firms had been Related-Constrained in 1959. This change accounts for almost all of the discrepancy between the actual and projected populations of these categories.

(3) In the second decade, the rate of transition into the Unrelated-Passive category increased, and some firms already among the 500 adopted Acquisitive Conglomerate strategies. In contrast, the only Acquisitive Conglomerates appearing between 1949 and 1959 had entered the 500 in that period.

This analysis also sheds some light on the size of the Dominant category.

TABLE 2-7. TRANSITION RATES FOR 1949–1959 PROJECTED THROUGH 1969.

| Category | Percentage of 1969 Top 500 Firms in Each Category | |
	Actual	Projected Using 1949–59 Rates
Single	6.2	7.5
Dominant	29.2	30.5
Related	45.2	46.7
Unrelated	19.4	15.3
Dominant-Vertical	15.6	13.4
Dominant-Constrained	7.1	7.7
Dominant Linked	5.6	4.3
Dominant-Unrelated	0.9	5.1
Related-Constrained	21.6	31.3
Related-Linked	23.6	15.4
Acquisitive Conglomerate	10.9	8.4
Unrelated-Passive	8.5	6.9

In Table 2-2 the estimated percentage of firms in this category rose during 1949–1959 from 35.4 to 37.3 percent and then dropped to 29.2 percent by 1969. Even if the transition rates had not changed between decades the Dominant category would have become smaller, dropping to 30.5 rather than 29.2 percent. From Table 2-4 it is apparent that entry-exit phenomena explain only 3.3 percentage points of this drop. Thus, the reason the Dominant category became smaller during 1959–1969 was simply that there were fewer Single Business firms in 1959 to move into the Dominant category, while the rate of transition out of the Dominant category remained virtually unchanged. This type of phenomenon is typical of systems characterized by largely one-way flows between categories with fairly stable transition rates. At the start the upstream category is full (the Single group) and the others nearly empty. As time passes, the downstream categories increase in size, but, since the upstream categories are not being fully replenished, eventually the sizes of all but the last category drop to low levels.

This analogy suggests that the Related group may also decrease in size in the future, if transition rates into the Unrelated category remain the same. Table 2-8 shows the projected sizes of the four major groups in 1979, 1989, and 1999, under the assumptions that the 1959–1969 transition rates and the entry-exit patterns are repeated each decade. The projections show a continuing decline in the Dominant group as it feeds the Related and Unrelated categories. The Related group itself would begin to shrink as firms move to the Unrelated category and fewer enter it from the Single and Dominant catego-

TABLE 2-8. Projected Strategic Class Distributions.

	Percentage in Category			
	Single	Dominant	Related	Unrelated
1979	3.3	22.6	46.0	28.1
1989	2.4	18.3	45.3	34.0
1999	2.1	15.7	44.3	37.9

ries. These projections should not be considered to be forecasts, since *cetabus parabus* assumptions are almost certainly not valid. Rather, the projections clarify the basic nature of the 1959–1969 transition pattern by showing what would happen if the identical pattern were repeated.

Paths to diversification. The data presented so far indicate that the management of a great many large firms saw the opportunity or felt the need to diversify during the past twenty years. Of all firms that were Single Businesses or Dominant Businesses in 1949 and were still among the largest 500 in 1969, 79 percent of the former and 45 percent of the latter had moved to categories of greater diversification by 1969. But *which* firms diversified, and what strategies of diversification did they employ?

It is estimated that 52 Single Business firms among the 500 in 1949 had diversified by 1959, 41 moving to the Dominant, and 11 to the Related category. The sample evidence on 1959–1969 is more scanty, but the estimate is that 27 Single Business firms diversified in this period, 17 becoming Dominant, 8, Related, and 2, Unrelated.

Obviously, most of the firms that moved from Single Business to Related or Unrelated Business strategies passed through the Dominant category at some point. Therefore, it might be thought that the distinction between Single Business firms that, ten years later, obtained more than 30 percent of their revenues from new business areas and those that had not diversified to this degree is rather arbitrary. Perhaps, for example, most of the firms that shifted from Single to Dominant postures between 1949 and 1959 were simply "diversifying," having been caught in mid-stream in 1959. The evidence does not support such a conclusion. Leaving aside the special case of vertically integrated firms, 33 firms in the sample were among the top 500 in both 1949 and 1959, and Dominant in 1959 (except Dominant-Vertical).[4] Of these, 15 had been Single Businesses in 1949 and 18 had been Dominant. In the next decade, 1959–1969, these groups moved as follows:

---

[4] Of the firms in the 500 in 1949 and 1959 that appeared in the sample, 30 were Dominant-Vertical in 1959, one having come from the 1949 Single Business category. None of these moved out of the Dominant-Vertical category by 1959.

Group	Stayed Dominant	Became Related	Became Unrelated	Merged or Acquired
1949–1959: Single-Dominant	8	4	1	2
1949–1959: Dominant-Dominant	7	7	2	2

The numbers of firms involved in these movements are not sufficient to produce any statistically valid inference. It does appear, however, that firms that went from the Single to the Dominant categories in the first decade were no more likely, and perhaps even less likely, to move on to the Related category in the next decade than firms that were Dominant in both 1949 and 1959. The hypothesized existence of this phenomenon was, in fact, one of the major motives for defining the Dominant category in the first place. As the managers of many Dominant Business companies seem either unwilling or unable to undertake further diversification, this category cannot be simply viewed as consisting of companies that are on their way to full diversification.

Most of the Single Business diversifiers during both decades stayed close to home, entering only businesses that were closely related to ongoing activities. Of Single Business diversifiers in the first decade, 14 percent moved into the Dominant-Vertical, 35 percent into the Dominant-Constrained, and 17 percent into the Related-Constrained categories. In the second decade, 38 percent of Single Business diversifiers were oil companies that moved heavily into petrochemicals, plastics, fertilizers, and sometimes uranium production and coal mining; another 38 percent consisted of firms entering the Dominant-Constrained and Related-Constrained categories. Table 2-9 gives a list of the Single Business diversifiers in both decades.

Dominant Business diversifiers also showed a very strong tendency to stay close to their major areas of competence in the first decade, but in the second decade the majority eschewed constrained diversification and moved into the Related-Linked and Unrelated categories. Shown below are the percentages of Dominant diversifiers that entered each Related and Unrelated subcategory during both decades.

Decade	Estimated Number	Related-Constrained	Related-Linked	Unrelated-Passive	Acquisitive Conglomerate
1949–1959	32	86%	0%	14%	0%
1959–1969	42	33%	38%	17%	12%

Most Dominant diversifiers came from the Dominant-Constrained subclass. During both decades about 44 percent of firms starting in this subclass (and not leaving the 500) had diversified out of the Dominant category by the end of the decade. There were too few firms in the Dominant-Linked and Unrelated subclasses to warrant any conclusions about their propensity to diversify.

TABLE 2-9. SINGLE BUSINESS DIVERSIFIERS.

Firms Leaving the Single Business Category Between 1949 and 1959	Category Entered
Calumet & Hecla Continental Oil Richfield Oil	Dominant-Vertical
Container Corp. of America Dana Deere Ford Motor General Cable Pet Royal McBee White Motor	Dominant-Constrained
American Enka Carrier Genesco Handy & Harmon	Dominant-Linked
Chrysler General Host Philip Morris	Dominant-Unrelated
Eaton Yale & Towne Lockheed Aircraft Mead USM (United Shoe Machinery)	Related-Constrained
Kelsey-Hayes	Related-Linked

Firms Leaving the Single Business Category Between 1959 and 1969	Category Entered
Atlantic Richfield Gulf Oil Marathon Oil Mobil Oil Standard Oil of Ohio	Dominant-Vertical
Brown Shoe Mohasco	Dominant-Constrained
Hershey Foods	Dominant-Linked
Ashland Oil Cluett, Peabody Coca-Cola	Related-Constrained
Ward Foods	Related-Linked
Champion Spark Plug	Unrelated-Passive

NOTE: Corporate names are those in use in 1969 or at the time of acquisition or merger if the firm was no longer in existence by 1969.

Very few vertically integrated firms were able to move into the Related or Unrelated categories in the period under study. In the first decade only 10 percent of Dominant-Vertical firms moved out of the Dominant category. The three firms in the sample that accomplished this were General Mills and CPC International—both integrated grain millers that diversified into a broad spectrum of packaged foods, and AMAX, which was described in Chapter 1. In the second decade Boise Cascade was the only firm observed to leave the Dominant-Vertical group. It entered the Unrelated category through an aggressive program of acquisition and internal development, which took it away from timber and lumber into a wide range of construction-related activities as well as education, office supplies, contract engineering, recreational products, and computer software.

AMAX was the only one of the "heavy" vertically integrated firms in the sample that achieved full diversification. None of the other *integrated* primary metals, oil, or rubber manufacturers moved beyond the Dominant-Vertical group. Significantly, the only major oil company to become Related was not integrated; Ashland, buying most of its crude and chemical feedstocks on the open market, had by 1969 expanded its petrochemical business and its activities in stone, gravel, and other road construction materials to 47 percent of revenues. A list of the Dominant Business diversifiers in both decades is provided in Table 2-10.

ORGANIZATIONAL STRUCTURE

It has been well documented that by the late 1960s most large corporations had adopted product-division forms of organization. Wrigley estimated that 86 percent of the 500 largest industrials in 1967 had product-division organizations, and Fouraker and Stopford found that 89.4 percent of 170 large United States firms with direct investments abroad were organized along divisional lines.[5] In addition, Chandler's study, although not quantitative, showed that the earliest product-division organizations appeared in the United States during the first decade of this century and that the long-term trend was toward the adoption of this structure by increasing numbers of large firms.[6] Nevertheless, the data in Table 2-11 and Figure 2.2 represent what is believed to be the first quantitative study of this phenomenon over a significant period of

---

[5] Lawrence E. Fouraker and J. M. Stopford, "Organizational Structure and Multinational Strategy," *Administrative Science Quarterly* (June 1968), p. 59. As previously noted, the Wrigley sample, although *a priori* fair and unbiased, contained disproportionately few vertically integrated firms. Hence, his estimate of the percentage of product-division structures is higher than the weighted estimates presented here.

[6] Chandler, *Strategy and Structure*.

TABLE 2-10. DOMINANT BUSINESS DIVERSIFIERS.

Firms Leaving the Dominant Category Between 1949 and 1959	*Category Entered*
ABEX	
AMAX	
American Optical	
Bell	
Borden	Related-Constrained
CPC International	
General Mills	
Gillette	
National Cash Register	
North American Rockwell	
Owens-Illinois	
Pillsbury	
Curtiss-Wright	
Midland-Ross	Unrelated-Passive

Firms Leaving the Dominant Category Between 1959 and 1969	*Category Entered*
Addressograph-Multigraph	
Pet	
Procter & Gamble	Related-Constrained
Stevens (J. P.)	
Stokely-Van Camp	
White Motor	
ACF	
Genesco	
Handy & Harmon	
Harsco	Related-Linked
Libby-Owens-Ford	
Times Mirror	
Time	
Air Reduction	
Boise Cascade	Unrelated-Passive
Martin	
Brunswick	
General Host	Acquisitive Conglomerate

NOTE: Corporate names are those in use in 1969 or at time firm was acquired or merged if it was no longer in existence by 1969.

TABLE 2-11. ESTIMATED PERCENTAGE OF FIRMS IN
EACH ORGANIZATIONAL CATEGORY.

Organizational Category	1949	1959	1969
Functional	62.7	36.3	11.2
Functional with Subsidiaries	13.4	12.6	9.4
Product Division	19.8	47.6	75.5
Geographic Division	0.4	2.1	1.5
Holding Company	3.7	1.4	2.4
Number of Firms Used to Derive the Estimates	189	207	183

time. The results were unexpectedly dramatic: between 1949 and 1969 the estimated percentage of firms among the largest 500 having product-division organizations rose from 20.3 to 75.9 at a nearly constant rate of about 14 firms out of the 500 per year.

The necessary result of increasing numbers of product-division firms among the 500 largest firms was, of course, decreasing numbers of functionally organized companies. Between 1949 and 1969 the percentage of functionally organized firms dropped from 62.2 to 11.2. As will be shown in the section on sources of change, most of this decrease was due to functionally organized firms adopting product-division organizations rather than leaving the top 500.

The previously unstudied functional-with-subsidiaries category did not change sharply in size during the twenty years under study. It accounted for about 13 percent of the 500 in 1949 and 1959, then shrank to 9 percent in 1969. As expected, the geographic-division category proved to be virtually unpopulated, accounting for only about 10 firms out of the 500 when at its maximum size. Also quite small, the holding company category decreased in importance in the first decade as managers moved to build true headquarters offices, then increased slightly in the 1960s as several Acquisitive Conglomerates with very "thin" top management groups entered the 500.

Sources of Change

Changes in the percentage of firms in each organizational category were divided into two portions corresponding to two major effects: entry-exit and organizational "shifting." This analysis demonstrated that the vast preponderance of the change in the distribution of organizational forms among the 500 was caused by firms changing their form of organization rather than exiting and being replaced by firms with different structures. The calculations are shown in Table 2-12.

FIGURE 2.2. Estimated Percentage of Firms in Each Organizational Class, 1949–1969.

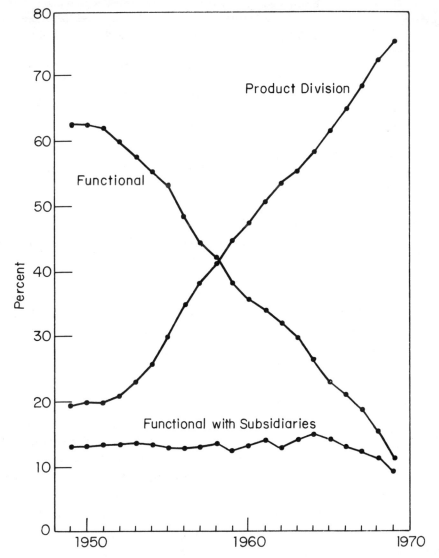

Table 2-13 parallels Tables 2-5 and 2-6, providing estimates of the acquisition rates, entry rates, and intercategory transition rates for the organizational categories. The rate of flow into the product-division category increased in the second decade, although it was substantial in both. The estimate that 1.2 percent of nonexiting product-division firms reverted to functional structures between 1959 and 1969 is based on but a single observation: American Motors. There were no other cases in the sample of firms abandoning the product-division structure.

The two firms in the sample that changed from functional- to geographic-division organizations in the first decade (Continental Oil and Foremost

TABLE 2-12. STRUCTURAL CHANGE AMONG THE TOP 500.

	Functional	*Functional with Subsidiaries*	*Product Division*	*Geographic Division*	*Holding Company*
1949–1959 Net Change	−26.0	−0.8	+27.3	+1.7	−2.3
Due to Entry-Exit	−7.4	+0.1	+6.0	0	0
Due to Shifting	−18.6	−0.9	+21.3	+1.7	−2.3
Percent Due to Shifting	71.5	111.0	77.9	100.0	100.0
1959–1969 Net Change	−25.0	−3.2	+27.9	−0.7	+1.03
Due to Entry-Exit	−7.9	0	+6.7	−0.7	+1.73
Due to Shifting	−17.1	−3.2	+21.2	0	−0.70
Percent Due to Shifting	68.3	100.0	76.0	0	0

Dairies) created divisions based on areas of the United States. In the second decade, the two sample firms that entered this category formed worldwide geographic divisions. In 1967 Caterpillar Tractor split its functional organization into four major divisions, each responsible for a similar product line in a different region of the world. Dow Chemical had what is best described as a functional-with-subsidiaries structure until the mid-1960s, when it created a mixed structure, with geographic, product, and functional divisions that were classed as worldwide geographic divisions.

All the firms in the sample that fell into the holding company category in 1949 developed true headquarters offices and strengthened administrative control over the divisions, moving to the product-division category by 1969. These companies were AVCO, ABEX (American Brake Shoe), Borg-Warner, Genesco, Pullman, Questor (Dunhill), and Rockwell Manufacturing. Entering the top 500 firms between 1959 and 1969, Bangor Punta had been a holding company when its sole business consisted of Cuban sugar plantations and its more recent strategy of being an Acquisitive Conglomerate did not alter the purely financial interest top management took in its holdings. Also in the holding company category in 1969 was Ling-Temco-Vought. In 1959 LTV was classified as a product-division firm, but in 1967, at the zenith of its acquisition program, it was judged to have crossed the line and become a holding company—its acquisition of the Greatamerica Company, itself a holding company, being the deciding factor.

The functional-with-subsidiaries category did not change radically in size during the twenty years of observation; although many of its members shifted to product-division organizations, the flow of firms moving into the category from the purely functional group kept the net change small. While it is tempting to think of the functional-with-subsidiaries structure as a transition adopted by firms in the process of moving from functional- to product-division structures, such a view is not borne out by the data. Of all firms that were in the

TABLE 2-13. STRUCTURAL CATEGORY TRANSITION RATES.

Starting Category	Percentage		Percentage of Non-Exiting Firms Ending in Each Category				
	Acquired	Displaced	Functional	Functional with Subsidiaries	Product Division	Geographic Division	Holding Company
1949–1959 Transition Pattern							
Functional	9.1	14.8	59.8	7.4	31.8	0.9	0
Functional with Subsidiaries	8.5	8.8	4.0	60.3	35.7	0	0
Product Division	28.0	5.6	0	0	100.0	0	0
Geographic Division	0	0	0	0	0	100.0	0
Holding Company	0	0	0	0	62.2	0	37.8
New Entries to the 500			31.1	10.1	53.6	5.3	0
1959–1969 Transition Pattern							
Functional	22.4	9.4	27.3	8.9	62.1	1.8	0
Functional with Subsidiaries	4.0	5.5	3.9	48.7	43.6	3.9	0
Product Division	17.4	6.5	1.2	0	98.8	0	0
Geographic Division	32.1	0	0	0	61.7	38.3	0
Holding Company	36.4	0	0	0	100.0	0	0
New Entries to the 500			14.2	4.8	71.4	0	9.6

top 500 in both 1949 and 1969 and dropped functional structures in favor of product-division organizations in this period, it is estimated that only 3 percent used the functional-with-subsidiaries organization as an intermediate stage in the change (e.g., American Enka and Philip Morris). The vast majority of firms that moved from the functional-with-subsidiaries category to the product-division category in this period had been in the functional-with-subsidiaries category in 1949. Of course, if the study had encompassed a time span longer than twenty years it is quite possible that the role of the functional-with-subsidiaries structure as an intermediate stage of organizational development would have been more evident. Nevertheless, if it is an intermediate and ultimately transient structure, it was little used as such during 1949 to 1969 and is remarkably stable, the median time to exit for firms in this category being at least thirteen years.

The data on entrance rates in Table 2-13 indicate that in both decades the proportion of firms *entering* the top 500 firms with product-division structures was roughly similar to the proportion of firms already among the 500 with product-division structures. This tends to suggest that firms smaller than those in the 500, and in particular those growing at above average rates, were undergoing the same pattern of transition from functional to product division organizations as those in the 500.

The data on exit rates appear interesting because of the disproportionate number of firms with product-division structures that merged or were acquired in the first decade. Out of the 11 firms in the sample that left the top 500 in 1949–1959 through merger or acquisition, 5 had product-division structures. If the likelihood of any firm being merged or acquired were independent of its structure, this result would have less than a 5 percent chance of occurring because of the random nature of the sample. The acquired firms with product-division structure were Clinton Foods, Mengel, and Pacific Mills, and the merging firms were Sperry and Remington Rand. Because the merging firms merged with *each other,* forming Sperry Rand, it can be argued that there were only four net exits from the product-division class attributable to acquisition or merger. Such a result would *not* be statistically significant. Since in the second decade the acquisition rate for product-division firms is not unusually high, there seems to be little to conclude from the anomaly of the first decade acquisition rate other than the danger of reasoning from a very few data points.

STRATEGY AND STRUCTURE

A growing body of theory and empirical evidence supports the idea that organizational structure is intimately related to a firm's strategy of expansion. The concepts and data developed by the major contributors to this field of study were reviewed in the Introduction and Chapter 1. The issues addressed in this section are not new; the data to be presented, however, do provide the first quantitative portrayal of the strategy-structure interaction over a period of time.

Between 1949 and 1969 most of the largest 500 corporations became significantly diversified and adopted product-division structures. It remains, however, to show that these changes were not separate parallel trends but reflect a cause and effect relationship between expansion strategy and organizational structure.

Table 2-14 shows the estimated percentage of the firms in each strategic class that fell in each organizational category in 1949, 1959, and 1969. The figures in this table are independent of the number of firms in the strategic classes and can be interpreted as indicating the likelihood of a firm having a particular type of structure, *given* its strategy. To simplify the discussion, Table 2-15 was constructed from these data.

In Table 2-15 the holding company and product-division categories have been combined. Although the two categories have differing amounts of control over divisions by headquarters, both represent specialization on the basis of product-market activity rather than function or geography. They are similar as well in their functional and geographic categories. Also combined in Tables 2-14 and 2-15 are the Dominant-Linked and Dominant-Unrelated categories. These classes were pooled because sufficient data were lacking for separate organizational breakdowns.

Two distinct patterns are clearly visible in Table 2-15. First, in each year the greater the diversification of the firm the more likely it was to have a multidivisional structure. Second, with only two exceptions, the likelihood that a firm with a given strategy had a multidivisional structure increased with time for all strategies. Thus, *combined with a definite positive association between diversification and divisionalization was a secular trend toward divisionalization that affected firms in all strategic categories.*

The total rise in the number of multidivisional firms among the top 500 can therefore be ascribed to two different trends: Since more diversified firms tend to be more likely to divisionalize, the trend toward diversification increased the number of multidivisional firms among the 500, and the trend toward divisionalization per se had a parallel effect. By projecting what would have happened if either trend had not occurred, it can be estimated that of the total increase in divisionalization among the 500 between 1949 and 1969, amounting to 256 firms, 53 percent was due to increased diversification and 47 percent to the secular trend toward divisionalization.

In the case of Single Business firms there is some doubt as to the existence of the secular trend toward divisionalization. Between 1949 and 1959 the two Single Business firms in the sample that had product-division structures (Ford

TABLE 2-14. STRATEGY AND STRUCTURE AMONG THE TOP 500.

Strategic Class	Percentage in Each Structural Class				
	Functional	Functional with Sub-sidiaries	Product Division	Geo-graphic Division	Holding Company
1949					
Single	90.7	4.0	2.7	1.3	1.3
Dominant	56.8	23.2	17.1	0	2.9
DV	61.9	25.3	12.9	0	0
DC	53.1	18.8	22.4	0	5.6
DL + DU	50.0	50.0	0	0	0
Related	42.2	14.2	40.3	0	3.3
RC	49.0	17.8	30.9	0	2.3
RL	26.2	5.5	62.7	0	5.5
Unrelated	0	0	61.2	0	38.8
UP	0	0	61.2	0	38.8
AC	—	—	—	—	—
1959					
Single	90.6	5.8	0	3.6	0
Dominant	36.4	22.4	34.5	4.2	2.5
DV	41.7	20.8	34.5	3.0	0
DC	46.1	20.9	25.6	4.3	3.1
DL + DU	0	29.5	56.9	6.8	6.8
Related	20.1	8.3	71.6	0	0
RC	26.1	9.9	64.0	0	0
RL	4.0	4.0	92.0	0	0
Unrelated	0	0	93.3	0	6.7
UP	0	0	91.8	0	8.2
AC	0	0	100.0	0	0
1969					
Single	62.3	14.2	14.2	9.3	0
Dominant	20.7	17.5	60.3	1.5	0
DV	32.2	22.6	45.2	0	0
DC	14.2	6.2	73.5	6.2	0
DL + DU	0	17.8	82.2	0	0
Related	2.9	6.6	89.5	1.0	0
RC	4.1	9.7	86.3	0	0
RL	1.9	3.7	92.5	1.9	0
Unrelated	0	2.3	85.3	0	12.4
UP	0	5.2	94.8	0	0
AC	0	0	77.8	0	22.2

TABLE 2-15. INCIDENCE OF MULTIDIVISIONAL STRUCTURE.

| | Percentage of Firms in Strategic Category Having Product-Division or Holding-Company Structures | | |
Strategic Category	1949	1959	1969
Single Business	5.3	0.0	14.2
Dominant-Vertical	12.9	34.5	45.2
Dominant-Constrained	28.1	28.7	73.5
Dominant-Linked or Unrelated	0.0	63.7	82.2
Related-Constrained	33.2	64.0	86.3
Related-Linked	68.2	91.9	92.5
Unrelated-Passive	100.0	100.0	94.8
Acquisitive Conglomerate	–	100.0	100.0
All Categories	23.9	49.0	78.4

and Continental Container) moved out of the Single Business category. In 1959 none of the Single Business firms in the sample had product-division structures. By 1969 the Single Business group was quite small and the two firms observed to have product-division structure (Donnelly and Interstate Brands) constituted 14.2 percent (weighted) of the entire class. Both had divisionalized in 1968–1969. Donnelly was particularly difficult to classify and its placement in the Single Business group was somewhat arbitrary. Donnelly's 1969 divisionalization was not in response to increased diversification; its management simply decided that the company's book printing and commercial printing activities would be carried out more effectively under separate general managements. Interstate Brands, a bread and cake producer, had announced a diversification program in 1967 and by 1969 had acquired a number of firms in the packaged and canned foods business. However, over 95 percent of its 1969 revenues still came from bread and cake. Instead of absorbing acquisitions into its functional structure or moving to a functional-with-subsidiaries structure, Interstate created separate divisions for bread, cake, and each of its acquisitions, apparently reacting more to the anticipation of further diversification than to the amount already achieved in 1969. Thus, great credence should not be placed on the correctness of the value 14.2 percent. Both cases, however, might be taken as indicative of an increasing propensity of firms to divisionalize even when product variety is low or when one product is still overwhelmingly dominant.

Among Dominant Business firms the trend toward increased use of the product-division structure was especially pronounced. In 1949 only 17 percent of Dominant Business companies were divisionalized, while by 1969 60 percent had adopted this form of organization. Table 2-14 shows that many vertically integrated firms moved from functional to divisional structures, although the proportion of Dominant Businesses having functional-with-subsidiaries structures remained fairly constant.

Most of the vertically integrated firms that adopted product-division structure were in the rubber, forest products, and aluminum industries. Firms like Goodrich, Firestone, Kimberly-Clark, Scott, Kaiser Aluminum, and Reynolds, despite their basic commitment to the processing of a particular material, tended to emphasize the fabrication and sale of a variety of specially designed products. Having a scale sufficient to permit duplication of facilities, strategies of fabricating almost all output, and aggressive marketing to a variety of customers led the managements of these firms to choose a product-division structure. On the other hand, most of the vertically integrated oil and steel producers had functional or functional-with-subsidiaries structures.

The oil industry differs in so many essentials from other industries that often little is gained by comparing oil companies with other firms. In no other industry are such vast, vertical processing chains almost entirely dedicated to producing a single virtually undifferentiated product that is sold directly to consumers. Most oil companies have employed functional or geographic-division structures in 1969. The exceptions were Ashland (refinery products, petrochemicals, road construction and material), which was not integrated, and Continental Oil, which had divided its petroleum operations into East Coast and West Coast divisions and had coal, chemicals, plastics, and fertilizer divisions as well—actually a mixed geographic/product structure.

Steel firms have tended to move to more centralized structures for their basic businesses, having subsidiaries carry out fabrication and marketing tasks that are not included in the primary activity of converting ore and coke into mill products. Armco Steel and Keystone Steel, both of which sold relatively small amounts of standard mill products (52 percent and 20 percent of revenues in 1969 respectively), were the only steel companies observed to have product-division structure in 1969.

Thus, those vertically integrated firms that chose to emphasize product rather than process or belonged to industries that required such an emphasis, have been the ones to adopt product-division organizations.

Structure and Diversity

In a statistical sense, diversification strategy explains a good deal of the variation in organizational forms observed among the leading 500 firms. To what degree do firm-to-firm variations in diversity explain the differences in structure, and how much is gained by using strategy as the predictor of structure rather than simple diversity?

As a general measure of diversity the firm's specialization ratio is a useful index. Table 2-16 shows the mean specialization ratios for firms in each of

TABLE 2-16. AVERAGE SPECIALIZATION RATIOS.

Structure	*1949*	*1959*	*1969*
Functional	0.842	0.832	0.811
	(114)	(62)	(17)
Functional with Subsidiaries	0.700	0.643	0.675
	(27)	(22)	(14)
Product Division	0.562	0.492	0.469
	(31)	(75)	(118)

NOTE: Figures in parentheses are the numbers of data points used in calculating each average.

the major organizational categories. The geographic division and holding company categories are not considered here, because of insufficient data.

The table shows the general trend toward diversity over time and the tendency for more diverse firms to have product-division structures. A two-way analysis of variance of this data reveals that the relationship between structure and diversity is statistically significant at the 1 percent level. Holding the effect of time constant, it was found that functional-with-subsidiaries firms had specialization ratios that averaged 0.152 less than those of functional firms and product-division firms had specialization ratios that on average were 0.326 below those of functional firms.

To compare the explanatory power of strategic categories to that of a straight specialization ratio, the following question was asked: If all one knew was each firm's strategic class, how many mistakes would be made in guessing whether or not each firm had a product-division structure, and how many mistakes would be made if one had to guess knowing only the specialization ratio of each firm? In guessing structure from strategy, Table 2-14 was used. For a given strategy in a given year, if the table entry was greater than 0.5 it was predicted that a firm with that strategy had a product-division structure. In 1949, this procedure would have resulted in 17.6 percent misclassifications; in 1969, 16.2 percent. In guessing structure from specialization ratios, the detailed distributions of specialization ratios were examined and the value found that minimized the expected number of errors. For 1949 and 1969 these values of *SR* were 0.725 and 0.57 respectively, giving percentage misclassifications of 30 percent and 27 percent in the same order. In other words, the best possible dividing line between product-division and functional forms of structure was an *SR* of 0.725 in 1949, which, if used as such, would have resulted in 30 percent of all firms being erroneously classed as either functional or divisionalized.

For both 1949 and 1969 predicting structure using only specialization ratios would have produced about 70 percent more errors than predictions using strategic categories. Consequently, in predicting structure the strategic categories are significantly superior to measures based only on the amount of diversity.

Strategic and Structural Change

If structure and strategy are causally related, not only will certain structures be associated with certain strategies of expansion, but strategic change will tend to be matched by structural change. A simple test of this proposition is provided by Table 2-17. The criterion used in this table is the percentage of all functional, functional-with-subsidiaries and geographic-division firms that switched to a product-division structure by the end of the decade. The evidence shows that in the first decade firms that moved to more diversified postures were more likely to divisionalize than similar firms that did not increase their degree of diversification. In the second decade, the pattern continued to hold for firms that started in the Single Business category, but Dominant Business firms seemed to divisionalize at the same rate whether or not they further diversified.

Since many of the 1959–1969 Dominant Business diversifiers moved out of the Dominant category in the last few years of the decade, a time lag between strategic and structural change might be the explanation for the apparent lack

TABLE 2-17. PERCENTAGE OF NONDIVISIONALIZED FIRMS SHIFTING TO MULTIDIVISIONAL STRUCTURES.

Category	Nondiversifiers	Diversifiers	Significance of Difference
1949–1959			
Single Business	0	15.1	.01
Dominant Business	34.7	88.0	.10
Related Business	55.7	—	—
1959–1969			
Single Business	19.8	41.7	.05
Dominant Business	52.0	61.2	Not Significant
Related Business	79.9	—	—

NOTE: Nondiversifiers are firms that did not move out of their major strategic category. Diversifiers are Single Business firms that moved to the Dominant or Related categories and Dominant Business firms that moved to the Related category. Tests of significance used were the Chi-square and exact binomial. The level of significance is the probability that a true condition of no difference could have produced the observed difference by chance.

TABLE 2-18. PERCENTAGE OF FIRMS HAVING MULTIDIVISIONAL STRUCTURES
AT THE START OF EACH DECADE.

Category	Nondiversifiers	Diversifiers	Significance of Difference
1949–1959			
Single Business	0	13.2	.005
Dominant Business	6.7	33.1	.025
1959–1969			
Single Business	0	0	No Difference
Dominant Business	32.0	37.3	Not Significant

NOTE: Comments appended to Table 2-17 also apply to this table.

of increase in divisionalization with diversification. As Chandler noted, after reviewing the organizational histories of General Motors, Du Pont, Standard Oil of New Jersey, and Sears Roebuck, "structure often failed to follow strategy. In each of the four companies, there was a time lag between the appearance of the administrative needs and their satisfaction. A primary reason for delay was the very fact that responsible executives had become too enmeshed in operational activities." [7] On the other hand, since there were only 13 Dominant diversifiers during 1959–1969 in the sample, there is a good chance that even if a relationship between diversification and divisionalization did exist for this group, a larger sample would be required to reveal it.

In addition to the effect of strategy on structure, there is the possibility that structure affects strategy. If a Single or Dominant Business firm adopts a product-division structure, perhaps in response to relatively minor variations in products, it might be more likely to diversify further than if it had not reorganized. The general managers in the headquarters office, freed from responsibility over day to day operations, may gain the objectivity required to look for opportunity beyond the current scope of their business. Furthermore, if diversification is attempted, it may proceed more rapidly within the administrative climate of the divisionalized firm. Table 2-18 was constructed to test this hypothesis. As in Table 2-17 the major strategic categories have been split into diversifiers and nondiversifiers, but here the criterion shown is the percentage of each group that had multidivisional structures at the *start* of each decade.

The evidence shows a strong connection between divisionalization and subsequent diversification in the first decade, but none in the second decade. Since

---

[7] *Strategy and Structure,* p. 389.

no Single Business firms in the sample had product-division structure in 1959, there is no way to measure the effect of divisionalization on Single Business diversification during 1959–1969. In the first decade divisionalized Dominant Business firms were more likely to shift to the Related class, but, as in the case of the strategy-structure relationship, in the second decade this association between structure and strategy was absent.

In conclusion, divisionalization and diversification were strongly associated during 1949–1959. In the next decade the evidence suggests that Single Business firms again were likely to divisionalize upon diversifying. During 1959–1969, however, the pattern of Dominant Business diversification changed, and interdependence with structure and structural change—if in existence—was not evident within the sample. This suggests that until the early 1960s the adoption of product-division structures was strongly contingent upon the administrative pressures created by diversification but that in more recent years divisionalization has become accepted as the norm and managements have sought reorganization along product-division lines in response to normative theory rather than actual administrative pressure.

SUMMARY

During the period 1949–1969 basic changes took place in the diversification strategies and organizational structures of large industrial firms. Many companies that had previously had narrow product-market scopes elected to diversify into new businesses related to their past strengths; in the latter portion of this era the tendency increased for such firms to move into lightly related or unrelated businesses. The only major exception to this pattern was the vertically integrated corporation. While many of the large vertically integrated industrials developed new business activities based upon by-products and the further processing of their main products, few chose to diversify into activities that did not make direct use of their raw material resources or primary production capacity.

The trend toward divisionalization paralleled the increase in diversification but was not wholly dependent upon it. While diversification and divisionalization were closely linked in the 1950s, during the 1960s the link was less clear, although both trends continued unabated.

The effects of both types of change have been profound. In 1949 the typical large firm followed a Single Business strategy and was functionally organized. By 1969, the modal strategy was Related-Linked and more than three quarters of large firms had product-division structures. This change has a dual nature: diversification serves to insulate the firm from the risks associated with each separate product-market activity but divisionalization places a particular unit of the firm in a close relationship with each business area. The result is a new type of industrial structure that is not adequately described by the traditional bureaucratic, oligopoly, industry structure, or competitive models of corporate behavior and influence.

Financial Performance

THIS CHAPTER PRESENTS AND INTERPRETS the results of an analysis of the average financial performance of firms in each of the categories of diversification strategy and structure. The focus will be on differences in performance among the categories, with membership in a category taken to be a relatively stable and continuing property of the firm.

The strategy of diversification, although creating complex problems of planning and administration, is generally thought to provide more than compensating benefits. Writers have theorized that diversification should decrease the variability of a firm's earnings, permit the pursuit of both growth and profit without conflict, expedite adaptation to change, and provide economies of scale in general management expertise and research and development. Accordingly, one would expect that the financial performance of diversified firms would be superior to that of nondiversified firms. Although this is true in a very general sense, there are several important exceptions and qualifications. In particular, the Unrelated-Passive group has experienced below average rates of profit and growth, and the nonvertically integrated Single and Dominant Business firms have, in some respects, outperformed diversified corporations in the Related Business category. In addition, although most of the differences in financial performance among categories can, in a sense, be attributed to a strong association between a firm's industry and its strategy, the association is so strong that it is virtually impossible to separate their relative effects. Diversification strategy cannot therefore be viewed simply as the result of management action but must be seen as bound up with the technological, economic, and competitive characteristics of the industry or industries of which the firm is a part.

Before the empirical data is presented, the nature of the anticipated results will be reviewed. While several of these conjectures were not supported by the data, the hypotheses and the conceptual schemes that underlie them provide starting points for analyzing the data and also offer a framework for distinguishing between the expected and surprising empirical results.

Theory and Hypotheses

Before the empirical portion of this study was begun a number of *a priori* expectations or hypotheses were developed concerning the relative financial characteristics of the categories. Most were derived from five different, but not necessarily exclusive, views of diversification and the behavior of diversified firms. They were (1) the portfolio concept of diversification; (2) the theory that diversification is a response to declining rates of profit and growth in a firm's original business; (3) the theory that diversification and divisionalization are associated with high returns to scale in the general management function and the area of research and development; (4) the conjecture that diversified divisionalized corporations possess control, reward, and resource allocation systems that are basically different from those of undiversified firms; and (5) the observation that in certain circumstances the strategy of an acquisitive conglomerate has proved startlingly successful, at least in terms of the growth achieved.

(1) *Portfolio Risk*. One of the simplest and most often used arguments in favor of diversification is that it reduces the total risk or variability in earnings that comes from spreading investment funds and effort among several businesses. Just as a mutual fund reduces the risk inherent in purchasing a single security by holding many, management can employ diversification to reduce the total risk borne by a corporation.

Until fairly recently it was commonly assumed that the smaller the commitment made to any particular security (or business) the more perfect the diversification.[1] The application of the modern Markowitz diversification theory to the securities market has shown that the best possible diversification is achieved by portfolios consisting of a few carefully selected securities (often less than ten).[2] The key requirement for efficient diversification is that negatively correlated returns be sought—if one goes up the other goes down. This result suggests that "too much" diversification can increase the risk faced by a corpo-

---

[1] Federal tax law, for example, gives tax benefits only to those mutual funds which have less than 5 percent of their assets in any particular security.

[2] Harry M. Markowitz, *Portfolio Selection: Efficient Diversification of Investments* (New York: John Wiley & Sons, 1959).

ration and that optimal diversification, in the statistical sense, is *not* necessarily obtained by investing in completely unrelated areas. For example, the ultimate diversified company, participating in all sectors of the economy would, by definition, have an average return and still bear the risk associated with major economic cycles. A firm active in military, space, and consumer electronics might earn an equal or better return and obtain superior protection against economic cycles.

There are, however, variations in sales and earnings that are of greater interest to the business manager than those caused by economic cycles: the secular shift in demand due to product obsolescence is the major business risk of this type, since the "cycle" in this case promises no recovery from the downward slide. Thus American Car and Foundry's diversification away from railroad cars to escape the "cyclical nature of the business" and moves of the major dairy companies into chemicals and packaged foods can be seen as attempts to reduce the evident risk of remaining totally committed to a declining or stagnant product-market area. It is hypothesized that the risks associated with product life-cycles, rather than with variability per se, provide the primary motive for diversification and are those from which diversification can provide the most important relief.

The value of negatively correlated returns implies that the best defense against a declining market is not a new unrelated activity but a new product that is functionally related to the reasons for the declining sales or profitability of the old. Thus, the optimal response to a declining demand for, say, textbooks is not to emphasize fiction or move into electronics but to create a product that should grow for the very reason textbooks are declining. If, for example, college instructors are making greater use of original sources, one might offer a scholarly paper reprint service along with collected excerpts from primary sources. This type of strategy, one of response rather than escape, requires two conditions: (1) a strategy of defining one's business in terms of a function rather than a product; and (2) the possession of sufficient managerial, technological, and marketing breadth and experience to permit rapid innovation and successful implementation of innovation.

The corporate characteristics that best mitigate the risks associated with the product life-cycle are those most closely represented by the Related Business group, and, in particular, those Related Business firms that have not diversified to such an extent that successes as well as failures are averaged out. Therefore, *it was hypothesized that the Related-Constrained category would experience the lowest risk in earnings and have an average rate of return at least as large as those of other categories.* In addition, it was conjectured that the ranking of the categories, in order of increasing riskiness relative to return, would be: Related-Constrained, Related-Linked, Unrelated, Dominant and Single.

(2) *The Escape Paradigm*. For a great many firms, diversification is the means employed to escape from declining prospects in their original business areas. Poor absolute performance is often the result of participation in a highly competitive noninnovative slow growth industry, or is simply due to failure to cope with competition in a potentially promising area. For example, both American Car and Foundry and American Brake Shoe, moved away from the railroad equipment industry in the 1950s; Armour has attempted to diversify away from meat packing; Borden, Pet, and Fairmont have developed a program to decrease their dependence on low margin dairy staples; General Foods has moved away from flour milling; and Republic Steel and U.S. Steel have ventured into housing.

If such firms can develop a strategy of diversification that builds on skills already possessed, namely a type of Dominant-Constrained or Related-Constrained strategy, it is expected that there would be a greater chance of success than if tenuously related or unrelated businesses are entered. Firms with few exploitable skills that are seeking escape through diversification, are most likely to adopt Dominant-Linked, Dominant-Unrelated, and Unrelated strategies, and will almost unavoidably use acquisition as the means of change. Since there is no *a priori* reason to expect acquisitions that do not build on current businesses to provide more than an average return, and, at least in the Dominant category, the original poorly performing business will outweigh new activities, it is expected that Dominant-Linked, Dominant-Unrelated and Unrelated firms will generally have less than average returns on investment.

The above conjecture must be somewhat qualified for the science-based industries. In industries such as chemicals, electronics, and complex business and industrial machinery, Linked and Unrelated postures may well be the result, perhaps the unexpected result, of science-based research. In such cases high performance would follow from the proprietary benefits that are typically associated with technological innovation. Consequently, the hypothesis offered is that *firms (excluding members of science-based industries) that adopt Dominant-Linked, Dominant-Unrelated or Unrelated-Passive strategies will experience returns on equity that are significantly lower than those achieved by firms in the same industry but with other strategies.*

(3) *Organizational Scale*. In a study of the organizational preconditions for direct investments abroad, Stopford found a close association between research and development intensity, product innovation, the product-division structure, and the degree of direct foreign investment.[3] In a subsequent paper, Fouraker and Stopford theorized that this relationship was due to the competitive advantage of innovative firms in foreign markets and the superior ability of product-division organizations to train and use general managers and to bring a diversity of staff specialists, technologies, and managerial experience

---

[3] Stopford, "Growth and Change in the Multinational Firm."

to bear on opportunities in several areas. They concluded that "the growth of foreign markets and opportunities requires diversification, reorganization, and the training of many more general international managers. The organizations that have been most successful in meeting this new challenge have been those Type (3) [product-division] organizations that had already developed the ability to produce general managers capable of controlling and guiding a heterogeneous, diverse enterprise." [4]

While foreign investment behavior is not investigated in this study, Fouraker and Stopford's conjecture that the product-division structure provides special advantages in innovative activity and develops the general management skills necessary to exploit these advantages is of interest. A further elaboration on this theme was provided by Vernon, who noted that such advantages could be seen as economies of scale. Arguing that large firms are better at the whole process of innovation—not necessarily at the act of innovation itself, but at the development and marketing activities which must be carried out to realize the benefits of innovation—Vernon suggested that the product-division structure is the key to gaining these advantages. The "constant process of search and adaptation, a process which continually pushes the firm into new products and new markets while permitting it to slough off the more senescent activities in which it has been engaged" he stated, was best carried out in a product-division framework because of its openness to change, explicit procedures for resource allocation, and heavy emphasis on localized coordination across functions. [5]

These observations suggest that the performance advantages of diversified divisionalized corporations, if such advantages exist, will be greater in environments calling for and producing relatively rapid technological change. More formally, it was hypothesized that *the effects of the product-division structure on growth and profitability will be more favorable in environments that require or encourage relatively rapid technological change.* This hypothesis does not imply that product-division firms necessarily have growth and profit rates higher than those of functional firms. It merely states that the effects of the product-division structure on performance will be *relatively* more favorable in environments characterized by change.

(4) *Systems Effects.* Systems of reward, control, and resource allocation influence behavior and performance. If, as several writers have pointed out, diversified divisionalized firms employ systems that are significantly different from those used by low diversity, functionally organized corporations, the effects of the difference might be observable in their respective records of financial performance.

As noted in Chapter 1, Scott's model of corporate development calls attention to many of the ways in which diversified divisionalized firms differ from

---

[4] Lawrence E. Fouraker and J. M. Stopford, "Organizational Structure and Multinational Strategy," *Administrative Science Quarterly,* June 1968, p. 64.

[5] Vernon, "Organization as a Scale Factor," p. 63.

simpler forms of enterprise. Goals, he suggests, become increasingly quantitative and oriented toward return on investment as the firm becomes active in diverse markets. While objectives such as obtaining the largest market share, the most sales, or the highest margins may be useful in a oligopolistic environment, objective comparison between businesses that also compete internally for corporate funds requires a standard that is uniform and directly related to the efficient use of resources—return on investment. The explicit and quantitative nature of the goals employed by divisionalized firms is matched by the creation of more formal systems of reward that tie promotion and bonuses to economic performance. The effects of these changes are compounded by the increase in the number of general management roles that comes with diversification and divisionalization. The ultimate general manager in a functional firm is the chief executive; for him promotion is irrelevant and only disastrous performance or age can usually unseat him. The division managers of a diversified firm, on the other hand, compete directly with one another as well as with outside firms, may receive substantial rewards in terms of money and status for outstanding performance, and are subject to transfer, dismissal or bonus reduction if their performance is below par. Scott states:

> . . . ease of measurement by the numbers (profit numbers) gives high visibility for good performance, hence the potential for rapid promotions in competition with others. A manager thus has the opportunity to make his way by "getting results" as much as by getting on well with his immediate superiors. A divisional organization with its open competition moves to another way of life, as removed from the functional organization and its bureaucratic traditions as the functional is from the family-like organization of the entrepreneurial stage.[6]

This internal socioeconomic system, which creates pressure for the efficient use of capital, also possesses the important property of being easily expandable. It is often simpler to create a new division to handle a new business than to merge its operations with those of a functional structure. Of course, diversification by acquisition almost always requires a product-division structure. The economic significance of these two structural attributes is that the conflict between the goals of high return and high rates of growth may be resolved by the divisionalized corporation.

Traditional microeconomic theory predicts a negative relation between a firm's rate of growth and its profitability. High rates of growth are achieved by accepting lower rates of return on incremental investments. While the normative theory of growth is not sufficiently well developed to determine the optimal growth rate for a particular firm, many researchers have suggested

---

[6] Scott, "Stages of Corporate Development," p. 35.

that business executives often seem to be overly concerned with growth. Baumol notes that: "economists who have spent time observing the operations of business enterprises come away impressed with the extent of management's preoccupation with growth. Expansion is a theme that (with some variations) is dinned into the ears of stockholders and is constantly reported in the financial pages and the journals devoted to business affairs. Indeed, in talking to business executives one may easily come to believe that the growth of the firm is the main preoccupation of top management." [7]

Whether the pursuit of growth in a Single Business firm stems from oligopolistic competition or simply from the desire to preside over an ever larger enterprise, it must be at the expense of profit. The divisionalized firm, by contrast, may be able to separate these goals to a much greater extent, pushing for maximum return in its current areas of operation and achieving growth through continuing diversification. The hypothesis that is offered to summarize this argument states: *Among firms with product-division structures, the relationship between growth and return on investment will not be as strong as among other types of firms.*

This hypothesis does not imply that product-division firms have, on average, either growth rates or rates of profit that are higher than those of other types of firms. While they may outperform functional firms, there are special problems associated with diversification and divisionalization that could easily depress the overall performance of these firms. To many executives, Gerald Loeb's advice "to put all your eggs in one basket—and then watch the basket" is still sound. While the product-division structure is based on the logical principle of having several "watchers" for several "baskets," the necessary emphasis on short-term measures may result in short-term performance. Furthermore, independent strategies to optimize the performance of each division do not necessarily produce optimum corporate performance. A large corporation has the capacity to bear risk and engage in long-term development projects that exceeds that of each division considered separately. As Berg notes:

> The divisions can no doubt judge what is in their own best interest better than the corporation can, but this ability is of little help to a corporate management interested in spending the limited resources available to the corporation in *its* interest. In addition, asking the divisions to take a broad corporate viewpoint when striking a balance between their own project expenditure and current profit is asking them to do a job which men at the corporate level themselves find exceedingly difficult to do (and which the divisions are ill-equipped to attempt). [8]

---

[7] William J. Baumol, *Business Behavior, Value and Growth* (New York: Harcourt, Brace & World, 1967), p. 87.

[8] Norman A. Berg, "Strategic Planning in Conglomerate Companies," *Harvard Business Review*, May–June 1965, p. 86.

The administrative difficulties associated with resource allocation in the diversified firm are compounded by the conceptual problem of defining suitable criteria for guiding the direction of diversification. Naïve schemes based on investing in industries that have high rates of growth and profit ignore the facts that if these profits are based on proprietary skills there is little reason to expect that they will accrue to an inexperienced entrant or that existing firms can be purchased for less than their fair value. Furthermore, if an area's profitability and growth are due to a supply-demand imbalance, it probably will act as a "cash trap" as capital investment matches growth and prices drop to equilibrium levels. As many of the firms that diversified into the computer industry discovered, IBM's performance was not an "industry" phenomenon and quite a few other diversifiers learned in the mid-1960s that the apparently lucrative chemical fertilizer and plastics chemicals businesses all too often absorbed large amounts of capital only to have margins drop drastically as total capacity exceeded demand. Clearly, a strategy of diversification cannot eliminate the need for careful consideration of the firm's special competences.

While certain advantages connected with economies of scale in research, general management depth, openness to opportunity, and performance-oriented control systems may be available to diversified divisionalized firms, the exploitation of these advantages is a major strategic and administrative challenge. Whether or not the average diversified firm has met and overcome this challenge to the degree necessary to produce superior performance is, at this point, a moot issue and more appropriately resolved by analysis of empirical data than further discussion. Thus, the following hypothesis represents a question to be tested rather than an expectation: (1) *Related Business firms will, on average, have higher profitability, higher rates of growth, and higher price-earnings ratios than other categories of firms;* (2) *Related-Constrained firms will outperform Related-Linked firms in the above areas;* and (3) *divisionalized Related Business firms will outperform those that are functionally organized.*

(5) *Conglomerate Growth.* Acquisitive conglomerates are a fairly recent phenomenon; most of the firms adopting this strategy of expansion did so in the decade 1960–1969. Both their mechanics of growth and the question of their ultimate economic efficiency have been subjected to scrutiny by researchers, the investment community, and U.S. Senate subcommittees without definitive conclusions being reached on either issue.[9]

One explanation of the conglomerate's ability to maintain a rapid pace of acquisition is a variation of the "bigger fool" theory of common-stock valua-

---

[9] For a spectrum of views see Harry H. Lynch, *Financial Performance of Conglomerates* (Boston: Division of Research, Harvard Business School, 1971); Statement of Dr. Irwin Stelzer, Hearings before the Senate Committee on the Judiciary, Subcommittee on Antitrust and Monopoly, *Economic Concentration*, Part 1, 88th Cong., 2d sess. (Washington, D.C.: Government Printing Office, 1967), pp. 181–202; and Thomas O'Hanlon, "The Odd News About Conglomerates," *Fortune*, June 15, 1967, pp. 175–177.

tion—if dividends are zero the security is still worth what the next bigger fool will pay for it. More formally, if the investing public acts as if it determines the value of a share of common stock by multiplying earnings per share by a price-earnings ratio and takes the price-earnings ratio to be some increasing function of recent earnings-per-share growth, then the firm can establish positive feedback between price-earnings ratio, acquisition rate, and growth in earnings per share. No value has to be created and early stockholders benefit at the expense of later investors because, once the growth rate slows, equity prices must drop to levels warranted by current earnings. Lynch has shown that if investors do look only at growth of earnings per share, such a strategy is possible and indeed seems to have been used by at least several conglomerates.

Another explanation rests on the idea that while the market feedback effect plays a role in conglomerate growth, value can be created. If (1) the return on capital of acquired firms can be improved, (2) if the capital structure of acquired firms can be rationalized, or (3) if there are any economic returns to scale through conglomeration, then the conglomerate's growth rate and price-earnings ratio may be warranted. As a very simplified example, suppose that a firm currently earning $1 million annually has a price-earnings ratio of 10, giving a market value of $10 million. If this firm's management can convince the public that it has the ability to acquire firms earning a total of, say, $20 million and to produce a 10 percent improvement in performance, the value of that extra potential $2 million per year, capitalized at a price-earnings ratio of 10 is $20 million. If this is added to the firm's current worth of $10 million it produces a current price-earnings ratio of 30, which, in turn, enables the company to carry out its acquisition program. Whether or not the acquired firms grow themselves is immaterial—it is the improvement in return that creates value. While such improvements may be possible, the public is not well equipped to decide which potential conglomerate will be able to deliver on its promises.

The question of the ultimate economic efficiency of a conglomerate also involves the degree to which improvements in acquired firms can be affected but excludes the larger issue of administrative control. Once growth slows, will the multi-industry Unrelated Business firm be able to operate efficiently and set strategy effectively in all its constituent areas? The same pro and con arguments that were discussed for the case of Related Business firms apply in even starker terms to the conglomerate. In addition, there is the very real problem of holding on to and attracting superior general management talent when the atmosphere of explosive growth gives way to stability. Unfortunately, the very newness of the conglomerate phenomenon prevents us from being able to bring much empirical evidence to bear on this question. While a few firms in the Unrelated-Passive category could be described as Acquisitive Conglomerates that have moved past their rapid growth phase, most of the Unrelated-

Passive firms never were Acquisitive Conglomerates. Instead, some became unrelated quite slowly and others became unrelated through a single merger that was not followed by further important unrelated acquisitions.

The hypotheses to be tested are designed to provide information on the degree to which conglomerate growth is related to abnormally high price-earnings ratios and the ability of Acquisitive Conglomerates to operate efficiently. It is hypothesized *that Acquisitive Conglomerates had price-earnings ratios that were significantly higher than those of other firms and that conglomerate price-earnings ratios were strongly related to the growth in earnings per share achieved. Both Acquisitive Conglomerates and Unrelated-Passive firms had average returns on capital that were not significantly different from the overall average of other types of firms.*

THE ANALYSIS OF FINANCIAL DATA

The financial data used in the analysis of the performance characteristics of the categories of diversification strategy and organizational structure were obtained from a modified version of the *Compustat* data bank. This computer disk file contained financial histories for the period 1951–1970 for almost all of the firms in the sample that had survived through 1970 as well as data on about 1,500 other corporations. The *Compustat* data, as well as data files containing information generated in this study, were accessed in a time-sharing mode through computer programs written expressly for this research. The programs contained routines for the manipulation of data, computation of simple averages, growth rates and standard deviations, multivariate regression, analysis of variance, and other statistical procedures.

The following variables were studied. The abbreviations are used to identify them in tables and graphs.

(1) *GSALES:* annual rate of growth in net sales.

(2) *GERN:* annual rate of growth in earnings after taxes and preferred dividends.

(3) *GEPS:* annual rate of growth in earnings per common share.

(4) *SDEPS:* relative standard deviation of year-to-year variation of earnings per share about the average long-term uniform growth trend. *SDEPS* is best thought of as the measure of the variability of annual growth rates.

(5) *PE:* price-earnings ratio of common stock.

(6) *ROC:* after-tax return on invested capital (net income plus interest divided by invested capital).

(7) *ROE:* after-tax return on equity (net income less preferred dividends divided by book equity).

(8) *E/C:* ratio of book equity to invested capital.

(9) *IFR:* internal-financing ratio defined as the ratio of the market value of added equity to earnings after taxes (annual retained earnings plus market value of new shares issued divided by earnings after tax and preferred dividends).

(10) *RPR:* risk-premium ratio for earnings per share defined as $(GEPS - 0.015)/SDEPS$ where 0.015 is taken as the available risk-free, after-tax rate of return. *RPR* is a measure of the degree to which growth above and beyond the risk-free rate is matched by increasing variability in earnings.

More detailed definitions of these variables together with descriptions of the computational procedures used to determine their values are given in Appendix B.

Although financial data were available on an annual basis from 1951 to 1970, knowledge of the firms' strategic categorization was limited to three points in time: 1949, 1959, and 1969. If a firm stayed in the same strategic category throughout a decade it is clear that its financial performance during that decade can be associated with that particular category. However, if a firm moved between categories, say from the Single Business category in 1949 to the Related-Constrained category in 1959, there is no unambiguous way of associating its financial performance during that period with any particular category. Not only is the precise date of transition unknown, if such a concept is even meaningful, but the very fact that a firm was moving between categories suggests that its performance might not be representative of the long-term characteristics of firms in any category. Consequently, the analyses presented in this chapter are based only on data pertaining to firms that stayed in the same category throughout a decade. For example, the average growth rate in earnings per share (*GEPS*) of Single Business firms is estimated from 1950–1959 data on firms that were in the Single Business category in both 1949 *and* 1959, and from 1960–1969 data on firms that were in the Single Business category in both 1959 *and* 1969. Thus, the category averages presented in this chapter include only firms whose product-market scopes remained stable for at least ten years.

One exception to the requirement of at least a ten-year residence in a category was made: the characteristics of Acquisitive Conglomerates were estimated by averaging data on all firms that fell in this category by the *end* of a decade. Because of the relative newness of this strategy, only two firms in the sample qualified as Acquisitive Conglomerates in both 1959 and 1969 (Colt and Grace), while twelve other firms adopted this strategy by 1969. Thus, it would have been impossible to obtain reasonable estimates of this category's average financial characteristics unless this modification in the rules for inclusion were made.

The elementary data points used in analyses were decade averages rather than annual observations. After the annual values of a financial variable for a firm had been found, two summary averages were obtained—one for 1951–1959 and one for 1960–1969. Category averages were then calculated by combining the appropriate decade averages and making corrections for time trends in average values (see Appendix B for details). While this procedure reduced the number of data points by a factor of ten, the existence of fairly long-lasting "firm effects" prevents the direct use of annual data.[10]

In calculating the decade averages, growth rates were obtained by making least-squares fits to a uniform growth model, simple arithmetic averages were used for the other variables, and both procedures included rules for omitting meaningless values and dealing with missing data points. Details are given in Appendix B.

Category Averages

Tables 3-1, 3-2, and 3-3 show the estimated mean values of the ten financial variables for the major strategic categories, all the strategic categories, and the organizational categories respectively. These results were obtained by regression analysis with "zero-one" variables used to represent the effects of the different categories and time. The estimated mean values displayed are *trend corrected,* and their absolute magnitudes have been referred to the 1960–1969 period. It must be emphasized, however, that it is the differences between category means that are important, and to which tests of significance apply, not their absolute magnitudes.

It was not necessary to display both the 1951–1959 and 1960–1969 means because interaction effects were not significant. That is, time trends in the financial variables seemed to affect all categories equally so that the 1951–1959 estimated means differ from those shown only by a constant amount for each variable, leaving the category differences unchanged.

F-ratios test the degree to which the entire set of category means differ from one another. More precisely, they provide a test of the hypothesis that all of the category means are actually equal. The level of significance of each F-ratio is shown in the tables. Note that the F-ratios may not be significant even when certain pairs of estimated category means differ significantly. This is because the F-ratios take into account the idea that with, say, eight categories there are twenty-eight possible pairable comparisons and random error will probably cause one of them to appear significant at the 5 percent level even if the true means are all equal.

In Table 3-2 F_1-ratios test the hypothesis, "all true category means are equal," and F_2-ratios test the hypothesis, "all true category means other than that of the Acquisitive Conglomerate category are equal." This distinction was necessary because Acquisitive Conglomerates were, in part, selected

---

[10] In other words, ten separate observations of Xerox's growth rate are not statistically equivalent to observing the growth rates of ten different office equipment companies.

TABLE 3-1. FINANCIAL CHARACTERISTICS OF THE MAJOR STRATEGIC CATEGORIES.

	GSALES	GERN	GEPS	SDEPS	PE	ROC	ROE	E/C	IFR	RPR
Est. Category Means:										
Single	7.17⁻⁻	4.81⁻⁻⁻	3.92⁻⁻	16.13⁻	14.60⁻⁻⁻	10.81	13.20	0.781	0.580⁻⁻	0.378⁻⁻
Dominant	8.03⁻⁻	7.95	5.99	22.40⁺	15.74⁻⁻⁻	9.64⁻⁻	11.64⁻⁻	0.752⁻	0.640	0.424⁻⁻
Related	9.14	9.39	7.64	16.43⁻⁻⁻	19.21⁺⁺⁺	11.49⁺⁺	13.55⁺⁺	0.799⁺⁺⁺	0.714	0.669⁺⁺⁺
Unrelated	14.24⁺⁺⁺	13.86⁺⁺⁺	7.92	31.19⁺⁺⁺	15.75	9.49	11.92	0.696⁻⁻⁻	1.322⁺⁺⁺	0.437
Est. Overall Mean	9.01	8.72	6.57	20.11	17.02	10.52	12.64	0.769	0.732	0.516
Partial R^2 (percent)	14.7	6.3	2.6	6.1	9.0	2.8	2.7	2.4	16.9	7.0
Sig. F_1-Ratio Test	.001	.001	.1	.005	.001	.05	.1	.1	.001	.001
Sig. F_2-Ratio Test	.05	.05	.1	.1	.001	.05	.1	.01	–	.001
Sig. F_3-Ratio Test	.001	.005	–	.1	–	.001	.001	.001	.001	–

NOTE: Estimated mean values of E/C, IFR, PE, and RPR are expressed as ratios; all others are expressed as percentages. The plus or minus signs following an estimated category mean indicate that it differed significantly ("+" for a positive deviation, "−" for a negative deviation) from the overall mean (t-ratio test). One sign indicates a deviation significant at the 0.1 level, two signs indicate the 0.05 level and three signs the 0.01 level. The partial R^2 shows the percentage reduction in variance due to category effects (as distinct from time effects). The F_1-ratio was used to test the hypothesis that category effects were absent (all category means are equal). The F_2-ratio was used to test the hypothesis that category effects, other than that of the Unrelated category, are absent. The table shows the levels of significance at which these hypotheses could be rejected.

TABLE 3-2. FINANCIAL CHARACTERISTICS OF THE STRATEGIC CATEGORIES.

	GSALES	GERN	GEPS	SDEPS	PE	ROC	ROE	E/C	IFR	RPR
Est. Category Means:										
Single	7.17^{--}	4.81^{---}	3.92^{-}	16.13^{-}	14.60^{---}	10.81	13.20	0.781	0.580	0.378^{--}
Dom.-Vertical	7.42^{--}	7.34^{-}	5.14^{-}	22.79	15.68^{--}	8.24^{---}	10.18^{--}	0.724^{---}	0.662^{--}	0.329^{---}
Dom.-Constrained	9.48	9.08	7.60	23.15	15.92	12.71^{+++}	14.91^{++}	0.807^{+}	0.609^{--}	0.658^{++}
Dom.-Linked-Unrelated	6.93	8.10	6.11	16.63	15.41	8.69	10.28	0.758	0.601	0.221^{-}
Related-Constrained	9.62	10.39^{++}	8.56^{+++}	15.91^{--}	19.19^{+++}	11.97^{+++}	14.11^{+++}	0.800^{++}	0.729	0.775^{+++}
Related-Linked	8.06	7.15	5.57	17.58	19.27^{+++}	10.43	12.28	0.798	0.681	0.451
Unrelated-Passive	6.10^{-}	7.78	5.96	20.90	13.77^{--}	9.40	10.38^{-}	0.830^{+}	0.616	0.357^{-}
Acquisitive-Conglom.	20.64^{+++}	18.64^{+++}	9.46^{+}	39.28^{+++}	17.43	9.56	13.13	0.591^{---}	1.970^{+++}	0.516
Est. Overall Mean	9.01	8.72	6.57	20.11	17.02	10.52	12.64	0.769	0.732	0.516
Est. Residual σ	6.06	8.73	8.02	18.63	5.45	5.05	5.33	0.142	0.400	0.456
Partial R² (percent)	20.00	11.40	5.50	8.80	10.30	9.40	9.60	13.00	36.40	7.40
Sig. F_1-Ratio Test	.001	.001	—	.005	.001	.005	.001	.001	.001	.015
Sig. F_2-Ratio Test	.05	.1	—	—	.001	.001	.005	.025	—	—

NOTE: Refer to the note to Table 3-1 for definitions of symbols. The F_1-ratio was used to test the hypothesis that category effects were zero (all category means are equal). The F_2-ratio was used to test the hypothesis that category effects are zero if the Acquisitive Conglomerate category is excluded. The table shows the significance levels at which these hypotheses can be rejected.

TABLE 3-3. FINANCIAL CHARACTERISTICS OF THE STRUCTURE CATEGORIES.

	GSALES	GERN	GEPS	SDEPS	PE	ROC	ROE	E/C	IFR	RPR
Est. Category Means:										
Functional	8.55	6.76---	5.08---	20.13	14.86---	10.28	12.28	0.774+	0.634--	0.329---
Functional-with-subs.	6.49--	9.57	8.32	23.90	16.60	9.49	11.09	0.766	0.671	0.485
Product Division	9.77+++	10.66+++	8.63++	19.82	18.73+++	10.75	12.90+	0.743-	0.762++	0.667+++
Est. Overall Mean	8.98	9.17	7.37	20.47	17.21	10.43	12.45	0.756	0.713	0.531
Est. Residual σ	5.22	8.18	7.71	19.88	6.27	5.10	5.02	0.144	0.429	0.700
Partial R² (percent)	8.2	4.5	4.6	0.5	4.5	0.5	4.1	1.4	1.4	4.7
Sig. F_1-Ratio Test	.025	.01	.05	—	.05	—	.05	—	—	.005

NOTE: Refer to the note to Table 3-1 for definitions of symbols. The F_1-ratio was used to test the hypothesis that category effects are zero and the table shows the significance levels at which this hypothesis can be rejected.

on the basis of their high rates of growth so that a significant F_1 for growth variables due to a high mean in the Acquisitive Conglomerate category is virtually meaningless. Hence F_2, testing the differences among the other means, is the relevant statistic for the growth variables. When an F-ratio is significant, the hypothesis of equality can be *rejected* and the conclusion can be drawn that true category differences actually exist.

Readers who are unfamiliar with some of these concepts and those who prefer a more detailed discussion of the techniques employed are referred to Appendix B.

Preliminary Evaluation

Without going too deeply into the nature and implications of the empirical data at this point, an overall appraisal of the results leads to several general but important conclusions. Table 3-2 indicates that differences in diversification strategy accounted for significant amounts of the variation in all of the financial variables except growth in earnings per share. Furthermore, it is evident that while the Acquisitive Conglomerate category, which was known in advance to be a special case, was an important contributor to the total discriminatory power of the categories, financial differences among the other categories were significant for seven of the ten variables. It is especially noteworthy that the variables providing the best measures of economic efficiency and overall investor appraisal of performance—return on equity, return on capital, and price-earnings ratio—were strongly related to diversification strategy.

The performance differences revealed by Table 3-2 show a high degree of consistency; strategies that are associated with high profitability tend also to be associated with high rates of growth, lower amounts of variability, and higher price-earnings multiples. This pattern of consistency allows three clusters of strategies to be identified:

Performance
————————

High	Medium	Low
Dominant-Constrained	Related-Linked	Dominant-Vertical
Related-Constrained	Single	Unrelated-Passive

Acquisitive Conglomerate

The heterogeneity of these clusters is particularly striking. There is no evidence to suggest that performance varies smoothly with the degree of diversity. Rather, two "losing strategies" stand out: among undiversified and lightly diversified companies, the strategy of vertical integration has tended to be associated with poor performance, and among diversified firms the Unrelated-

Passive product-market posture has produced distinctly below-average results. The dissimilarity of the two low-performing strategies is intriguing and the reasons for the below-average performance of these categories will be examined in Chapter 4.

The fact that the categories are associated with significantly different levels of financial performance, regardless of the specific pattern of the differences, is itself an important finding. In one of the most careful and comprehensive studies of corporate diversification in the United States, Gort tried to relate growth in assets (1939–1954) and return on equity (1947–1954) to a composite measure of diversification based on a 4-digit product count and a type of specialization ratio, but he found only very small and nonsignificant correlations.[11] In a more recent study, Eslick regressed return on equity for the period 1956–1965 against 4-digit product count for 450 of the firms in the *Fortune* 500. Again, no association was found.[12] Since there appears to be no relation between profitability and overall measures of diversity, the connection between profitability and diversification strategy shown in Table 3-2 takes on extra importance. In addition to representing managerially meaningful distinctions among corporate diversification postures, the strategic categories and the "top down" approach to measurement reveal a consistent pattern of strategy associated performance differences that are not discernible when traditional measures of diversification are employed.

Why does the category technique reveal a relationship between diversification and performance when simple measures of diversity do not? The answer is twofold. First, the categories are actually a crude approximation to a multidimensional measure that takes into account several factors in addition to diversity per se. Second, the pattern of differences observed indicates that it is not diversity itself but the central organizing principle used to manage diversity that is the critical factor in explaining performance differentials.

Neither return on equity nor return on capital, for example, seems to show any regular pattern of increase or decrease as one moves from the less to the more "diversified" categories. Table 3-1 indicates that profitability tends to be higher in the Single and Related major groups and lower in the Dominant and Unrelated groups, but that even this "down-up-down" pattern explains only 30 percent of the total variability explained by the subcategories. The story told by the profitability pattern of the subcategories (Table 3-1) seems to be: among Dominant Businesses, those that stayed close to home do well and those that are vertically integrated or have moved into linked and unrelated areas do relatively poorly. Again, among Related Businesses, those that

---

[11] Gort, *Diversification and Integration,* pp. 74–77. Gort did find, however, a moderate relation between the rate of asset growth and the *rate* of entry into new 4-digit industries, though the association is hardly surprising.

[12] Statement of Donald F. Eslick, *Economic Concentration,* Part 8, pp. 4996–5026. Eslick's conclusions emphasized the existence of a moderate negative relation between return on equity and the 4-digit product count between 1959–1967, but since the association was not evident in the longer period 1956–1965, his argument is somewhat perplexing.

have gone further afield have done less well than those that have chosen or been able to limit their product-market scope. Unrelated Businesses have experienced lower than average returns on capital, but the Acquisitive Conglomerates have employed high leverage to boost their return on equity. A similar pattern can be seen for the growth variables, except that Acquisitive Conglomerate growth, without a per-share adjustment, is very much greater than that of any other category.

The degree to which the pattern of price-earnings ratios does *not* correspond to the profitability and growth variables is interesting. Although the Dominant-Constrained group has experienced higher returns and growth than the Related-Constrained group, its price-earnings ratio is not only below that of the Related-Constrained group, but below the overall average. The Related-Linked group, on the other hand, has consistently underperformed both the Dominant-Constrained and Related-Constrained groups but has the highest average price-earnings ratio of all. Why this is so cannot be determined from the financial data alone. This issue will be brought up in a subsequent section, however.

The structure categories also divided the companies into groups with significantly different levels of financial performance. The product-division firms, in general, outperformed functional and functional-with-subsidiaries firms, significant differences being found for six of the ten variables tested. The two types of functional firm, however, did not display similar patterns. The functional-with-subsidiaries type had relatively low rates of sales growth but high growth rates in earnings, while for true functional firms the opposite was true. In addition, while the profitability of true functional firms was close to that of product-division firms, the average return experienced by functional-with-subsidiaries firms was lower than either. Although the reasons for these differences are not clear, it does seem that between them the two functional types can match either the earnings growth rate or profitability of the product-division firms, but not both simultaneously.

THE QUESTION OF INDUSTRY

Given the association of different strategies with different financial consequences, it is natural to inquire whether such differences remain, disappear, or change when each firm's major industry membership is taken into account. For example, while Related Business firms outperformed Dominant Business firms in aggregate, the opposite might be true within some industries. Or, perhaps the aggregate difference is solely the result of unequal membership in industries with different average performance levels.

In the first attempt to develop industry-corrected category differences, each firm was assigned a 3-digit SIC code that was the most representative of its major business activities. Firms so diversified that their primary industry was not determinable were placed in a special group. The value of the financial variables for each firm was then adjusted by subtracting from each decade average the overall decade average of the industry to which the firm belonged. Thus, the financial variables were converted into industry relatives. For example, two firms with returns on capital of 10 percent and 13 percent might belong to industries with average returns to capital of 8 percent and 14 percent, so that their industry relatives become 2 percent and −1 percent respectively. The industry averages were obtained from an analysis of all 1,700 firms in the *Compustat* data bank.

The results of the analysis were negative; industry relatives did not differ significantly by category. Several problems with the procedure, however, cast doubt on the meaningfulness of the result. First, in some cases the average of all *sampled* firms in a given industry fell below the 1,700 firm average and in other cases it was greater. This was essentially due to the small number of sampled firms in each 3-digit industry and meant that the average industry relatives of the categories were not strictly comparable. Second, the sparseness of the *total* number of firms in certain industries when combined with extreme values of particular variables produced spurious relatives. The business equipment group, for instance, had so few firms in it that Xerox's high growth rate gave all the other firms in the group, including IBM, below average relatives. While perhaps true in some strict technical sense, calling Hygrade's performance "relatively" better than IBM's seemed too much of an artifact of the sample to warrant serious attention.

In the second attempt to control for industry effects 2-digit industry groups were used. While the sample firms engaged in a total of twenty-one different 2-digit industries (including a special "conglomerate" group), the chemical group (28) was split into basic chemicals and pharmaceutical-toiletries groups and the transportation group (37) was split into land-based and aviation-aerospace groups to give a total of twenty-three distinct industries. Then, rather than use the industry relatives method, the industry effects and category effects were both represented by zero-one variables in regression analyses.

Theoretically, the regressions should have delivered measures of the relative effects of the categories on performance; measures that would be independent of industry associated differences. However, numerical problems arose that were traced to multicollinearity [13]—the effects of industry and diversification strategy were not separable. At this point, Table 3-4 was constructed and it

---

[13] Operationally a near singular regression matrix. For a discussion of this problem see John R. Meyer and Robert R. Glauber, *Investment Decisions, Economic Forecasting, and Public Policy* (Boston: Division of Research, Harvard Business School, 1964), Chap. viii.

became obvious that industry corrected results were not only elusive, but essentially unattainable and possibly meaningless.

Table 3-4 shows the number of sampled firms in each major industry group that fell in each strategic category in 1969; Table 3-5 displays the same information for 1949. The idea behind industry corrections is to compare firms with similar technological-market environments that have adopted different strategies. But Table 3-4 indicates that most firms have responded similarly to their industry environments. Paper (26), oil (29), rubber (30), and primary metals (33) firms have, for the most part, followed strategies of vertical

TABLE 3-4. FREQUENCY OF DIVERSIFICATION STRATEGY BY INDUSTRY, 1969.

SIC Industry	Single	Dominant-Vertical	Dominant-Constrained, Linked, Unrelated	Related-Constrained	Related-Linked	Unrelated
10 Mining, Metals		1				
20 Food	6	4	3	8	4	2
21 Tobacco			1			
22 Textiles				2		
23 Apparel				1	1	
24 Lumber and Wood Products		1				1
25 Furniture and Fixtures			1			
26 Paper and Containers	1	6	1	1	1	
27 Printing and Publishing	1		1		3	
28 Chemicals			1	4	7	5
283–4 Drugs, Soap, Toiletries			1	9	3	
29 Petroleum		7		2		
30 Rubber and Plastics		4		1		
31 Leather and Shoes			1			
32 Stone, Clay and Glass	1		1	1	4	
33 Primary Metals	1	7			1	
34 Fabricated Metals			2	1	1	1
35 Machinery, Exc. Electrical			7	8	4	4
36 Elect. Mach. and Electronics	1			2	8	3
37 Transportation Equipment	1		4	2	5	3
372 Aircraft and Aerospace			2	1		6
38 Instruments				1		2
39 Miscellaneous					1	
99 Multi-Industry					1	5

NOTE: Shown are the numbers of firms out of the entire sample that were in existence in 1969 and fell in each strategic class within each industry.

TABLE 3-5. FREQUENCY OF DIVERSIFICATION STRATEGY WITHIN INDUSTRIES, 1949.

SIC Industry	Single	Dominant-Vertical	Dominant-Constrained, Linked, Unrelated	Related-Constrained	Related-Linked	Unrelated
10 Mining (Metal & Coal)	2	1				
20 Food	15	8	9	3		
21 Tobacco	3		1			
22 Textiles	1		2	1		
23 Apparel	3					
24 Lumber and Wood Products		3				
25 Furniture and Fixtures			2			
26 Paper and Containers	7	5	1			
27 Printing and Publishing	1		5			
28 Chemicals	2		2	10	8	1
283–4 Drugs, Soap, Toiletries			2	9		
29 Petroleum	8	2		2		
30 Rubber and Plastics		4		1		
31 Leather and Shoes	2					
32 Stone, Clay and Glass	2		2	2		
33 Primary Metals	7	10				
34 Fabricated Metals	2			3		
35 Machinery Exc. Electrical	7		6	12	2	3
36 Elect. Mach. and Electronics	2		5	1	5	
37 Transportation Equipment	10		5	4	1	1
372 Aircraft and Aerospace	4		4	1		
38 Instruments	2		1			1
39 Miscellaneous	1					
99 Multi-Industry						

NOTE: Shown are the numbers of firms out of the entire sample that were in existence in 1949 and fell in each strategic class within each industry.

integration. Textile (22), apparel (23), chemical (28), drug (283), electrical machinery (36), and instrument (38) companies are almost all in the Related Business categories. A closer look at the exceptions shows that they are chiefly due to the broadness of the industry categories. Of the three nonvertical forest products companies, two are really in building materials rather than paper. In the petroleum industry (29), one of the two diversified firms is not an oil company but a paving and roofing materials (asphalt) manufacturer. Consequently, none of these industries really provides enough examples of similar environments and dissimilar strategies to be statistically useful.

The only industries that contain anything approaching a spectrum of strategies are food processing (20), machinery (35), transportation (37), and aerospace (372)—and these are among the most heterogeneous. Food processing includes vertically integrated soybean processors, beer companies and firms with diverse lines of packaged foods like General Foods. "Machinery" is a catch-all industry that includes firms as disparate as Addressograph-Multigraph and Deere. The nonaviation transportation industry (37), while seemingly containing both diversified and nondiversified firms, really splits into Dominant Business vehicle manufacturers and Related Business parts and equipment companies. The case for heterogeneity is not as strong in the aerospace industry (372), where the primary distinction is between firms that have *not* diversified out of the industry and the surprising number that have moved on to Unrelated strategies (e.g., AVCO, North American Rockwell, Martin, TRW and Whittaker).

The situation in 1949 (Table 3-5) was similar, except that the food industry had not yet developed many diversified firms, and Unrelated Business firms were few in number.

From one point of view the net result of this situation is that only the food processing and perhaps the aerospace industries have within them a sufficient number of firms in different categories to permit a controlled comparison. Such a comparison would, however, require a sample directed specifically at these industries and even then the results would hardly be of general interest. In addition, a more realistic 3-digit definition of industries would further strengthen the connection between industry and diversification strategy, making it close to impossible to control for industry. Taking a broader point of view, it seems evident that most of the strategy-related performance differences are due to industry differences, but that the two effects are simply not separable. The higher performing industries tend to consist of mostly Related Business firms, and Related Business firms tend to belong to higher performing industries. Which came first? The answer seems to be that they came together; the same conditions that produce above average performance—science-based proprietary strengths, growth in markets served along with rapid product innovation—produce diversified firms. The strategies that were successful in the early part of the century—mass production of basic durable goods and vertical integration to achieve control over primary industrial materials—produced large firms committed to single businesses that are now faced with mature, slowly growing, highly competitive nonproprietary product-market areas.

Implications

A definition of industry that is detailed enough to permit the comparison of close competitors is of no use when the effect of diversification is of primary interest. A diversified firm is not a close competitor with any one nondiversified firm. Broader definitions of industry reveal that diversification strategy and the general technological-market environment tend to be alternate aspects of the same phenomenon. Thus, one cannot "eliminate" the industry effect on performance without also eliminating the effects of diversification strategy. The two are inextricably mixed.

This observation implies that a strict normative interpretation of performance differences is, in general, highly questionable. The empirical evidence that Related-Constrained firms outperform Dominant-Vertical firms does not mean that Dominant-Vertical companies *should* attempt to follow Related-Constrained strategies. Both may be reasonable responses to different technological and economic environments. Since there are no diversified steel companies or vertically integrated electronics companies, a recommendation that the steel companies diversify because diversified firms are more profitable would be based upon false logic. In a sense, it is as valid to think of the electronics company as being diversified *because* it is in a profitable science-based business as the reverse.

TESTING THE HYPOTHESES

To what extent do the empirical results on financial performance support the hypotheses advanced in the first section of this chapter? In answering this, the hypotheses will be dealt with one at a time, to be followed by a summary synthesis.

Portfolio Risk

Regarding the relative degrees of risk and return experienced by firms in various categories it was hypothesized: *Related-Constrained firms would experience the lowest variability in earnings and have an average rate of return at least as large as that of other categories. In addition, the rank order of the categories in terms of increasing variability relative to return was conjectured to be: Related-Constrained, Related-Linked, Unrelated, Dominant, and Single.*

In developing a measure of return one must answer the questions "Return to whom?" and "Return on what investment?" While the stockholder can be used as a reference, returns to stockholders can depend as much on market swings and changing expectations as on performance. In addition, the market is essentially a device for equilibrating uncertainty, not passing on returns. If, for instance, it were known with certainty that a firm would increase its earnings at a rate of 20 percent per year for the next five years, the current price of the company's stock would reflect that knowledge, and returns over the next five years to stockholders would (theoretically) be quite low. Rapid price increases are the result of *unexpected* improvements in a firm's prospects.

Annual values of return on book capital or equity can be equally misleading. Fluctuations in these rates can reflect capital investment programs as much as changes in profitability and book-value figures are sensitive to inflation and capital turnover rates. In addition, growing firms can have marginal rates of return substantially in excess of their average rates of return.

In the light of these considerations, and in view of the fact that the mechanisms that were hypothesized to lie behind risk-return variations with diversifications were based on flexibility in resource allocation, the firm's average rate of growth in earnings per share was taken as the measure of "return." Under uniform growth assumptions, *GEPS* is proportional to the firm's incremental return on investment and it also serves as a market-free proxy for stockholder benefit.

Ideally, "risk" should measure the potential variability in a firm's earnings. Unfortunately, the empiricist must make do with observed variability. We take as our measure of risk the standard deviation of annual growth rates in earnings per share about the uniform growth trend (*SDEPS*). More formally, *GEPS* and *SDEPS* are obtained through a least-squares fit of the following expression to annual earnings per share data:

$$\text{Log } (EPS_t) = A + (GEPS)t + \tilde{\epsilon}_t$$

where t is an integer that measures time in years, and $\tilde{\epsilon}_t$ is the annual deviation from the uniform growth model. *SDEPS* is the estimated value of the standard deviation of $\tilde{\epsilon}_t$ and may be thought of as the variability in the *rate* of earnings per share growth. The estimated mean values of these measures for each category are shown in Table 3-2.

As can be seen from the *F*-ratios in Table 3-2, neither variable was found to be significantly affected by diversification strategy. Even though the Related-Constrained category had an average growth rate in earnings per share that was 3.42 percentage points above that of the Dominant-Vertical category ($p = 0.025$),[14] the very high overall variability in *GEPS* kept the total results of classification from being significant. Similarly, though the value of *SDEPS* for the Related-Constrained group was lower than the overall average ($p = 0.025$), the high total variability in *SDEPS* again kept the overall fit from being significant (if the Acquisitive Conglomerate category is omitted). However, the fact that the *direction* of the deviation of the Related-Constrained category was as hypothesized for *both* variables suggested that a composite measure of risk and return might prove more sensitive to category effects.

The risk premium ratio (*RPR*) that was used as a combined measure is adapted from a ratio suggested by Sharpe.[15] While subject to the usual weak-

---

[14] This notation refers to the level of statistical significance of the statement just made.

[15] William F. Sharpe, "Mutual Fund Performance," *Journal of Business,* January 1966, pp. 119–138.

nesses of a single measure of a multifactor situation, the risk premium ratio at least provides a consistent way of measuring return relative to risk. The ratio is defined for the purposes here as

$$RPR = (GEPS - 0.015)/SDEPS$$

where 0.015 (1.5 percent) is taken as an approximation to the "risk-free" (government bonds) after tax return (and hence growth rate if all funds are retained) available to corporations. In essence, *RPR* measures the risk associated growth per unit of variability in growth. Leaving aside considerations of risk-return preference, the bigger *RPR* is, the better.

Table 3-2 shows that the average *RPR* for Related-Constrained firms was 0.775, significantly above ($p = 0.001$) the overall average of 0.516. Thus while Related-Constrained firms did not significantly surpass the others in growth in earnings per share or variability considered separately, their average growth rate relative to variability, *RPR*, was considerably superior, as predicted.

Contrary to the hypothesis, the Dominant-Constrained category also had a very high *RPR* (0.658) that did not differ significantly from that of the Related-Constrained category. In fact, the picture that emerges from the risk premium ratio data is of two distinct and internally homogeneous groups: a high-performing group consisting of the Related-Constrained and Dominant-Constrained firms and a low-performing group that includes *all* other categories (see Table 3-6). The two groups differ at a high level of significance ($p = 0.001$) and none of the mean *RPR*s of the categories within either group differ significantly from one another.

Diversification in itself has not served to reduce the relative variability of the firm's earnings stream. Dominant Business firms have shown less relative variability than Unrelated Business firms, and Dominant-Constrained firms have outperformed Related-Linked firms in this measure. What has been

TABLE 3-6. RISK-PREMIUM RATIOS.

High-Performing Group	
Related-Constrained	.775
Dominant-Constrained	.658
Pooled Average	.741
Low-Performing Group	
Acquisitive Conglomerate	.516
Related-Linked	.431
Single	.378
Unrelated-Passive	.337
Dominant-Vertical	.329
Dominant-Linked and Unrelated	.221
Pooled Average	.374

important is the way in which the firm's businesses are related. It is the companies that have at least some product-market diversity but have a strategy of restricting these activities so that a central strength or skill spans all of their activities—the Dominant-Constrained and Related-Constrained firms—that have shown the lowest variability in earnings relative to growth. The absolute levels of *GEPS* for these firms provide assurance that the result is not due to stability associated with abnormally low growth.

While the superiority of Related-Constrained firms was predicted, the hypothesized ordering of the other categories was not supported. Recalling the major theoretical argument, it seems that rather than being wrong, the concept was not extended far enough. It was argued that the ability of a firm to "ride the product life-cycle," substituting new products for old was critical in reducing risk relative to return, and that this could be accomplished most effectively in firms in which variety was closely controlled. Such firms are not *so* diversified that they cannot avoid the total systematic risk of the economy, and they are diverse enough to compensate for declining prospects in one product-market area with new products that are functional substitutes for the old product. This line of reasoning led to the hypothesis of Related-Constrained superiority in return relative to risk. The fact that the Dominant-Constrained (but not the Single) category shared this superiority may mean that the need for diversity was overestimated and the value of controlled or channeled diversity in mitigating risk was underestimated.

A further interesting point is the poor risk return performance of the Dominant-Vertical firms. Although these firms often appear "Related-Constrained" in terms of their end products (e.g., Goodyear, Alcoa, and the like), it is obvious that their average risk premium ratio is drastically below that of true Related-Constrained firms ($P = 0.001$). In addition to justifying the classification applied to these firms, this demonstrates that the commitment to a single material overrides the possibly beneficial effects of end-product variety on risk-return performance.

The Escape Paradigm

Consideration of the motives and mechanism for escape through diversification from stagnant business areas led to this hypothesis: *Firms that are not members of science-based industries that adopt Dominant-Linked, Dominant-Unrelated, and Unrelated strategies will experience returns on equity that are significantly lower than those achieved by firms in the same industry but following other strategies.* The reasoning was that low performance was the cause for adoption of these strategies, not the result.

As noted in the section on industry effects, industry and strategy are closely related, and there are too few firms in the sample to permit a detailed definition of industry. Accordingly, the hypothesis was tested by dividing all firms into two large groups: those in science-based industries and those in all other industries. The science-based industries were chemicals (28), business machines (357), electrical machinery and electronics (36), aerospace (372), and instruments (38). Two regressions were then computed, and in each a zero-one variable was used to indicate membership in a science-based industry. The variable, *SCI,* was assigned a value of *one* if the firm's major businesses were in any or all of the science industries and *zero* otherwise. The first regression simply served to remove the relative premium in return gained by science-based firms. The equation was

$$ROE = A + B_1 (SCI) + B_2 (DLU) + B_3 (U) + B_4 (TIME) + \tilde{\epsilon},$$

where B_1, B_2, B_3, and B_4 represent the effects of science-based industry, Dominant-Linked or Unrelated strategy, Unrelated strategy and time on return on equity.

The results were:

Coefficient	Value	*t*-Ratio	*P*
A (Intercept)	11.90	—	—
B_1 (*SCI*)	3.70	6.00	0.001
B_2 (*DLU*)	−1.17	−1.11	—
B_3 (*U*)	−2.13	−2.04	0.02
B_4 (*TIME*)	0.08	0.02	—
$R^2 = 0.116$			

where *P* is the level at which the *t*-ratio is significant,[16] and R^2 is the proportion of variance explained by the regression.

The science-based industries clearly receive a return on equity premium, estimated here as 3.7 percentage points. The regression shows that when the science industry premium is removed, Unrelated Business firms have significantly lower returns on equity. This is in contrast to the results of Table 3-1 (where the science premium is not removed) in which the Unrelated category does not differ significantly from the average in return on equity. Thus, if the fact is taken into account that Unrelated Business firms are generally members of science-based industries, their relative profitability is seen to be poor. The Dominant-Linked and Dominant-Unrelated (hereafter *DLU*) firms, on the other hand, are not significantly below the average return on equity when science premiums are removed.

The second regression was similar in format to the first but split the Unrelated and *DLU* groups into those in science-based industries and those that were not. The resulting coefficients of interest are shown in Table 3-7. The startlingly high coefficient for *DLU* firms in science-based industries is based

---

[16] Here the *t*-ratios test the hypothesis $B_i = O.$

TABLE 3-7. EFFECTS ON RETURN ON EQUITY (*ROE*).

Strategy	Science-Based Industries	Other Industries
Unrelated	−3.82	−1.20
(*t*-Ratio)	(−1.68)	(−1.02)
Significance	0.05	−
DLU	12.61	−1.66
(*t*-Ratio)	(2.48)	(−1.55)
Significance	0.005	0.1

on only one company: Xerox. While significant in a strict statistical sense, it would be foolish to generalize from such a result. Unrelated Business firms in science-based industries are seen to have returns on equity that are lower than those of other firms when the usual premium received by science-based firms is taken into account. Although there is a tendency for Unrelated and *DLU* firms in nonscience industries to have lower returns on equity, neither coefficient is significant.

The original conjecture was that nonscience-based firms adopting Unrelated or *DLU* strategies did so because of low profitability and that this poor performance would not be entirely remedied by the diversification strategy. The evidence, however, indicates that the performance of these firms was somewhat lower, but not by enough to support the hypothesis. While it was *not* expected that *science-based* firms in the Unrelated and *DLU* categories would have unusual rates of return, the data in Table 3-7 show that they did: *Unrelated* science-based firms have significantly lower returns on equity than other science-based firms. Which are the science-based Unrelated firms? Companies like AVCO, Air Reduction, Curtiss-Wright, FMC, GAF, Grace, Lear, Litton, LTV, Martin Marietta, North American Rockwell, Olin, TRW, and Whittaker. These firms have an average return on equity of 11.87 percent, which is near the average of all other firms. But the average science-based company has a return on equity of 15.68 percent. Evidently, the strategy of moving from a science-based business to an Unrelated Business posture has, on the average, either been due to or resulted in relatively poor profitability.

Testing the Effect of Divisionalization

The flexibility in resource allocation, the economies of scale in the general management function, and the openness to change that theorists ascribe to multidivisional organizations would be of the greatest relative benefit in environments subject to fairly rapid, particularly technological, change. Specifically, it was hypothesized that the effects of product-division structure on growth and profitability would be relatively more favorable in environments that require or encourage rapid technological change.

To test this hypothesis, return on equity (*ROE*) and growth in earnings per share (*GEPS*) were chosen as measures of growth and profitability. The science-based industries were taken as most representative of environments subject to technological change: chemicals (28), business machines (357), electrical machinery and electronics (36), aerospace (372), and instruments (38). In more specific terms, the hypothesis states: *The difference between the average return on equity (and growth in earnings per share) of product-division firms and the average of nondivisionalized firms will be greater in science-based industries than in other industries.*[17]

Table 3-3 can be used to find the average return on equity and growth rate in earnings per share for *all* product-division and *all* nondivisionalized firms:

Structure	Average ROE	Average GEPS
Product Division	12.90	8.63
Nondivisionalized	11.93	6.02
Difference	0.97	2.61
Significance	Not Significant	0.025

In aggregate, product-division firms have an average growth rate in earnings per share that is substantially higher than that of nondivisionalized firms; both types of firms, however, appear to have about the same level of overall profitability.

Turning now to the question of relative performance in science-based and other industries, the data for return on equity (Table 3-8) not only do not support the hypothesis, but tend to indicate that the converse may be true. The results show that science-based firms receive substantial profit premiums regardless of their type of organization. In addition, we find that product-division and nondivisionalized firms have equal profitability in nonscience-based areas, and that product-division firms in science-based industries have, if anything, lower profitability than other firms in these areas, although the difference is not statistically significant. So few of the sampled firms in science-based industries had nondivisionalized structures over a ten-year period that statistically significant results on this hypothesis are virtually out of the question. It would require about 85 (rather than 8) observations in the nondivisionalized science-based category to make the observed difference significant.

---

[17] Nondivisionalized firms consist of those with functional or functional-with-subsidiaries structures.

TABLE 3-8. RETURN ON EQUITY (*ROE*) BY INDUSTRY TYPE AND STRUCTURE.

	Science-Based Industries	Nonscience-Based Industries
Product Division	14.56	11.60
Nondivisionalized	16.26 [a]	11.55
Difference	−1.70	0.05
Significance	Not Significant	Not Significant

[a] Based only on 8 data points.
Estimated product-division effect = −0.23 (not significant).
Estimated science-industry effect = +3.12 ($p = 0.001$).
NOTE: Critical level of significance is 5 percent. Tests on differences and estimated effects are for equality with zero. Estimated product-division and science-industry effects obtained by two-way analysis of variance.

The results for growth in earnings per share (Table 3-8) also suffer from too few nondivisionalized science-based firms, but in this case it is clear that the overall superiority of product-division firms in growth is not just due to membership in science-based industries. The averages shown in Table 3-9 can be closely replicated if a growth rate premium of 1.73 percent per year is associated with product-division structure and an independent premium of 2.29 percent with membership in a science-based industry. Again, however, there is no evidence that product-division structures are *especially* beneficial in a science-based environment. In summary, it appears that:

(1) Firms in science-based industries have average rates of return on equity and growth in earnings per share that are higher than the average rates of firms in other industries. A science base is associated with estimated return and growth per year premiums of 3.12 percent and 2.29 percent respectively.

(2) The vast preponderance of science-based firms have product-division structures. There are too few nondivisionalized science-based firms to permit a statistically meaningful comparison with product-division firms in these industries.

(3) When the effects on performance of structure are separated from the effects of industry membership, the product-division structure appears to be associated with higher growth rates in earnings per share, but has no particular impact on return on equity.

Although the original hypothesis was not supported, there is not enough data on nondivisionalized science-based firms to consider it refuted. The real problem, however, is that the original hypothesis was based on a rather naïve view of the relationship between environment, strategy, and structure. Clearly, the nondivisionalized firms in science-based industries, although few, are not suffering: they have an average return on equity of 16.26 percent and an average annual rate of growth in earnings per share of 8.42 percent, both of which are respectably above the overall averages. These are firms like Abbott Labs (49–69), Addressograph-Multigraph (60–69), Kodak (49–58), National Cash Register (49–69), Pfizer (49–59) and Rohr (49–59), which, while having various degrees of diversity, also have developed particularly successful major product lines: antibiotics, speciality business machines, cameras and film, accounting machines, and aviation and aerospace power equipment respectively. *There were no examples in the sample of surviving science-based firms that followed their major product line into the maturity and decline phase of its life-cycle without diversifying further and adopting a multidivisional structure to manage the more complex enterprise that resulted.* This suggests that in science-based industries diversification is not simply one of several alternative strategies for expansion, but an eventual necessity for long-term survival. As long as a firm has a "winner" on its hands, it can make high returns and grow rapidly within the framework of a relatively simple product-market scope and organizational structure. However, if prospects in its major area decline, alternative sources of profit and growth must be sought. Similarly, if research and development efforts produce results, their application often lies in areas other than those with which the firm is familiar.

One of the implications of this view is that a comparison between product-division and nondivisionalized firms in science-based industries can shed little light on the question of the value of a product-division structure—what is actually being compared are firms in different stages of development with differing organizational requirements. Thus, as managers of science-based firms seem to act purposefully and avoid the "wrong" strategies of staying with a declining business until the bitter end, or diversifying without divisionalizing, the relative merits of these options are not empirically measurable.

TABLE 3-9. GROWTH IN EARNINGS PER SHARE BY
STRUCTURE AND INDUSTRY TYPE.

	Science-Based Industries	Nonscience-Based Industries
Product Division	9.79	7.57
	(60)	(56)
Nondivisionalized	8.42	5.81
	(8)	(92)
Difference	1.37	1.76
Significance	Not Significant	Not Significant

Composite fit significant at the 0.025 level. Average product-division effect = 1.73.
Average science-industry effect = 2.29.
NOTE: Average effects obtained from a two-way analysis of variance. See note to Table 3-8 for other comments.

Viewing strategy and structure as effects of performance rather than causes also brings into question the degree to which the observed "science premium" can be considered to be independent of the strategies and structures of firms in science-based industries. One could argue that technologically based products enjoy a sort of temporary miniature monopoly status and thereby produce superior performance and that this effect has little to do with the fact that most science-based firms are diversified and divisionalized. On the other hand, it could equally well be claimed that the continued health, growth, and risk-taking ability of firms in these industries have been dependent upon management's ability to institutionalize the process of innovation. Continuous innovation, in turn, may not require diversified divisionalized firms for its initiation, but they are its certain eventual result.

Testing for Systems Effects

One of the more subtle hypotheses advanced was that among product-division firms the relationship between growth and profitability would not be as strong as among other types of firms. Economic theory predicts that growth and profits will tend to be negatively related because, in an economy in equilibrium, an increase in a firm's long-term growth rate can only be obtained by accepting a lower rate of return on marginal investments.

Taking growth in sales (*GSALES*) and return on equity (*ROE*) as the measures of growth and profit, Figure 3.1 shows the hypothesized situation. While divisionalized firms may have a negative relation between growth and profit, their special control, reward, and resource allocation systems should act to reduce the marginal amount of return they must sacrifice in order to gain a unit of growth.

Theoretically, the lines in Figure 3.1 represent the average marginal *opportunity-sets* over growth and profit faced by the two groups of firms. Unfortunately, there is no way of observing an individual firm's growth-profit opportunity-set. Following the practice of past research in the area, it was assumed that some general growth-profit relationship exists for large groups of firms, and that each company's growth-profit performance can be thought

FIGURE 3.1. Hypothesized Relationship.

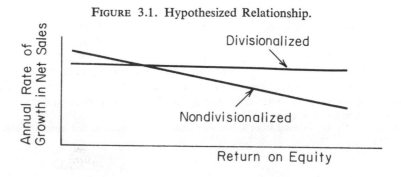

of as a particular point in the overall relationship. Thus, regression can be used to estimate the general growth-profit relationship from single observations of growth and profit for individual firms.

In setting up the regression it is important to determine both lines simultaneously so that the difference between them can be subjected to direct tests of significance. If the two growth-profit relationships are assumed to be

$$GSALES = \alpha_0 + \beta_0(ROE)$$

for divisionalized firms, and

$$GSALES = \alpha_1 + \beta_1(ROE)$$

for other firms, they can be combined by introducing a zero-one variable, *PD*, where

$$PD = \begin{cases} 1 \text{ for product-division firms} \\ 0 \text{ for other firms} \end{cases}$$

giving

$$GSALES = \alpha_0 + \alpha_1(PD) + \beta_0(ROE) + \beta_1(ROE)(PD) + \beta_2(TIME) + \tilde{\epsilon}$$

where the *TIME* variable has been included to represent changes in the overall level of growth rates and $\tilde{\epsilon}$ is the random error term. The individual data points on *GSALES* and *ROE* that were used were the 1951–1959 and 1960–1969 averages for each firm. Thus, *TIME* is also a zero-one variable.

Several regressions were computed, all based on this type of equation. It was found that (1) *GSALES* and *ROE* were positively rather than negatively related for all firms and for each subgroup; (2) that industry terms did not improve or change the regression, and the coefficients of such terms were not significantly different from zero; and (3) that when a strategy variable corresponding to "Related Business" and "other" was added, the structure terms were the only ones that were significant. In other words, product-division structure, or its absence, was a much more important contributor to the explanatory power of the regression than Related Business strategy or its absence. Once the product-division variable was included, the additional information supplied by the Related Business variable was insignificant. The results of the best regression obtained are shown in Figure 3.2.

The overall relationship between growth and profit for all firms was estimated to be

$$GSALES = 4.80 + 0.455ROE \text{ (at 1960–1969 levels)}$$

with $R^2 = 19.1$ percent. The *t*-ratio of the *ROE* coefficient was 6.87. Why was a positive relationship found rather than the negative one predicted by economic theory? Clearly the estimated relationship does not represent the opportunity-set available to an individual firm: management cannot *choose*

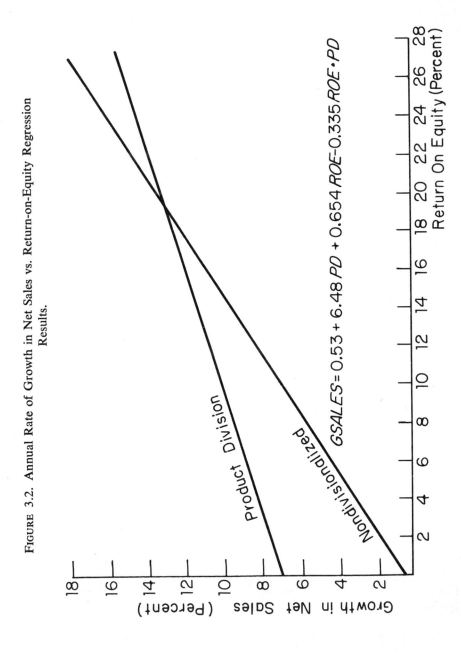

FIGURE 3.2. Annual Rate of Growth in Net Sales vs. Return-on-Equity Regression Results.

$GSALES = 0.53 + 6.48\,PD + 0.654\,ROE - 0.335\,ROE \cdot PD$

to increase both growth and profit at the same time or there would be no firms at the low end of the spectrum. Instead, the relationship seems to indicate that firms do not have homogeneous opportunity-sets and that the same situations that produce above average profit also are associated with above average growth, and vice versa. Then, even if there is a marginally negative relationship between growth and profit within a number of special groups of firms considered separately, the aggregate effect is a positive relationship. This is illustrated in Figure 3.3.

Each group, of course, could consist of only a single firm, in which case what we are observing are the relative degrees to which firms have been able to insulate themselves, through proprietary skills, invention, or simple market power, from equilibrating economic forces. The implication is that the results shown in Figure 3.2 cannot be used to test the original hypothesis and must be evaluated in the context of a positive growth-profit relation among firms.

The regression shown in Figure 3.2 was quite significant and indicates (1) that the average product-division firm has both a higher rate of growth in sales and a higher rate of profit than the average firm with another type of structure; and (2) that growth and profitability are less closely related among product-division firms than among other firms.

Among nondivisionalized firms, a difference in rate of return on equity of 1 percent is usually associated with a difference in sales growth rates of 0.53 percent, while among product-division firms the same difference in profitability is associated with a 0.32 percent difference in sales growth rates. The difference in slopes, estimated to be −0.21, was negative at the 0.006 level of significance.

Another way of looking at the data is that among firms with low levels of

FIGURE 3.3. Aggregate vs. Marginal Effects.

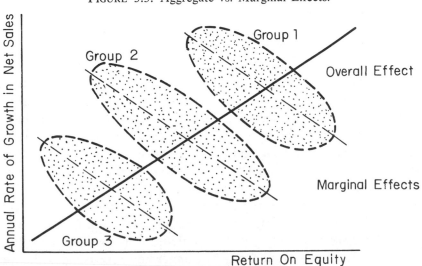

return on equity, product-division firms have higher rates of sales growth and among firms with high rates of return on equity, nondivisionalized firms tend to have the highest rates of sales growth. The crossover point in return on equity is estimated to be 19 percent, but has a very large standard error.

Removing the Acquisitive Conglomerates from the regression does not change the signs of any coefficients or alter their significance, though the estimated crossover point drops to 12 percent. This is because the Acquisitive Conglomerates have uniformly high rates of sales growth but the full spectrum of profit rates and consequently affect only the size of the intercept of the product-division growth-profit line, not its slope.

In conclusion, the general concept behind the original hypothesis seems to be supported. Among product-division firms, sales growth is less closely associated with profitability than among firms with functional or functional-with-subsidiaries structures.

Testing Overall Performance

In addition to the hypothesis of relative growth-profit independence, it was hypothesized that:

(1) *Related Business firms will, on the average, have higher profitability, higher rates of growth, and higher price-earnings ratios than other categories of firms.*

(2) *Related-Constrained firms will outperform Related-Linked firms in these measures.*

(3) *Divisionalized Related Business firms will outperform those that are functionally organized.*

It has already been noted in the preliminary evaluation of the financial data that the Related category does outperform other firms in most measures and that the Related-Constrained subgroup has performance levels generally higher than that of the Related-Linked subgroup. Table 3-10 displays results for all three hypotheses: average values of *ROC*, *ROE*, *GSALES*, *GEPS*, and *PE* for each group in question were computed (some were obtained directly from Tables 3-1 and 3-2), and the values shown in Table 3-10 are the differences between category averages and the significance of tests on these differences.

As can be seen, the Related group as a whole has higher profitability and higher price-earnings ratios than other firms. In addition, its average growth rate in earnings per share tends to be higher, though its sales growth is no different from the average of other firms. Looking inside the Related category, we find the Related-Constrained group significantly outperforming the Related-Linked group in growth in earnings per share, and tending to have a higher level of profitability. Further investigation shows that the difference in growth in earnings per share directly reflects a difference in earnings growth and is not due to differential dilution effects. Somewhat surprisingly, the relative

TABLE 3-10. RELATED BUSINESS PERFORMANCE.

	ROC	*ROE*	*GSALES*	*GEPS*	*PE*
Difference Between Related Businesses and All Others	+1.61 (0.01)	+1.51 (0.02)	+0.20	+1.63 (0.10)	+3.71 (0.001)
Difference Between Related-Constrained and Related-Linked Businesses	+1.54 (0.10)	+1.83 (0.10)	+1.56	+2.99 (0.05)	−0.08
Difference Between Divisionalized Related Businesses and Functionally Organized Related Businesses	+0.30	+0.80	+3.10 (0.05)	−1.86	+1.08

NOTE: Figures shown are differences between estimated mean values of the variables. *ROC*, *ROE*, *GSALES*, and *GEPS*. They are expressed as percentages so that the differences are in terms of percentage points. Figures in parentheses indicate the level of significance of the difference. Levels of significance less than 0.10 are omitted.

underperformance of the Related-Linked group is not reflected in its average price-earnings ratio, which tends to be somewhat higher than that of the Related-Constrained category.

Comparison between Related Business firms with product-division structures and Related Business firms with functional or functional-with-subsidiaries structures reveals only one significant difference: the divisionalized group has a higher rate of sales growth. Other differences also favor the divisionalized Related Business firms but are not large enough to be statistically meaningful.

In summary, the first two hypotheses are strongly supported and the third, except for the case of sales growth, is not.

Conglomerate Performance

As a partial test of the theory of conglomerate growth it was hypothesized that:

(1) *Acquisitive Conglomerates will have price-earnings ratios that are significantly higher than those of other firms, and conglomerate price-earnings ratios will be strongly related to the growth in earnings per share achieved.*

(2) *Both Acquisitive Conglomerates and Unrelated-Passive firms will have average returns on capital that are not significantly different from the overall average of other firms.*

Table 3-11 shows the tests of these conjectures. Average values of *ROC*, *ROE*, *E/C*, *GSALES*, *GERN*, *GEPS*, *IFR*, and *PE* for the Acquisitive Con-

TABLE 3-11. UNRELATED BUSINESS PERFORMANCE.

	ROC	ROE	E/C	GSALES	GERN	GEPS	PE	IFR
Difference Between Average of Unrelated Category and That of Other Firms	−1.15	−0.81	−0.082 (0.005)	+5.85 (0.001)	+5.75 (0.001)	+1.51	−1.42	+0.657 (0.001)
Difference Between Average of Acquisitive Conglomerate Category and That of Other Firms	−1.02	+0.52	−0.189 (0.001)	+12.36 (0.001)	+10.54 (0.001)	+3.07 (0.10)	+0.43	+1.310 (0.001)
Difference Between Average of Unrelated-Passive Category and That of Other Firms	−1.17	−2.31 (0.10)	+0.064 (0.05)	−3.05	−0.99	−0.64	−3.42 (0.025)	−0.122

NOTE: Figures shown are differences between estimated mean values of the variables. *ROC*, *ROE*, *GSALES*, *GERN*, and *GEPS*. They are expressed as percentages so that the differences for these variables are in terms of percentage points. Figures below differences are levels at which they are significant. Levels of significance less than 0.10 are omitted.

glomerate category, the Unrelated-Passive category, and the Unrelated category as a whole are compared to the average values for all other firms and the differences are presented and tested to determine if they differ significantly from zero.

The data make it obvious that the two subgroups of the Unrelated Business category have radically different financial policies and levels of performance. The conglomerates achieve very high growth rates in sales and earnings, have average or slightly below average returns to capital, but employ high leverage to boost their return on equity (and to finance their rapid growth). The Unrelated-Passive firms, by contrast, have below average growth in sales, have slightly below average returns to capital, but have unusually *low* leverage, driving their average return on equity well below that of other firms.

The conglomerates tend to be well known, but which are the Unrelated-Passive firms? A partial list includes American Standard, Bell Intercontinental (previously Bell Aircraft), Boise Cascade, Champion Spark Plug, Curtiss-Wright, DiGiorgio, GAF, Martin Marietta, Midland-Ross, North American Rockwell, Olin, Pullman, Stewart-Warner, Sybron, TRW and USM (previously United Shoe Machinery). These firms derived more than 30 percent of their revenues from activities unrelated to their largest group of related businesses but failed to qualify as Acquisitive Conglomerates in either 1959 or 1969. To be classified as an Acquisitive Conglomerate an Unrelated Business firm had to (1) have a five-year average growth in earnings per share of at least 10 percent per year; (2) have made at least five acquisitions in the past five years, three or more of which took the firm into new unrelated businesses; and (3) have had a five-year average *IFR* greater than one. If the firm met these requirements any time during the five years immediately prior to the classification date, it was placed in the Acquisitive Conglomerate category. Many of the Unrelated-Passive firms diversified so slowly or so long ago that they did not meet the requirements. Others became Unrelated Business firms as the result of one or two major acquisitions but did not follow up these initial moves with further unrelated acquisitions.

Turning to the hypotheses, we find that Acquisitive Conglomerates have an average growth rate in earnings per share that is higher than that of other firms, though the difference is only marginally significant, and an average price-earnings ratio that is no different from the average of other firms. Related Business firms have an average price-earnings ratio that is markedly higher than that of the conglomerates. This result is somewhat surprising because the usual theories of conglomerate growth are based on the use of a high price-earnings ratio to obtain favorable share exchange ratios in noncash acquisitions.

That Acquisitive Conglomerate price-earnings ratios have been, on the average, quite ordinary was also found by Weston and Mansinghka, who concluded that:

A dilemma confronted the conglomerate firms with depressed price/earnings ratios. If they merged with firms with higher price earnings [ratios], the conglomerates would suffer dilution in earnings per share which would at least initially depress growth rates in earnings per share. The disadvantage of a differentially lower price/earnings ratio in merger activity, can be offset by offering non-equity forms of securities in exchange or utilizing delayed equity forms such as convertibles and warrants.[18]

The high leverage employed by conglomerates (average 40 percent debt or preferred) certainly suggests that this may be the case, particularly as Weston and Mansinghka also found that a high proportion of conglomerate debt consisted of convertible securities.

But what about the "feedback" effect between growth in earnings per share, price-earnings ratio, and acquisition rate that is supposed to enable conglomerates to bootstrap their way to growth? Figure 3.4 shows a scatter plot of price-earnings ratio and growth in earnings per share, both averaged over 1960–1969, for the thirteen Acquisitive Conglomerates in the sample for which

FIGURE 3.4. Price-Earnings Ratio vs. Growth in Earnings Per Common Share for Acquisitive Conglomerates.

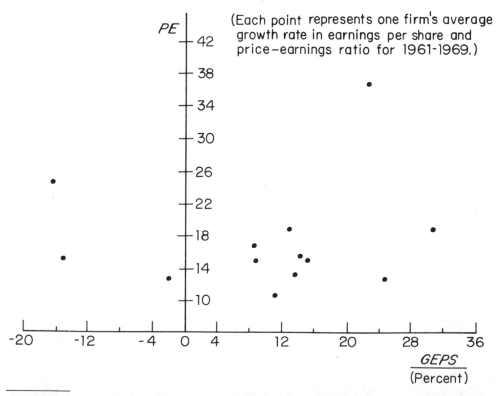

[18] J. Fred Weston and Surenda K. Mansinghka, "Tests of the Efficiency Performance of Conglomerate Firms," *Journal of Finance*, September 1971, p. 926.

meaningful values could be calculated. The coefficient of correlation between price-earnings ratio and growth in earnings per share for these firms is 0.10 and is not statistically significant. If similar data for 1962–1967 is studied, the same lack of correspondence between earnings-per-share growth rate and price-earnings ratio is evident.

It can only be concluded that not all Acquisitive Conglomerates relied on high price-earnings ratios to power their growth. Some, such as Litton, Whittaker, and Grace certainly correspond to the popular view. But many others, such as Bangor Punta, Colt, LTV, U.S. Industries and White Consolidated achieved quite rapid growth of earnings per share with below average price-earnings ratios. LTV, for example, had an average *PE* during 1962–1967 of 10, and during the same period Colt achieved an average annual increase in earnings per share of 41.4 percent with a price-earnings ratio of 13.4, and U.S. Industries experienced an 81 percent annual growth rate with a price-earnings ratio of 10.4. Apparently, this was accomplished by heavy use of convertible securities, concentrating on the acquisition of firms with very low price-earnings ratios or firms whose stock was not publicly traded, and the use of "incentive" purchase arrangements in which the seller's compensation is deferred and based on future growth.

In summary, the first hypothesis was not supported, and the second, concerning profitability, was only partially supported. Acquisitive Conglomerate profitability does not differ from that of other firms, but Unrelated-Passive companies had a decidedly lower return on equity. While it may be a means of avoiding exceptionally poor performance, the Unrelated Passive strategy of expansion has not, on average, proved to be a means of achieving above average growth or profitability. Indeed, as noted in a previous section, many Unrelated-Passive firms are primarily active in science-based industries, and in comparison to other firms in these industries, their performance has been inferior.

A QUESTION OF PRICE

The price of a corporation's stock not only represents the investing public's evaluation of management quality and future prospects for earnings and dividends, but, in itself, is an important element of a firm's ability to diversify. Several writers have noted the strong statistical relationship between bullish stock markets and merger activity.[19] The mechanisms that allow firms with

---

[19] See Jesse W. Markham, "Survey of the Evidence and Findings on Mergers," *Business Concentration and Price Policy* (Princeton, N.J.: Princeton University Press, 1955), p. 157, and Ralph L. Nelson, *Merger Movements in American Industry: 1895–1956* (Princeton, N.J.: Princeton University Press, 1959), p. 64.

relatively high price-earnings ratios to obtain immediate improvements in earnings per share by acquiring firms at a price that implies a lower multiple are well known to both theorists and executives. Since the ease or difficulty with which a firm can manage the financial aspects of moving into a new business area through acquisition depends in part upon its market-determined price-earnings ratio, the degree to which the price-earnings multiple varies with diversification strategy, either as cause or effect, deserves scrutiny.

In Table 3-2, and elsewhere in the text, it was shown that firms in the Related Business category had an average price-earnings ratio that was much higher than that of other categories. In addition, the fact that the Related-Linked category underperformed the Related-Constrained category in terms of growth, stability, and profitability, yet had an equal or higher *PE* multiple, has been noted. In order to test the validity of this impression and put the argument in more precise terms, a simple valuation model was developed, and predicted versus actual results were examined on a category by category basis.

Regression equations employing a number of different combinations of variables as predictors of price-earnings ratios were tested, and the one that had the best overall predictive power is shown below.

$$PE = 10.97 + 4.8(TIME) + 0.127(GEPS) - 0.075(SDEPS) + 3.72(RTN)$$

(*t*-ratios):   (7.5)   (3.22)   (−3.58)   (1.64)

$R^2 = 0.48$; F-ratio $= 24.9(4, 337)$.

Here, *TIME* is a zero-one variable that is set to *zero* for the period 1951–1959 and *one* for 1960–1969. *PE, GEPS,* and *SDEPS* are the previously defined decade averages of the price-earnings ratio, growth rate in earnings per share, and relative standard deviation in growth of earnings per share, and are expressed as percentages. *RTN* stands for the corporate retention rate—the ratio of retained earnings to earnings after taxes and preferred dividends.[20]

All coefficients were significant at the 0.05 level and the *GEPS* and *SDEPS* coefficients were significant at the 0.001 level. Since the purpose of the regression was to obtain a general valuation formula, rather than follow the rule of omitting firms that moved between categories (a rule used for other computations in this chapter), all sampled firms for which data were available were included. Decade averages were used because comparability with other data was desired. The fact that *GEPS* is a fitted rather than ratio measure of growth makes the use of ten-year averages more acceptable than it would be otherwise.

Since the regression formula is linear, it can be used to predict category means as well as individual data points. By substituting the category mean value for *GEPS* and *SDEPS* shown in Table 3-2 into the regression equation (along with mean values for *RTN* which are not shown), and setting *TIME* = 1,

---

[20] *RTN* had an overall mean value of 0.513 and the only category which had a mean *RTN* significantly different from this was the Acquisitive Conglomerate group (mean *RTN* = 0.754).

predicted mean *PE*s for each category were obtained. They are shown in Table 3-12 along with the actual average category *PE*s, the difference between these two, and the significance of the differences.

The results confirmed what had been suspected. Even when the effects of the earnings-per-share growth rate, stability, and retention rate are taken into account, the Related Business category has an unusually high mean price-earnings ratio, and the "*PE* gap" is most prominent in the Related-Linked category. Only the Single Business category had a significant negative "*PE* gap." Dividing the regression residuals by strategy increased the total R^2 from 0.48 to 0.58 and the resulting decrease in variance was significant at the 0.5 percent level.

Why does the Dominant-Constrained group, which outperforms the Related-Linked group in every measure (though both are above average), have an average price-earnings ratio of 15.9 while the Related-Linked category's average is 19.3? One could argue that the price-earnings ratio is a measure of expected rather than past performance, but the use of decade averages would remove all but the most persistent disparity between historical and expected performance. The only plausible explanation for the continuing existence of this difference over twenty years is that investors believe the Related-Linked firms to be more likely to maintain their performance over the long term. Whether or not this belief is justified cannot be determined, but the idea that performance based chiefly upon a single major business is ultimately more transient than that growing from diversity does seem reasonable.

Another conclusion to be drawn from the analysis of price-earnings ratio differences is that an unusually high multiple is not necessary in order to play the conglomerate game of trading shares for earnings. Single Business firms can be a tempting target for many would-be conglomerates: with price-earnings multiples well below average, average returns on capital, and conservative attitudes toward debt, even many Dominant-Vertical firms could gain both profitability and higher earnings per share by acquiring companies in this group. That the executives of Single Business firms realize this may be one of the reasons why the category is rapidly shrinking toward nonexistence.

SYNTHESIS

The most important single finding was that the categories did separate firms into groups that displayed significant and consistent differences in financial performance. This result not only established the validity of the specific set of categories but also provided support for this approach to the study of diversification and organizational structure. That an admittedly approximate system

TABLE 3-12. PRICE-EARNINGS MULTIPLE GAP.

	Single	Domi-nant-Vertical	Domi-nant-Con-strained	Domi-nant-Linked and Un-related	Related-Con-strained	Related-Linked	Unre-lated-Passive	Acquis-itive Con-glomerate	All Firms
Actual Price-Earnings Ratio	14.60	15.68	15.92	15.41	19.19	19.27	13.77	17.43	17.02
Calculated Price-Earnings Ratio	17.02	16.64	16.84	17.19	17.50	16.94	16.55	16.89	17.02
Difference	−2.42	−.96	−.92	−1.78	+1.69	+2.33	−2.78	+.54	0.00
t-Ratio	−2.44	−1.15	−.81	−.81	+2.34	+2.11	−1.59	+.33	−
Level of Significance	.02	−	−	−	.01	.02	.06	−	−

for capturing the essence of top management's goals and conception of a corporation's business might be superior to traditional measurement techniques in detecting the implications of diversification implies that the growing understanding of the general management task can be usefully brought to bear on issues best studied by nonclinical methods.

Although many of the performance differences among the categories could be thought of as reflections of industry differences, the close connection between strategy, structure, and the firm's economic environment makes it difficult to separate these effects, either conceptually or mathematically. Is the steel industry a poorer performer than the chemical industry because of inexorable economic laws, or has the strategy of vertical integration itself helped to bar steel firms from opportunities to apply their skills to new businesses based on other materials, markets, or technologies? Have Related Business firms performed well because they tend to be active in science-based industries, or do science-based industries owe their continued health to the strategic and structural attributes of the firms that constitute them? These questions cannot be answered yet, but in their asking we are proposing that in the long run firms create their environments as well as react to them.

Although performance differences existed among the major categories of diversification strategy, breaking the major categories into subcategories more than doubled the explanatory power of the model. In most cases, performance differences between Dominant-Vertical and Dominant-Constrained firms, between Related-Constrained and Related-Linked firms, and between Unrelated-Passive and Unrelated-Acquisitive firms were greater than those among the nondifferentiated major categories. That we were surprised by this finding makes it all the more important: it implies that the firm's economic performance is more closely associated with the type rather than the extent of its product-market scope, and with the way in which businesses are related to one another rather than their number.

The heterogeneity of the major categories and the pattern of several important subcategory differences are clearly visible in Figures 3.5 and 3.6. These graphs also serve to illustrate the finding that the Related-Constrained and Dominant-Constrained categories were the top performers in almost all measures. While the Acquisitive Conglomerates exceeded all other categories in terms of both absolute and per-share growth, their profitability was average and their relative stability extremely poor. The dismal performance record of the Unrelated-Passive group also casts some doubt on the conglomerate's ability to maintain its profitability, much less its growth, once it ceases being "acquisitive."

The Dominant-Constrained and Related-Constrained firms are both based on *controlled diversity*. Neither committed to a single business nor fully diversified multi-industry firms, their strategies reflect a managerial decision to undertake only those business activities that relate to and can draw strength

Figure 3.5. Category Means: Risk-Premium Ratio vs. Return on Invested Capital.

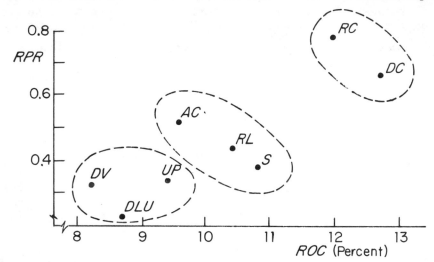

from some product, skill, or market characteristic that is common to all; these are firms that need not resort to metaphysics to define their strategies yet are diverse enough to make the allocation of resources among competing uses a continuing challenge.

From the data presented in Chapter 2 we know that the Dominant-Constrained and Related-Constrained categories together account for about one third of the largest 500 firms and that 74 percent of the first category and 86 percent of the second had product-division structures by 1969. The Related-Constrained group has been quite stable in size while the Dominant-Constrained category has diminished in size since many of its members moved to more diversified postures—most of them having entered the Related-Constrained category. Few of the firms that joined the diversification movement of the 1960s entered either category, although a fair number of Related-Constrained firms adopted Related-Linked strategies during this period.

Why have these firms been consistently high performers? Andrews has suggested that "diversification is often an illusory diversion from the opportunities a company is best able to capitalize," and their postures of controlled diversity certainly reflect a rejection of the mutual fund concept of general management.[21] Still, it would be foolish to constrain a firm's product-market scope to a dying industry, and the apparent success of the Dominant-Constrained and Related-Constrained firms might depend to a large extent upon a process of self-selection: poorly performing companies in these categories may well elect to adopt Linked or Unrelated strategies of diversification, leaving behind those who remain successful. Therefore, controlled diversity is probably not the

---

[21] Andrews, *The Concept of Corporate Strategy*, p. 40.

cause of high performance; it is rather that high performance eliminates the need for greater diversification.

Some support for this view comes from the performance of the Dominant-Vertical firms. Like the Dominant-Constrained firms, the Dominant-Vertical companies have remained largely committed to a single business—in practice a single raw material. Unlike Dominant-Constrained firms, however, Dominant-Vertical firms create such huge concentrations of assets devoted to the processing of raw materials and build organizations that are so internally interdependent that escape from poor performance through diversification becomes exceedingly difficult.

One of the more surprising findings was the poor performance of the Unrelated-Passive firms. Before the data-gathering portion of the research was undertaken, it had been assumed that Unrelated Business firms and "conglomerates" were pretty much one and the same. Even after qualitative evidence began to show that many Unrelated Businesses were neither highly diversified nor aggressive acquirers of other firms, it was believed that the distinction between Unrelated-Passive and Acquisitive Conglomerates was obscure. The financial data, however, indicated that these two types of strategy were associated with radically different financial policies and levels of economic performance. The Unrelated-Passive category had the lowest rate of sales growth, very high variability in earnings per share, the next to lowest return on capital, and, curiously, the most conservative capital structure.

The true conglomerates, on the other hand, lived up to most expectations. Despite heavy rates of dilution, their rapid absolute growth gave this category the highest average growth rate in earnings per share, although it also had the

FIGURE 3.6. Category Means: Growth in Earnings Per Share vs. Return on Equity.

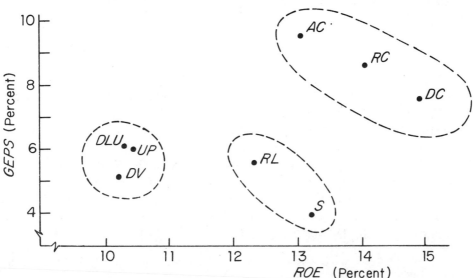

highest relative variability. Heavy use of debt levered a below average return on capital into an above average return on equity. The only unexpected results were that the Acquisitive Conglomerates' mean price-earnings ratio was quite average and that growth in earnings per share and price-earnings ratio were virtually uncorrelated for these firms.

Both types of Unrelated Business firms tended to be heavily involved in science-based industries. A direct comparison between Unrelated Business in science-based industries and other types of firms in these industries showed that they were significantly *less* profitable than most of the firms they compete with.

In organizational structure, firms with product-division structures significantly outperformed those with other forms of organization in all growth measures and in risk-adjusted growth in earnings per share. Their returns on capital and equity were about average. Although few firms in science-based industries were not divisionalized, there was some indication that the same patterns held in both science- and nonscience-based industries: product-division firms were equally profitable but faster growing.

The finding that product-division firms not only grow faster overall but have been able to separate growth and profitability to a greater extent than other types of firms was by far the most intriguing result for the area concerning structure. One could argue, as Reid does, that growth associated with low profits is the result of management emphasizing "its interests" at the expense of stockholders' interests.[22] The evidence, however, demonstrates that growth and profitability are positively related, and the special achievement of many product-division firms has been to increase total profits more rapidly than functional firms that have the *same* level of economic efficiency (return on capital). This ability is due to the special reward, control, planning, and resource-allocation systems used by product-division organizations. The control and reward system creates pressure for maximum return in current operations and it is the independent function of general management to allocate capital to areas that promise growth. Unlike many functionally organized firms, and particularly unlike a vertically integrated firm, the diversified divisionalized company does not have to reinvest in marginal activities just to "stay in the game"; its strategy permits, and its structure facilitates, a range of policies tailored to individual businesses. Some areas can be used as cash generators or even dropped entirely; others may provide stable long-term performance and still others may consist of risky, but potentially lucrative new ventures. As a result, there is less conflict on the corporate level between the goals of profitability and growth.

Finally, in the investigation of price-earnings ratios, it was found that Related Business firms, and especially Related-Linked firms, seem to have been given earnings multiples that were higher than would be expected from their

---

[22] Samuel Richardson Reid, *Mergers, Managers and the Economy* (New York: McGraw-Hill Book Company, 1968), p. 168.

performance. Of course, the result could be spurious—more sophisticated methods for computing expected price-earnings ratios might eliminate the apparent "*PE* gap." Still, the gap is considerable: Related-Linked firms had average growth rates and rates of return that were slightly lower than those of other firms, yet had the highest average price-earnings ratio. Whether this gift from the market is only apparent, due to consistent irrationality, or due to long-term and as yet unrealized expectations, cannot be determined. In any case, the Related-Linked firms' average price-earnings ratio of 19.3 *does not* seem to have tempted their managements to rely heavily on mergers or acquisitions. Their sales and earnings growth rates are average, their earnings-per-share growth rate is somewhat below average but quite stable, and their rate of issuance of new shares is quite normal.

CHAPTER 4

The Low-Performance
Strategies

TWO WIDELY DISPARATE LOW-PERFORMANCE STRATEGIES can be distinguished among the diversification categories: the vertical integration and the Unrelated-Passive product-market posture. The gap between the average level of performance of these firms and that of firms with other strategies was quite significant, and it cannot be attributed to simple variation. What makes this finding particularly important is that these two low-performing categories represent polar extremes of strategy—a complete commitment, not only to a single industry, but to controlling an entire sequence of processing stages, versus the operation of a set of unrelated business enterprises. This chapter will explore the reasons for the low performance of these two groups. In particular, it will examine the reasons Dominant-Vertical firms have so infrequently sought to improve their prospects through diversification and why the Unrelated-Passive strategy, which imposes few constraints on the pursuit of opportunity, has not produced even average levels of performance.

THE DOMINANT-VERTICAL PATTERN

Of the largest 500 United States industrials, about 15 percent have been vertically integrated Dominant Business firms during the twenty years under study. The size of these firms, however, magnifies the economic impact of their behavior and performance—44 percent of the Dominant-Vertical companies were among the largest 100 firms in 1969. Considering the maturity of the industries in which they participate and the relatively undifferentiated nature of the products they sell, it is not too surprising that the average growth rate and return on capital of Dominant-Vertical firms is well below the norm for large corporations. What is more difficult to explain is the reluctance or inability of these firms to change their strategies in the face of continued poor performance. In the period under study, only five Dominant-Vertical companies were observed to move on to Related or Unrelated Business strategies: two of them were grain milling and converting firms that moved easily into packaged foods; AMAX diversified into a variety of mining activities; Boise Cascade had less than the usual amount of timber holdings for a forest products company and expanded rapidly into construction and other businesses, and Di Giorgio moved by divestiture and acquisition from an integrated fresh fruit company to the production and sale of lumber, soft drinks, branded consumer products and other unrelated products. *None* of the vertically integrated oil, paper, primary metals, meat packing, or rubber companies in the sample managed to move into the Related Business (or Unrelated Business) category; firms in heavy industries have acted as if diversification and integration were incompatible strategies.

Like the Dominant-Vertical firm, the Dominant-Constrained company derived the preponderance of its revenues from a single major business. Unlike the vertically integrated firms, companies in the Dominant-Constrained category exhibited a strong tendency to abandon their one-business postures in response to deteriorating performance. A comparison of the 1951–1959 performance of Dominant-Constrained firms that stayed Dominant-Constrained during the *next* decade with that of Dominant-Constrained firms that moved to strategies of greater diversification during the next decade showed that lower levels of growth and profitability were closely associated with a subsequent decision to diversify. Nonetheless, the "low" performing Dominant-Constrained firms that sought a remedy in diversification were more profitable and faster growing than the average Dominant-Vertical company.

	1951–1959 Average	
Firms That Were Dominant-Constrained in 1949–1959	Return on Equity	Growth in Earnings Per Common Share
Stayed Dominant-Constrained During 1960–1969	17.4	11.7
Diversified Out of the Dominant-Constrained Group in 1960–1969	13.4	6.7
Significance of the Difference	0.02	0.10

In the sections that follow we will look at some of the reasons why Domi-nant-Vertical firms have not, as a group, meaningfully diversified. The major barriers to diversification are: mature industries and near-commodity products, problems in the transferability of skills, production-oriented management, complex functional organizations, and low performance itself. All of these affect other types of firms as well, but in the vertically integrated enterprise they come together with a combined impact that greatly diminishes the ability and willingness of management to undertake the task of strategic change.

The Strategy of Integration

By the first decade of the twentieth century, industrialization and corporate combinations had resulted in the formation of many large-scale integrated businesses. In the manufacturing sector, integration came earliest and most completely in industries that were extractive or agriculturally based: oil, lum-ber and paper, iron and steel, copper and nickel, rubber, meat packing, and fresh fruit. The creation of integrated firms was spurred by the economies of scale available from the creation of nationwide sales and marketing organiza-tions and the construction of ever larger manufacturing plants. Once a strategy of great size was adopted, the control of raw material sources became a major competitive weapon.[1]

Although the vertically integrated firms grew rapidly during the early dec-ades of the century, by the mid-1950s many of them faced problems of slow growth, eroded margins, and industry overcapacity. Usually the suppliers of basic materials to other manufacturers, these firms found themselves tied to strategies of efficient operation of complex capital-intensive processes in a time when consumer marketing, product innovation, engineering of special products, and science-based research were becoming the types of skills most highly rewarded by the marketplace. The steady growth in the demand for oil and refinery products is the only major exception to this pattern, though this has been an essentially fortuitous phenomenon; the oil industry neither foresaw nor developed the major markets for its products.

Requiring huge commitments of capital, the extractive industries can be among the most profitable in times of rapidly rising demand. However, products like sheet steel, paperboard, and petrochemical feed stocks are valued chiefly as raw materials in the manufacture of a vast variety of final products. Nondif-ferentiated because it is their economic function to be standardized, the profit-ability of these products is largely contingent upon the balance between capac-ity and demand. In a mature slowly growing industry, the constant oligopolistic struggle to be a low-cost producer and provide flexible and geographically

---

[1] For a detailed discussion of the development of the strategy of integration see Alfred D. Chandler, Jr., "The Beginnings of 'Big Business' in American Industry," *Business History Review,* vol. 32 (Spring 1959), pp. 1–31.

dispersed capacity almost ensures industry overcapacity (on the average) and poor profitability for all.

The steel industry's constant capacity problem is well known, and the aluminum industry, once considered a "growth industry," now shares the same problem. Commenting on the state of the aluminum business in 1971, *Forbes* magazine noted:

> The villain here is overproduction. "Inventories are at record levels and prices are terrible," summarizes analyst David Healy of Burnham & Co. "I calculate that on a Free World basis that aluminum consumption would have to increase 31% next year to use up excess inventory and return the industry to a 100% operating rate. No such increase is likely." Some analysts think supply could exceed demand for three more years.[2]

Economic theory explains and predicts the existence of such phenomena, indicating that these competitive patterns are not pathological—they are the results of mature industries producing near-commodity products by processes that require quantum investments of capital.

Of course, what is a problem for a firm's management is not necessarily a problem for society. Given a low level of technological change, there is no reason for the integrated extractive industries to earn more than a minimal return. What does cause concern and require explanation is the tendency for the managements of Dominant-Vertical firms to constantly reinvest in their low-return business. Bethlehem Steel, for example, recently completed the construction of its new Burns Harbor mill, representing an investment of more than a billion dollars. In money terms, this is a larger project than IBM's 360 venture. Yet, even if successful, analysts believe the new mill will do little more than arrest Bethlehem's *decreasing* earnings per share and push its return on capital back up to 6 percent.[3]

The lack of diversification by the steel industry stands out even among vertically integrated firms. Some Dominant-Vertical firms in other industries have embarked on diversification programs, but only a few companies have treated new businesses as strategically important, rather than as side ventures. Among oil companies, Standard Oil of Ohio, Continental Oil, and Phillips Petroleum derive substantial portions of their revenues from other than basic refinery products. In 1969 Continental Oil obtained 10 percent of its revenues from coal production (Consolidated Oil, acquired in 1965) and another 13 percent from plastics, chemicals and fertilizer. Ohio Standard almost slipped into the Related category in 1969 with 71 percent of its revenues coming from refinery products and crude oil, and the balance from coal, chemicals, fabricated plastic products, and metals. But, in January 1970, Brit-

---

[2] *Forbes*, January 1, 1972, p. 102.

[3] Interview with industry analysts at Paine, Webber, Jackson and Curtis, Boston.

ish Petroleum obtained effective control of Ohio Standard and the combined company had more than 80 percent of its sales in crude oil and refinery products.

Phillips Petroleum has devoted more research effort to developing specialty chemicals and plastic products than most other oil companies, and the effect on its sales mix has been significant. In 1969 Phillips derived 73 percent of its revenues from crude oil and refined products, 6 percent from natural gas, and 21 percent from synthetic fibers, synthetic rubber, fertilizer, plastic pipe and other molded products, vinyl sheet and a paperboard and plastic coated container business. If there is a pattern in the oil industry, it is that the larger worldwide integrated companies have been the least prone to diversify.

Among paper companies, neither the full-line paper and paperboard firms nor the cellulose wadding consumer products companies (e.g., Kimberly-Clark and Scott Paper) have attempted to move beyond the confines of their industry. Boise Cascade started as a lumber company and, rather than try to become another Weyerhaeuser, moved into building materials of all types and containers. The critical strategic difference exhibited by Boise was to then fully exploit the business implications of its product-market activities. It adopted a product-division structure in about 1959 and moved into factory-built homes, mobile homes, land development and recreation products. On the container side, Boise built up a business that included plastic, metal, foil, and paper containers. Finally, in a number of unrelated moves, the company moved into the engineering and construction of industrial plants, computer software, and the distribution of office supplies. Partly aided by its initial small size, Boise's rapid diversification also came from a willingness to look for opportunities beyond lumber and other wood-based products.

The major rubber companies have complex businesses that make classification difficult. Tires (and wheel rims) are the major product of each of the Big Four, and all have developed fairly large businesses devoted to selling the chemicals and yarns associated with the integrated manufacture of tires. Yet none have really devoted major resources to their two main opportunities to diversify: (1) to become full-line producers of automobile, truck and farm equipment parts or (2) to engage in real science-based research in order to become chemical innovators rather than just producers of bulk chemicals.

It is somewhat ironic that while Goodyear and Goodrich have tried to develop aerospace materials and electronics businesses, requiring skills far removed from their basic competences, several aerospace companies have diversified into the auto-parts field.

Nonextensible Technology

In Chandler's chronicle of the development of the first diversified firms in the early part of this century, the impetus supplied by new technologies and new markets was emphasized heavily:

> In those industries most affected by the new markets and new technology, growth came . . . by going overseas and still more by diversification. . . . Diversification came when leading companies in these technologically advanced industries realized that their facilities and the scientific know-how of their personnel could be easily transferred into the production and sale of new goods for new markets. For those enterprises whose energies were concentrated primarily in merchandising, diversification came because of the changing markets in the city and then in the suburbs.[4]

The technologically advanced industries (chemicals, electrical, and, later, electronic equipment and products based on the internal combustion engine) were not only science-based, but encompassed knowledge and techniques that were not related specifically to a single product, material, or process. This special property of extensibility was and still is a key influence on the ease with which a firm can diversify. The production of steel and paper and more recently the manufacture of spacecraft and atomic power plants are all dependent upon some scientific knowledge and complex technologies, but little of the vast store of know-how associated with these activities has proven applicable to other products. Extensible technologies, by contrast, have found wide application in areas far removed from those to which they were first applied. Electrical science was first concentrated in the business of creating capital goods for the generation of power. Widespread electrification led in turn to a proliferation of consumer and industrial products that utilized electric motors as power sources. The development of radio, television, transistors, radar, electronic control systems, and computers led firms that had skills in the electrical sciences into a vast array of related businesses. Similarly, chemical science has proven applicable to product areas as diverse as textiles and antibiotics. The crucial point is not so much that these technologies are science-based as that it is in these areas that science-based research has provided the greatest diversity of fruitful results. This fact has been one of the primary determinants of diversification strategy. A textile manufacturer, no matter how finely honed his skills, simply has fewer opportunities for transferring those skills to other product-market areas than the average producer of electronic devices.

Most vertically integrated firms embody an industrial pattern that predates the rise of the new technologies. The nature of the products and the strategy of integration both coincided with and supported the development of technologies that were based on process rather than product, and on improving the efficiency of production rather than changing the nature of the end product. While research efforts in the new technologies have continually blurred the boundaries between sciences, industries and products, the production-oriented inward-looking research in steel, oil, paper, and nonferrous metals companies has chiefly served to create less expensive or improved steel and other metals, gasoline, and paper.

---

[4] Chandler, *Strategy and Structure,* p. 51.

Still, the problem of relatively nonextensible technology has not proven to be an insuperable barrier to the diversification programs of many nonintegrated firms. When neither a firm's technology nor its markets have been particularly conducive to a transfer of skills or strengths to new areas, careful sequences of moves and more than the usual amount of imagination have enabled quite a few to move to Related Business product-market postures. For example, in 1949 American Chain and Cable had well over 70 percent of its revenues coming from the production and sale of chain, steel wire cable, and valves and other simple cast shapes. Almost as an incidental sideline, it also made a specialized type of hardness-testing instrument that was well respected but had a limited market. Its strategy of diversification during the next twenty years was threefold: (1) it integrated forward into the production of brakes, clutches, hoists, and overhead cranes as these products employed both its cables and its casting and foundry capabilities; (2) it exploited its growing position in hoists and cranes by moving firmly into stackers, palletizing equipment, conveyers, and other materials handling equipment; (3) it built on its reputation in the hardness-testing field by moving gradually into data-recording instruments, gauges, and data loggers, and eventually into industrial controls, telemetry, and other electronic instruments. Recently it has sought to draw on both branches of its diversification program by developing equipment and systems for automated warehouses.

Another example is Union Tank Car's (now Trans Union) diversification strategy. While its competitor, American Car and Foundry, made an unrelated and eventually abortive move into defense electronics, Union Tank exploited its experience in tank-car leasing by moving into truck leasing, the operation of truck and rail bulk terminals, built on its growing financial skills by entering the credit and loan field, and then combined its experience in transport and finance by taking a position in international trade services. At the same time it utilized its tank-car manufacturing skills by moving into the water and chemical tank business, entering the waste treatment and pollution control fields and introducing a line of home water conditioners. However, that the potential for expansion of corporate competence can easily fall short of management's ambitions is also illustrated by Union Tank's experience—an attempt to build missile silos under government contract was resoundingly unsuccessful, and eventually resulted in the resignation of the company's chief executive.

While these and other companies found it possible to diversify away from relatively nonextensible technologies, the complexity of the linking relationships made it anything but an easy task. For vertically integrated companies the problem is intensified by the process nature of their technologies and the illusion of diversification provided by forward integration into fabricated products.

For raw materials companies, the most obvious opportunities for transferring technological skills to other areas involves the production of products that are close substitutes for their original products. The strategy of vertical integration creates a large commitment of capital and human energy to a particular product, not to a product function. As a consequence, other products that perform the same function are not seen as logically related to the companies business but as threats to the firm's continued viability. For steel company executives, aluminum and plastics are not viewed as natural partners to steel in a structural materials business, but as competing substances which can undermine the economic performance of the ore-to-mill production system. For an oil company, petrochemicals are a way to increase the profitability of oil production and refining—the distillation of coal and petrochemical feedstocks is a technology to be feared rather than welcomed. This attitude is not irrational; it is a natural consequence of large-scale investment in capital-intensive and inflexible processing systems.

The same principle affects the strategy of forward integration into products that use the integrated firm's major product as a raw material. Dominant-Vertical companies frequently refer to this as "diversification," but in practice they look upon fabricated products as simply one way of insuring utilization of the firm's basic investments in raw material sites and processing capacity. Even at Boise Cascade, where a strategy of rapid diversification later took the firm completely out of the Dominant-Vertical category, the president, R. V. Hansberger, noted in 1963 that "the security of diversification came as a by-product of a plan to improve the use of our trees." [5]

Alcoa's strategy to increase primary demand for aluminum by demonstrating how it could be used to create a variety of products called for forward integration into cookware, wire, containers, branded foil and a number of other fabricated products. The goal of stimulating demand was achieved, but the company's so-called "diversification" posture has never served to insulate it from cycles in the demand for and supply of aluminum. As long as the final product businesses of the vertical chain have strategies of making *aluminum* pans and *aluminum* wire (or *steel* pipe or *rubber* gloves) rather than exploiting the full business potential of their product-market positions, the net result is merely an intensification of the firm's dependence on a single material. This occurs because each new fabrication activity creates a corresponding need for expensive, high fixed-cost, basic processing capacity.

By-product diversification can offer the integrated firm a means of moving into new business areas, but the scope of action is limited by the growth rate of the primary business. Steel firms were suppliers of benzene long before the oil companies began to produce this valuable chemical building block in volume. But a steel company's sales of by-product materials (in this case from coke ovens) are limited by its rate of steel production. Meat packers face the same problem in fully exploiting their chemical by-products, as do paper companies in the area of cellulose chemicals.

---

[5] Boise Cascade Corp., *Annual Report to Stockholders,* 1963.

Management and Organization

Barriers to diversification can also arise when a one-industry strategy is institutionalized through organizational structure and the values and attitudes of management.

The functionally structured organization, departmentalized on the basis of production stages, may be an aid to efficient operation, but it also severely limits the number of generalist roles and thus the number of executives who perceive and are responsible for the corporation as a whole. In addition, the partitioning of an integrated firm into departments (e.g., extraction, processing, milling, and converting) tends to promote a style of investment decision that focuses on capacity and "balance" rather than on rate of return and the consideration of alternate uses for capital. In a study of the investment decision process in both integrated paper companies and paper divisions of diversified divisionalized firms, Ackerman found that:

> Investment analyses in the integrated firm were carefully confined to one division and excluded the impact on profitability or the need for additional capacity in other divisions linked to it by product transfers. . . . In short, the corporate executives sought ways to isolate the effect of capacity changes to individual units. . . . A difficulty arose, however, if the desired balance between paper making and converting capability was upset by a major addition at the mill stage. The definition of converting plants was then encouraged by the corporation to restore an internal discrepancy. . . . Such behavior, by itself, does not make economic sense. It may, in fact, provide one explanation for the recurrent tendency in this industry to extend capacity additions to paper to converted products at the expense of prices and, ultimately, profitability at the converting end of the business.[6]

In contrast, Ackerman found that the "paper division" managers of the diversified firms tended to include subunit interrelationships in their analyses of major investments.

Allocation systems that promote reinvestment are, in turn, part of a more general tendency to judge investments in terms of their historical and industry performance. A new plant may seem justified if it promises a 10 percent return if alternative products yield only 9 percent, but even more lucrative returns from extra-industry investment may not even be considered. Thus, a steel firm may make the best possible use of its capital within the context of the steel business but may, in fact, be making a poor economic decision. This tendency is undoubtedly intensified by the heavy depreciation cash flows, often thought

---

[6] Robert W. Ackerman, "The Impact of Integration and Diversity on the Investment Process," unpublished paper, Harvard Business School, 1969, pp. 14–15.

of as representing "costless capital," that are available to capital intensive producers.

The one-industry strategy, in addition to promoting questionable reinvestment rates, is usually associated with the development of values and attitudes that assign significant existential worth to the products or processes themselves. One cannot read the literature on the steel, auto, oil, rubber, or paper industries without realizing that executives in these businesses look upon them as intrinsically exciting and worthwhile and take great pride in the process of production itself. The effects of this orientation on the propensity to diversify are obvious. In testimony before the U.S. Senate Subcommittee on Antitrust and Monopoly, Joel Dirlam, an economist, expressed the opinion that this value-set was a major reason for the lack of diversification in the steel industry:

> I would like to just mention an industry which has not diversified, which is vertically integrated, and yet has complained perhaps more vigorously than any other industry over a period of years before this committee and elsewhere about its low level of return and profits. I refer to the steel industry.
>
> The absence of diversification of large steel firms is, perhaps, surprising One of the motives for diversification is said to be that firms will endeavor to move from relatively low-return lines to more profitable businesses. Large firms in steel have been unwilling or unable to diversify out of steel, in spite of their sizable internal flows of funds, and in spite of the fact that the industry is characterized by excess and obsolescent capacity and by steadily increasing competition from substitutes. A partial explanation . . . may be that steel executives regard themselves not as having gone into a business but having adopted a way of life. . . . It is interesting that when one of the more profitable steel companies, National Steel, speaks of diversification, it means—not that it is going to move into other industries but that it will attempt to reduce the reliance on the automobile industry for outlets.[7]

Attitudes such as these are reminiscent of the situation that faced Alfred Sloan when he took over the management of the then struggling General Motors Corporation. In setting the future strategy of the concern he explicitly called into question the tendency for management to regard the company's purpose as selling a particular set of products: "The primary objective of the corporation, therefore, we declared, was to make money, not just to make motor cars." [8] Of course, loyalty to a product or industry may not be dysfunctional and may even be required for the effective operation of complex enterprise.

---

[7] Statement of Joel Dirlam, Hearings Before the Senate Committee on the Judiciary, Subcommittee on Antitrust and Monopoly, *Economic Concentration*, Part 2 (Washington, D.C.: Government Printing Office, 1965), p. 767.

[8] Alfred P. Sloan, Jr., *My Years With General Motors* (New York: Macfadden, 1965), p. 64.

However, such an attitude may also induce overinvestment and strongly inhibit strategic change.

Size and Performance

Even when the management of an integrated business decides to channel funds and energy into new areas, the absolute size of the original business can render invisible the impact of all but the most vigorous diversification programs. For example, several of the major oil companies that were classified in this study as Dominant Businesses have petrochemical, plastic, and fertilizer operations that, if split apart from the parent firm, would be among the largest 500 industrials in their own right. For the very largest corporations this is an almost insoluble dilemma. Piecemeal additions to the businesses of companies like United States Steel, General Motors, and Standard Oil of New Jersey can produce but insignificant changes in earnings and their rate of growth. In addition, the close scrutiny of the Federal Trade Commission virtually blocks the large merger route to diversification for these giant firms; even when unrelated businesses are entered, the public and the government may not permit the large increase in overall concentration of economic power implied by significant diversification of the industrial giants.

Size is also a problem for large, but not giant, enterprises. Not only may the financial effects of diversification be relatively small in comparison to the firm's major activity, but the organizational subunits dealing in diversified areas must operate in the shadow of the company's large functional structure. The most frequent structural form adopted by integrated firms with diversified activities is the functional-with-subsidiaries organization. While this structure allows diversified businesses to operate apart from the firm's main business, the general managers of diversified subunits are hierarchically on a par with the functional department managers of the major business. Not only must the general manager of a division compete for capital and top management attention with several large units that are really just parts of one business, but the general office remains wedded to the major business and is ill-equipped to objectively judge the merits of business projects in the diversified areas. Two distinct styles of appraisal and supervision are required of top management in a functional-with-subsidiaries structure—one for coordinating the functional departments and dealing with the strategic issues that affect the major business, often on a day to day basis, and another for dealing with general managers of diversified semi-autonomous divisions. It will be a rare top management team that can simultaneously serve both needs. More often, the diversified business must struggle to cope with resource allocation, appraisal, and control systems that were developed for the integrated business.

Coupled with large size, the relatively poor performance of the Dominant-Vertical firms makes strategies of diversification all the more difficult to implement. Low price-earnings ratios mean that the acquisition of attractive businesses will result in substantial dilution. This is, in turn, especially expensive to these firms; since their stock values are almost entirely based on dividend rates, dilution implies a substantial additional cash drain if current stockholders are to be satisfied. On the other hand, paying cash for acquired companies or investing cash in new business development projects requires very large commitments if diversification is to have any visible influence on total earnings. Yet the oligopolistic nature of competition in the integrated industries makes constant infusions of cash necessary just to maintain position. In a business where expensive raw material sites and costly plants are the key competitive weapons, it is difficult to disinvest—like the poker player who has so far matched the bets of others, the integrated business keeps reinvesting because although winning is improbable, loss is certain if it does not.

Summary

Although the strategy of vertical integration is a reasonable and rational response to certain technologies and market conditions, these very conditions have become associated with mature and less profitable industries. Escape from these industries, however, is particularly difficult for the large vertically integrated firm. Its technologies tend to be based on process rather than science or product function and are not readily transferable. Large size implies that the scale of investment in new businesses must also be large if noticeable changes in corporate performance are to be achieved, but low price-earnings ratios and high pay-out policies make such investments financially quite difficult. Finally, the integrated businesses train few generalists, and their attitudes and the organizational structure they preside over tend to inhibit strategic change. Thus, unlike nonintegrated firms, the Dominant-Vertical companies have not, in general, significantly diversified in response to low performance.

The Unrelated-Passive Strategy

Among diversified firms, those that followed the Unrelated-Passive strategy exhibited lower levels of profitability and growth and smaller risk premium ratios. While this category has not been a large one in numerical terms, it grew substantially in the ten years between 1959 and 1969. Since the Acquisitive Conglomerates have focused a great deal of attention on the concept of expansion into completely unrelated areas, the relatively poor performance of the Unrelated-Passive firms, which have developed unrelated product-market postures without the conglomerate's tactic of rapid and continuous acquisition, takes on special interest.

In general, an Unrelated Business firm was defined as one that derived less than 70 percent of its revenues from its largest group of somehow related businesses. This category was then further subdivided into Unrelated-Passive and Acquisitive Conglomerate categories. The Acquisitive Conglomerates were selected on the basis of their rates of growth, rates of acquisition, and rates of movement into new unrelated businesses. While it might therefore be thought that the Unrelated-Passive firms consist chiefly of conglomerates whose rapid growth phase is over, it was found that this simple screen split the overall Unrelated group into two quite distinct subgroups.

While Acquisitive Conglomerates have usually expanded by acquiring large numbers of individual companies over a relatively short period of time, an Unrelated-Passive firm tends to have developed in one of three other ways: (1) evolution from a pre-World War II holding company; (2) the merger of two or three already large and often diversified firms; or (3) a strategy of expansion into both related and unrelated areas, usually undertaken in order to diversify away from some major business area. In order to clarify these three types of development, several examples will be discussed.

Holding Company

Avco was started in the late 1920s to serve as a holding company for American Airways (now American Airlines) and several aviation equipment firms. By 1945 Avco controlled American Airlines, Pan American Airways, Consolidated Vultee, Lycoming, New York Shipbuilding, Crosley (electronics, broadcasting, and refrigerators), New Idea (farm equipment) and several other firms. This portfolio of unrelated businesses had been built partly as a result of war contracts but chiefly as a defensive investment against government action, which finally forced Avco to sell its interests in both airlines and Consolidated Vultee in 1945. Avco then bought Bendix (home washers), but suffered such losses in this area that it left the home appliances business by 1956, leaving electronics and aircraft engines and parts as its largest business. Avco's transition from holding company to operating company occurred during this period, and management's decision to drop all consumer products was followed by heavy internal investment in laboratories oriented toward military and space research and development. By 1959 Avco's largest business was contract research on advanced materials, electronics, and missile re-entry technology.

Between 1949 and 1964 Avco had followed an Unrelated-Passive strategy —operation of unrelated businesses with little or no growth by acquisition. In 1964, however, defense sales dropped sharply and management began to look outside the current product-market scope of the company for new opportunity. Delta Acceptance Company, a finance company, was acquired in 1964, followed by the acquisition of Bay State Abrasives in 1965. By 1969 Avco had moved by acquisition into life insurance, the credit card business, land development, motion pictures, and steel wire. Its largest single business in 1969 was the production of helicopter engines (31 percent of sales) and it was classified as an Acquisitive Conglomerate.

Pullman's early development was roughly analogous to Avco's. A holding company created in 1927 to control both Pullman-Standard, which manufactured railroad "sleeping cars" and freight cars, and the Pullman Company, a firm that operated the sleeping cars, providing maintenance and personnel on a contract basis. In 1947 the government ordered the sale of the sleeping car operations portion of the company's business and with the proceeds the firm acquired the M. W. Kellogg Company, which was engaged in the design, fabrication, and erection of plants and equipment for the oil and chemical industries. Between 1950 and 1959 Pullman moved into the truck-trailer business through acquisition, and into the production of plastic chemicals in plants built by its Kellogg division; still, the headquarters office remained small and Pullman was essentially a holding company. Between 1959 and 1963 Pullman became an operating company, creating a true product-division structure. In the process, it left the chemical business, sold off a small steel mill that had supplied steel to both divisions, and dropped several unprofitable Kellogg products—pressure vessels, heat exchangers, and rocket casings. Between 1963 and 1969 Pullman acquired a company that designed and built furnaces for the steel industry and developed, by internal investment, a number of new businesses related to plant construction and truck trailer and railroad car manufacture. Pullman was classified as Unrelated-Passive throughout the period 1949–1969. "Passive" only in the sense that it did not expand by rapid acquisition of new unrelated businesses, Pullman actually followed Related-Constrained strategies of diversification in two separate unrelated areas.

A third example is Rockwell Manufacturing. Formed to implement a depression survival plan of joining together a number of manufacturing companies, Rockwell Manufacturing retained a holding company structure until about 1960. It produced gas and oil meters, cash registers, taxi meters, pumps, and power tools for wood and metal working. A program of marketing rationalization by the combination of similar sales groups led to the combination of about twenty separate businesses into five divisions in 1960.

Large Merger

The 1961 merger of the Martin Company and American Marietta, one of the largest mergers in history, created an Unrelated-Passive firm of giant size. Martin was a manufacturer of airframes and missiles, while Marietta was itself a diversified company that sold lime, concrete, and pulverizing machinery, as well as paints, ink, coatings, dye, and other chemical products. The newly formed Martin Marietta quickly sold off most of Marietta's paint and chemical businesses and also divested itself of the pulverizing machinery and some other activities. The company's only major diversification move since the merger was the acquisition (through a tender offer) of Harvey Aluminum, a small but integrated aluminum company.

The Martin Marietta merger resulted in an Unrelated-Passive company that showed little of the dynamism that management had hoped for. Both sales and earnings showed *negative* rates of growth during 1961–1969, and the return on equity averaged about 11 percent.

Olin is another example of an Unrelated-Passive firm that was formed by merger (Olin Mathieson Chemical prior to 1969). Mathieson Chemical had been a producer of bulk, heavy chemicals that sought diversification in the 1952 acquisition of E. R. Squibb & Sons, a manufacturer of antibiotics and other ethical drugs. Olin Industries was itself an Unrelated Business company at the time of the merger, producing arms, ammunition, explosives, cellophane, lumber, flooring, copper and other nonferrous metals, and dry cells. After the merger the company initiated a venture in primary aluminum. Between 1954 and 1969 Olin made no further large acquisitions, though in 1968 Squibb was spun off and merged with Beech-Nut. Olin's return on capital has averaged about 7 percent since the merger, and growth has been both erratic and very low. While the reasons for Olin's poor record are not entirely clear, *Fortune* has suggested that top management had an exceptionally difficult time reaching agreement on corporate goals and in creating a suitable structure to control and coordinate the firm's activities.[9]

Two other firms that became Unrelated Businesses chiefly through one or two mergers are North American Rockwell and Sybron. The 1967 merger of North American Aviation and Rockwell Standard brought together a firm in the aerospace and electronics business, with one producing auto parts, machinery parts and light aircraft and textile machinery. Sybron was formed by the 1965 merger of Ritter and Pfaulder, producers of tanks and waste-treatment equipment, and dental and hospital equipment respectively.

At the risk of generalizing from too few examples, it seems that when a rapidly diversifying firm merges with another equally large firm, the degree of acquisition activity drops sharply and the managements turn to work on the problem of creating an administrative system to knit two large very different firms together.

Mixed Diversification

Until 1963, Champion Spark Plug was a single-product company. In that year, however, it began a diversification program with the acquisition of a

---

[9] *Fortune,* September 1958, p. 212.

producer of test equipment for quality control. In short order the firm acquired companies producing fire detection equipment, steel bar, paint sprayers and coating equipment, X-ray tubes, and cartridge tape recorders. More cautious than an Acquisitive Conglomerate, Champion seems to buy firms with highly proprietary products that may benefit from its financial resources or multinational skills.

American Standard began to diversify away from its plumbing, heating, and heat exchanger business in 1955 with establishment of a division to explore the commercial feasibility of products related to or based upon the use of atomic power. Management stated that fluctuations in the construction of residential housing were the primary reason for its decision to increase the "engineered products" portion of its business.

American Standard developed a line of military aircraft guidance-system components in the late 1950s but sold it in 1960 because of the "heavy capital requirements." During the 1960s the company relaxed its policy of internally generated diversification and acquired an instrument producer, a company making safes and office record-keeping materials, and Westinghouse Air Brake. The latter was by far the largest and contributed 14 percent of the firm's 1969 revenues.

Also following mixed strategies were Boise Cascade, Di Giorgio, Curtiss-Wright and USM (United Shoe Machinery). Some of the firms that became Unrelated Businesses via the mixed route displayed no consistent rationale behind their diversification moves. Others, however, seem to have had relatively clear strategies of diversification but also were willing to enter Unrelated areas if the right situation presented itself.

UNRELATED-PASSIVE PERFORMANCE

While not far from the overall average, the profitability and rates of growth of Unrelated-Passive firms were low in comparison to the averages of other diversified firms. In addition, as shown in Chapter 3, many Unrelated-Passive firms had the majority of their activities in science-based industries and, when compared to other firms in these industries, their performance was particularly poor. *Relatively* low profitability in science-based industries is also a characteristic of Acquisitive Conglomerates, and Unrelated-Passive firms have the additional problem of low rates of growth.

The type of data on which this study was based do not lend themselves to explanations of *why* the performance of the Unrelated-Passive firms has been relatively poor. The ways in which these firms developed and their special strategic and structural attributes do, however, suggest some hypotheses.

The attainment of higher than average profitability by an Unrelated Business firm would seem to call for at least three things: (1) careful selection of constituent businesses, (2) willingness to divest poor performers, and (3) an administrative structure that creates pressure for profit and contains generalists capable of making resource allocation decisions and intervening if problems arise. When the Unrelated-Passive firms are judged on these criteria, many, though not all, fail to measure up.

The Unrelated-Passive firms that developed from holding companies had usually operated for a length of time without any real central office or formal control and resource allocation systems. Significantly, when such firms made the transition to being operating companies with full product-division structures, the divestiture of several product lines or businesses was almost always an immediate consequence. Having little or no strategic direction from the top and with interdivisional transfers of cash made difficult by the holding company's legal status, each business entity of such a firm developed on its own. The managements of these holding companies and quasi-holding companies frequently cited the value of diversification as a defense against adversity, but apparently did not follow strategies of channeling funds from mature to growing businesses. Under such circumstances, it would be surprising if the overall corporate performance were anything but average.

In each case of the creation of Unrelated-Passive firms through large mergers, one of the merger partners had already been diversifying fairly rapidly through acquisition. When such a firm merges with another large firm whose businesses are unrelated to its own, severe strategic and administrative problems can result. Neither a pure "unrelated" approach (e.g., Textron) nor a single concept of relatedness suffices to guide the development of the firm, and administrative systems built around different clusters of core skills are difficult to combine. Not only are synergistic benefits of such a merger difficult to obtain, but the approximately equal size of the merger partners can produce complex struggles for influence and resources, and unlike a merger of firms in the same business, these tensions cannot be resolved by combining similar facilities.

Firms that became Unrelated-Passive by following "mixed" diversification strategies also had strategic and administrative problems similar to those faced by the "large merger" group. In addition, for many of these firms the low performance that was the initial motive for diversification was not alleviated by the acquisition of unrelated enterprises.

Thus, the Unrelated Business strategy seems to call for an approach that is essentially administrative rather than operations-oriented. When the enterprise consists of a set of disparate businesses, the basic task of general management is the "management of managers," and it requires special types of control, reward, and resource allocation systems. Because of the way they developed, however, most firms in the Unrelated-Passive group have either (1) weak administrative structures or (2) administrative systems designed for and bound to Related Business strategies. Unlike the Acquisitive Conglomerates, which tend to view each business as an independent unit, many of the Unrelated-Passive firms had tried to exploit tenuous synergies among unrelated businesses, or attempted to knit together groups of unrelated businesses that appeared to share a common rubric (such as the "amusement business," or the "consumer products" business).

CHAPTER 5

Summary of Findings
and Implications

T HE AIM OF THIS STUDY HAS BEEN to add to the store of knowledge concerning the development, form, and economic performance of large industrial corporations. In the preceding chapters data relating to diversification have been offered, and interpretations of the findings provided. Now the threads of evidence must be drawn together into a coherent set of conclusions.

SUMMARY OF FINDINGS

Seventy percent of the largest 500 firms fell into the Single or Dominant Business categories of diversification strategy in 1949. By 1969, over half of these firms had either moved to Related or Unrelated Business strategies or had been acquired and had their places in the top 500 taken by more diversified firms. At the same time, the product-division structure, employed by 20 percent of the large firms in 1949, moved to a position of predominance, being used by 75 percent of the large firms in 1969. Thus, the revolution in the form of the large American corporation, which was identified and traced in its early stages by Chandler, progressed rapidly toward its culmination during this period.

The change in the composition of the largest 500 firms came about through two distinct processes: strategic change by firms that were already members of the largest 500, and the entry of new firms into this group to replace those that had been merged, acquired, or had dropped below the size limit for inclusion. Data showed that, except for the case of Acquisitive Conglomerates, the effects of both of these processes were of about equal magnitude. In addition, it is worth noting that the role of major mergers (involving firms of approximately equal size) in the overall increase in diversification was negligible.

Few would dispute the very general conclusion that the average large firm became substantially more diversified and more than likely changed its structure from a functional to product-divisions structure during the period 1949–1969. Such a result could have been obtained with techniques much simpler than those employed. What insights, then, did the concepts of strategy and structure and the method of classification contribute that would not have been revealed by more primitive measures, such as the product count?

Diversification

First, although a strong and continual trend existed toward increased diversification, it was far from uniform. Some firms were more likely than others to increase the diversity of their product-market postures, and there was a degree of predictability about which strategy of expansion a diversifying firm would adopt. The number of Single Business firms among the top 500 decreased sharply between 1949 and 1959, dropping from slightly more than a third of all large firms to less than one fifteenth. Most of the Single Business diversifiers stayed close to their original areas of business competence, entering the Dominant-Constrained category. While the Dominant-Constrained group was itself experiencing an exodus to more diversified postures, the flow of new Dominant-Constrained firms from the Single Business group kept it from decreasing in size until the 1960s, by which time the Single Business category had become too small to provide a steady flow of newly diversifying firms.

The tendency for newly diversifying firms to stay close to home in their search for opportunity was also evident among Dominant-Constrained firms in the 1950s. Dominant-Constrained companies that diversified further between 1949 and 1959 strongly tended to enter the Related-Constrained category; although they decreased their dependence on their largest single business, these companies continued to restrict their scope of activity to businesses that built on some central skill or strength. In the 1960s, however, Dominant-Constrained diversifiers entered the Related-Constrained and Related-Linked categories with about equal frequency. This increased willingness to look farther afield for opportunity was one of the most obvious differences between the two decades. Firms diversifying from within the top 500 and those that entered it by growth were much more likely to adopt Related-Linked or Unrelated Business strategies during the 1960s than in the 1950s.

The most stable of the categories was the Dominant-Vertical group. Almost none of these large raw-materials processing companies moved into the Related or Unrelated Business categories, few were merged or acquired, and few of the firms that entered the top 500 were Dominant-Vertical. The poor economic performance of most of these firms suggests that their slowness to diversify was due more to the existence of special barriers to diversification than to complacency. In particular, their historical development and economic purpose have left these firms with technologies that are process- rather than product-oriented and attitudes and practices that favor selling rather than marketing. Their large investments in capital-intensive primary processing plants promote capacity utilization rather than return on investment analyses of new projects. Departmentalized but functional structures overshadow new business ventures and they encourage managerial attitudes that tend to discourage any search for opportunity that might take the firm outside of current industry boundaries. Because of these and similar factors, the vertically integrated firm tends to be a special case among large American corporations. If current trends continue, the years to come will increasingly show large firms as splitting into two camps: the majority of modern divisionalized firms following Related and Unrelated Business strategies, and the Dominant-Vertical holding on to an earlier pattern of industrial structure.

Among Related Business firms, in 1949 those that were Related-Constrained outnumbered Related-Linked companies by more than two to one. By 1969, the Related-Linked subgroup was slightly larger than the Related-Constrained. Though both subgroups of the Related category grew during these twenty years, most of the overall increase came in the Related-Linked group, and most of that came in the 1960s. During the 1950s, virtually none of the Related-Linked growth was due to changes in strategy by already large firms—its increase in this period was purely due to firms that broke into the top 500. During the 1960s, however, both factors were at work. Dominant and Related-Constrained firms moved frequently to Related-Linked strategies and 29 percent of all new entrants to the 500 were in this strategic category.

A similar but exaggerated pattern governed the growth of the Acquisitive Conglomerate category. There were no Acquisitive Conglomerates in the sample in 1949, but by 1969 they constituted 10.9 percent of the top 500 and most had entered the 500 in the 1960s. Of firms that were among the largest 500 in both 1949 and 1969, only 2.2 percent had become Acquisitive Conglomerates by 1969.

Thus, not only does a trend exist toward increased diversification but there is an increasing tendency for experienced diversifiers to adopt Linked rather than Constrained strategies of diversification and a definite change in the composition of the top 500 due to fast growing Acquisitive Conglomerates. Both of these changes in the expansion paths used by large corporations became more pronounced in the 1960s.

Structure

Of the five categories of structure defined for the study, only the functional, functional-with-subsidiaries, and the product-division groups contained significant numbers of firms. At its maximum extent during the period of study the geographic-division category only contained an estimated 10 of the largest 500 firms and the holding company category was only slightly larger with 19 firms. The functional-with-subsidiaries category was fairly stable in size, chiefly because many of the companies with this structure were in the Dominant-Vertical class, the most stable strategic class.

The data gave strong support to Chandler's proposition that "structure follows strategy," but forced the addition of "structure also follows fashion." Between 1949 and 1969 the relative numerical positions of the functional and product-division categories more than reversed: starting at 63 percent of the top 500 in 1949, the functional structure was only used by 11 percent of large firms in 1969 while the product-division organization increased in usage from 20 percent to 76 percent of the top 500 in the same period. Investigation of the association between strategy and structure showed (1) firms that are members of categories of diversification strategy that correspond to greater amounts of product-market diversity are more likely to have product-division structures; (2) during the 1950s, functional firms that shifted to categories of greater diversification were more likely to change to product-division structures than functional firms that did not change strategy; and (3) during the 1960s this relationship did not hold—while many firms changed from functional to product-division structures, those that underwent strategic changes were no more likely to divisionalize than other firms. The conclusion can only be reached that product-division structure has become so well known and understood that modern firms tend to adopt it more readily than the companies of a generation ago. The firms Chandler studied often adopted the divisionalized structure only after the old system began to collapse under the burden of diversified operations. By contrast, many corporations of the 1960s, even those that were not highly diversified, split their operations into semi-autonomous divisions without having suffered great administrative strains. Some divisionalized because they planned to diversify, others wanted to create greater accountability for product performance, even among closely related products, and still others simply believed that the product-division structure was a better form of organization.

Performance

The findings with regard to the population of the categories of strategy and structure are necessarily analytical—they cannot serve to validate the systems of classification because no other types of information were included in the analyses. In looking at the relative financial performance of the categories, however, we are also looking at the degree to which the categories provide a meaningful map of a portion of reality. If the categories serve to divide firms into groups that are internally more homogeneous than the sample as a whole, there is evidence that the information provided by the classification system extends beyond that which was used to classify the companies.

The two most important findings regarding the economic performance of different categories of diversification strategy were (1) that the system of classification revealed differences in financial results and policies that were not discernable if simple measures of diversity were employed to discriminate among firms; and (2) that performance differences among the strategic categories were more closely linked to the way in which the firm related new businesses to old than to overall diversity.

If measures of diversity, such as the product count, correlated with profitability or growth, one could easily argue that category-associated performance differences merely reflected a more basic correlation between profits or growth and diversity. No such correlation with simple measures of diversity has been found, however. We are led to the conclusion then that the system for capturing the essence of top management's goals and concept of the corporation's purpose and scope is a better predictor of financial performance than simple measures of diversification. This result helps to validate the system of categories used here because it provides assurance that at least a portion of reality has been captured.

Although performance differences existed among the major categories of diversification strategy (Single, Dominant, Related and Unrelated), the explanatory power of the system was more than doubled by breaking these categories into subcategories. This showed (1) that among Dominant Business firms, the Dominant-Vertical group was low performing while the Dominant-Constrained was among the highest performing; (2) among Related Business firms, the Related-Constrained subgroup was high performing while the Related-Linked was average or slightly below average; and (3) among Unrelated Business firms, the Unrelated-Passive subgroup was among the poorest performing and the Acquisitive Conglomerates were average in profitability and substantially above average in growth. The heterogeneity of the major categories indicates that performance differences are not really related to diversity per se, but are more a function of the firm's strategy for dealing with growth and diversity.

The Dominant-Constrained and Related-Constrained groups were unquestionably the best overall performers, and both strategies are based upon the concept of controlled diversity. Neither totally dependent upon a single business nor true multi-industry firms, these companies have strategies of entering only those businesses that build on, draw strength from, and enlarge some central strength or competence. While such firms frequently develop new products and enter new businesses, they are loath to invest in areas that are unfamiliar to management.

Although Dominant-Constrained firms tended to move on to Related Business strategies in response to deteriorating performance, Dominant-Vertical firms had, on the average, much poorer performance levels but were either unable or unwilling to employ diversification as a remedy. Scott calls these firms the "heavies" of American industry and the evidence here supports his conjecture that they face special barriers to diversification and are among the poorest performers.[1]

The distinction between Unrelated-Passive and Acquisitive Conglomerate strategies was found to correspond to two radically different sets of financial policies and levels of economic performance. Unrelated-Passive firms had the lowest rates of growth in sales, poor rates of return on capital, high variability in growth in earnings per share and also the most conservative capital structures. The Acquisitive Conglomerates, by contrast, had very high rates of growth in sales and earnings, experienced heavy dilution but still achieved above average rates of growth in earnings per share, and used leverage to boost a below average return on capital to an above average return on equity. Somewhat surprisingly, Acquisitive Conglomerate price-earnings ratios were quite average, with no correlation between conglomerate price-earnings ratios and growth rates in earnings per share. It seems that the "bootstrap" model of conglomerate growth, whereby the firm uses a high price-earnings ratio to make favorable acquisitions and the resulting rapid growth in earnings per share to keep its price-earnings ratio high, does not apply to most Acquisitive Conglomerates. Instead, many firms with low price-earnings ratios achieved rapid growth through acquisition by heavy use of convertible securities, deferred payments, and rationalization of the capital structures of acquired firms. By buying companies with their own excess debt capacities or with promises of future gains in earnings per share, these firms obtained rapid increases in size without abnormally high price-earnings ratios.

The low performance of the Unrelated-Passive firms came as a surprise, since many observers have grouped these companies with the Acquisitive Conglomerates. While they are active in several unrelated business areas, as are the true conglomerates, most of the Unrelated-Passive companies had neither the administrative structure nor the aggressive acquisition programs of the conglomerates. Many of the Unrelated-Passive firms were created by the merger of two already diversified, but unrelated, firms, and others developed patterns of business activities that were similar to those of the firms formed by merger. The way in which these firms developed has resulted in weak admin-

---

[1] Bruce R. Scott, "Stages of Corporate Development" (unpublished paper, Harvard Business School, 1970), p. 42.

istrative systems. The marriage of two large Related Business firms to produce
an Unrelated Business company results in control by managers who have spent
their careers dealing with related businesses and are used to systems of control,
information, and reward that presuppose a degree of similarity among businesses, as well as familiarity, on the part of top management, with the details
of many activities. In the combined firm, however, resource-allocation decisions may focus on "which side of the house" gets supported rather than on
individual investment proposals. Growth through future unrelated diversification moves is not easier for the Unrelated-Passive firm than for the Related
Business firm.

Firms with product-division structures had rates of growth that, on the
average, were significantly higher than those of firms with other type of organizational structures. Their rates of profit were at least as high as those of
other firms. More interesting was the finding that, among firms with product-
division structures, growth in sales was less directly related to profitability
than among firms with other types of structures. Stated somewhat differently,
differences in the growth rates of functionally organized firms can, to an extent, be explained by differences in their rates of profit; among product-
division firms, however, differences in rates of profit were associated with
much smaller differences in rates of growth. This seems to indicate that firms
with product-division structures do not rely as heavily on current profits to
power their growth as functionally organized firms. This result was possibly
due to the special systems of control, resource allocation, and reward used by
product-division firms, which allow a high degree of separation between the
goals of current profitability and growth. In fact, the two levels of general
management that characterize the product-division firm may be thought of as
concern with current return on investment (division management) and growth
through investment in new products and businesses (top management).

IMPLICATIONS OF THE FINDINGS

In the twenty years between 1949 and 1969 the structure of industry in the
United States underwent a remarkable change, a change that was not foreseen
by most observers. As in the earlier portions of the century, big business carried out the lion's share of industrial activity, but concentration in individual
industries did not increase appreciably. Instead, the boundaries between various
industries became more and more blurred as firms expanded their product-
market scopes to include several industrial sectors.

Many present day observers of the industrial situation still fail to recognize
either the extent or the impact of the revolution that has occurred in industrial

structure. In the important and widely read book, *The New Industrial State,* for example, J. K. Galbraith claims that the technological requirements of large modern industrial enterprise have created corporations that are inflexible, uncontrolled from the top, and that have superseded the competitive markets in their need to plan over long time spans, make vast capital commitments, and maintain production flow through long-linked production systems. In particular, Galbraith claims that the imperatives of technology and size have acted to vest corporate power in the *technostructure*. In his analysis of the modern corporation, Galbraith argues that: [2]

1. Modern technology requires an ever increasing time span between the conception of a product or project and its completion and the size of markets and enterprises implies the advance commitment of vast amounts of capital.

2. Technology is based on specialization, and specialization requires an increasingly complex administrative structure to coordinate the work of specialists. Furthermore, top level managers no longer have the expertise to directly influence or control the nature of the products or services that are produced by the corporation.

3. Because time spans are long, costs high, and because large scale organization is inflexible and difficult to redirect, uncertainty in the final outcome of a project cannot be tolerated. Hence the firm supersedes market uncertainty by planning, the manipulation of consumer tastes, interfirm agreements, and vertical integration.

4. The imperatives of technology and the ability of the firm to supersede the market make it necessary and possible for power over critical decisions to pass from the hands of owners and top management to the technostructure. The technostructure is the group of technically oriented personnel that engages in product planning and market planning, guides projects, and assures their final outcome.

5. The technostructure has no compulsion to maximize profits and, therefore, does not. Galbraith writes: "But with the rise of the technostructure, the notion, however tenuous, that a few managers might maximize their own return by maximizing that of the stockholders, dissolves entirely. Power passes down into the organization. Even the small stock interest of the top officers is no longer the rule. Salaries, whether modest or generous, are according to scale; they do not vary with profits.[3]

Because the technostructure does not seek to maximize profits, it naturally pursues the goal of perpetuating itself and increasing its power and influence. The important consequence of this, Galbraith claims, is that economic models, public policies, and attempts to exert macroeconomic control of the economy

---

[2] John K. Galbraith, *The New Industrial State* (Boston: Houghton Mifflin Company, 1967). Our analysis of Galbraith parallels that of Scott, "Stages of Corporate Development," pp. 45–47.

[3] Ibid., p. 116.

can no longer be based on the assumption of profit maximization on the part of corporations.

Whether or not forward planning and marketing techniques have the power to control the demand for products is a debatable point, but this study has not been addressed to that issue and is consequently not an appropriate forum for such a debate. Galbraith's propositions concerning the nature of planning within the firm and the locus of decision-making power are, on the other hand, directly relevant to this study. This view of corporate life ignores fifty years of evolution in the nature and structure of American industrial enterprise. That great size, economic stability, technology, and the increasing complexities of industry can create a phenomenon like the technostructure is hardly arguable. That it is ascendent and increasingly important is, however, quite a different matter. As early as 1920, managers at du Pont discovered that size, technology, and product diversity were producing administrative problems that threatened management's ability to guide and control the company. Their solution was reorganization—the birth of the multidivisional form of organization. Alfred Chandler described du Pont management's victory over the technostructure: "In September, 1921, the du Pont Company put into effect this new structure of autonomous, multidepartmental divisions and a general office with staff specialists and general executives. . . . Unencumbered by operating duties, the senior executives at the general office now had the time, information, and more of a psychological commitment to carry on the entrepreneurial activities and make the strategic decisions necessary to keep the over-all enterprise alive and growing and to coordinate, appraise, and plan for the work of the divisions. . . . [This structure] has served the du Pont Company effectively ever since." [4]

It is now known that neither du Pont's problem nor its solution was unique; the dominant form of large business enterprise in the United States today is the diversified multidivisional corporation. Unlike the firm that Galbraith describes, these firms have split their operations into separate businesses, each controlled by a division manager who is responsible for current profit as well as planning. The division manager in such a firm is *not* far removed from the goal of profit maximization—he is reviewed on his profit performance at least once a year and his compensation is typically dependent upon his performance. In a study of reward systems in product-division companies, Salter found that systems of review and control were more formal than in functional organizations and that division manager's bonuses, stock options, and eligibility for advancement were tied to the formal systems of control. [5] Thus, while a manager's salary may not be tied to his ability to maximize profit, his total compensation is, and—what is more important to most managers—so are his chances for promotion.

---

[4] Chandler, *Strategy and Structure*, p. 135.

[5] Salter, "Stages of Corporate Development."

The control and reward systems of product-division organizations allow top management to create great pressure for profit maximization. Pressure so created can, in fact, be greater than that caused by the competitive struggle among firms. Nothing prevents top management from setting goals for division managers that require performance above and beyond that normally expected from a Single Business firm in the industry. While such goals may not be met, their existence, or potential existence, can create a climate strongly conducive to profit maximization.

With regard to the superseding of markets, it is the *capital* markets rather than intermediate or consumer markets that have been absorbed into the infrastructure of the new type of corporation. While this may be no more preferable in a social and economic sense than control over product markets, it is an entirely different phenomenon. Both investment bankers and the market for equity securities now treat the firm as a whole and leave to top management the task of deciding which business, or even which industry, should receive new infusions of capital and which should be treated as cash generators. Furthermore, recent history shows that most large firms have infrequently approached the equity markets for new capital, preferring to depend upon reinvested earnings for growth. This means that the diversified, divisionalized firm is increasingly becoming the arbiter of intersectional shifts in funds.

If Galbraith's model does not accurately describe the modern corporation, what does it describe? Scott has observed that the type of firm that most closely matches Galbraith's model is the large, integrated Dominant Business corporation—our Dominant-Vertical firm.[6] These firms have *faced special barriers* to diversification and are increasingly becoming representatives of the "old industrial state."

The new type of firm has adapted to the imperatives of modern technology and modern markets—the need to meet demands for variety, to apply new skills and ideas to old products, to regularly rechannel resources into new product areas, to rapidly respond to new customer demands, and to have the ability to bring talented men, money, and equipment together to work on a project for a time and then to *disband* the project and find efficient uses for these resources elsewhere. The new linkages are not vertical—from raw materials to processors to factories—but horizontal and market related. A cheap, efficient microwave oven is developed, and firms engaged in food processing, packaging, oven equipment, and cooking utensils must all respond. The high density photo-storage library becomes possible, and firms that publish books, make paper and ink, sell microfilm equipment, as well as those involved in computers, educational technology, data transmission technology, copying equipment, and eventually even the telephone company, must all respond in some way.

---

[6] Scott, "Stages of Corporate Development," p. 48.

Implications for Management

The critical resource of the modern, diversified, divisionalized firm is general management skill, and the change from the old to the new industrial structure has multiplied several-fold the number of general management positions to be filled in industry. The training and effective employment of generalists must become the prime concern of any firm that has goals that include growth by diversification or participation in the new technologies that quickly produce a proliferation of new products.

Not only must top management train and make use of general managers, but it must learn how to fine tune the product-division form of organization. At a time when most large companies were merely experimenting with diversification and the product-division structure was an atypical curiosity, the progressive firm could gain a competitive edge in many industries merely by reorganizing along product-division lines. Such a move simplified the life of top management and provided for greater visibility of individual product performance. Now, however, most large firms have adopted the product-division structure and the competitive advantages that come from superior organization must be sought by fully exploiting the potentials of this structure. For example, it would be expected that highly diversified firms would greatly benefit from improved systems of strategic review and formal systems of intervening in divisional operations during crisis situations.

With regard to the efficacy of various strategies of diversification, it would be pleasant to report that the Dominant-Constrained and Related-Constrained are the optimal strategies and should be followed by all prudent firms. The data, however, only indicated that an *association* between these strategies and high levels of financial performance. While it may be that these strategies tend to produce good rates of growth and profit, it is more likely that firms that are already rapidly growing and profitable think it wise to restrict their scopes of activity to business that directly relate to their currently successful areas of competence. Nevertheless, the intensive cultivation of a single field has proven, on the average, financially more successful than bold moves into uncharted areas. While many consider them to be the most interesting and technologically powerful firms, the Related-Linked companies have experienced distinctly average levels of performance over the past twenty years.

The finding that Related-Linked and Unrelated-Passive strategies have not proven particularly rewarding to most firms should be of interest to managements that are planning to embark on programs of increased diversification. During the 1960s, many Related-Constrained and Dominant-Constrained firms moved to Related-Linked and Unrelated-Passive strategies only to discover, the data show, that expansion into new tenuously related or unrelated areas, though it makes good reading in annual reports, does not always produce the desired results. In particular, the formation of large Unrelated-Passive firms through the merger of two diversified but unrelated firms has been strikingly unsuccessful. Managements expecting to exploit the synergistic effects of bringing two such firms together should be warned that the organizational problems rising from this type of merger have, on the average, nullified any possible beneficial gains due to scale or synergy.

Managements that are responsible for the affairs of Dominant-Vertical firms are probably already aware that their companies face special barriers to diversification. While it would be foolhardy to suggest that fully integrated firms abandon their commitments to their major businesses and seek diversification, we can point out that increased integration will only heighten the barriers to diversification. Firms whose growth patterns have placed them at the decision point between increased integration and product-market diversification should realize that, although integration may provide temporary improvements in costs and permit an increase in size, other firms making similar decisions have eventually found themselves heavily invested in stagnant low-profit industries. While integration itself can make good economic sense, it implies a long-term commitment to an industry, a pattern of operations, and an administrative system that preclude rapid redeployment of resources and adaptation to change.

Finally, the findings on the variability in earnings experienced by firms following various strategies of diversification should be of interest to managers who expect product-market diversification to protect their firms from financial instability. Although the categories of diversification strategy did not differ significantly in earnings variability itself, there were significant differences in the ratio of earnings variability to growth rates in earnings—the risk premium ratio (RPR). This means that variability is strongly affected by growth, and the firm's *strategy of expansion* is the critical factor influencing the degree of variability. Firms that followed Dominant-Constrained and Related-Constrained strategies had the most favorable risk-premium ratios, and all other categories had poorer, and approximately equivalent, risk-premium ratios. The implication is that both very little and very great diversity produce equivalent variability in earnings, but carefully controlled diversity is the best form of diversification for reducing fluctuations in earnings. We suggest that the factor responsible for this result is the ability of the diversified, but "constrained," firm to employ the beneficial effects of negatively correlated returns by replacing products that are stagnant or declining, with close functional substitutes that are profitable and growing for reasons related to the decline of the original products. In other words, the "constrained" firm ties its fortunes to the satisfaction of a particular functional need (such as business-information processing, permanent-image making, or convenience foods). It then develops a variety of products that relate to this fairly constant need and continuously searches its product line for weak points, innovating to meet changing tastes and needs.

In contrast to this strategy, the firm that seeks stability through diversification into tenuously related or unrelated areas is merely *averaging* risks rather than exploiting negatively correlated returns. At the most, such a policy can only reduce uncertainty to the level experienced by the economy as a whole.

Public Policy Implications

If we assume that one of the important objectives of American economic public policy is to strengthen competition and foster market structures that are free and in equilibrium, assumptions regarding the behavior of the corporate sector must play an important role in the policy process. If models of business behavior that are based on Single Business firms are applied to the new industrial structure, the conclusions thereby derived will be wrong and the policies adopted will be ineffective. Of particular importance is the recognition that most large enterprises now employ decentralized administrative structures and control systems that strongly induce division-level managers to meet and exceed their profit targets. This means that policies designed to affect corporate behavior that are not translated into profit goals by the firm's control system will have little chance of influencing behavior. For example, corporate goals such as reducing pollution will probably never create more than rhetoric unless division-level managers are provided with incentives to curb pollution that are as strong as the rewards tied to profit and growth. As another example, Bower states that if "the goal of an anti-inflationary policy is a slowing of the rate of private investment, some means must be found to induce the corporate officers to take pressure for current earnings and growth off their divisions. As long as division managers will rise and fall on relative profit and growth in the short run, they will put great pressure on their top management to find investment capital. The pressure of the inside management on top management is then likely to be very strong to keep investing, no matter how severe outside pressure may become." [7]

Another area that should be of concern to economists and public policy makers is the behavior and fate of the Dominant-Vertical firm. The issue is not their economic power, but their lack of it in modern terms. As noted in Chapter 4, the single-industry strategies of these companies have left them tied to stagnant businesses, and the policy of vertical integration has deepened their commitments to particular materials and processes. Unless these firms can adapt to the new technologies, new types of competition, and new forms of organization, they will become the railroads of the future—necessary but weak and inefficient. A proposal to make these firms even larger through diversification may seem radical (or perhaps reactionary) in the light of current concern over the misuse of power by large firms, but we suggest that it may no longer

---

[7] Joseph L. Bower, "Planning Within the Firm," *Journal of the American Economic Association,* May 1970, p. 193.

be valid to assume that all large firms follow oligopolistic patterns of competition and tend to maximize sales, market share, or growth at the expense of return. The multidivisional firm can exert great pressure on division managers for current profit and the diversified firm can rechannel resources out of stagnant areas into ones that promise greater return and, presumably, in which new capital would produce social and economic benefits. It also may no longer be assumed that the total economic power of a firm is translated into an ideological and political commitment to a product. The multidivisional diversified company can bear economic, social, and legal change in isolated areas at a much lower cost than can a Single Business enterprise.

The "Dominant-Vertical Syndrome" should be of particular interest to European planners because many of their policies are designed to create just this type of firm. The all too frequent response of European businessmen and planners to American competition has been to assume that large and more financially powerful firms are needed. McArthur and Scott report that French planners are trying to extend ideas of economies of scale, ideas that apply most appropriately to industries like steel and oil, to the electrical equipment, chemical and consumer products industries. They state that: "The French prescription would probably result in domination of each industry by one or two companies. This would amount to the creation of a French 'champion' in each industry, on the pattern of Péchiney in aluminum. This French champion would face little if any competition from other French firms; instead it would carry the French colours against foreign competitors." [8]

While size may be a help to certain firms, without the diversity that allows cross-fertilization among business activities, or, more important, without the generalist skills necessary to manage a diversified firm, the results may be the creation of a set of Dominant-Vertical or Unrelated-Passive companies, ill equipped to face the realities of modern competition. More vital than size is the creation of firms that have organizational structures that encourage rapid innovation and economic performance at the product-market level; equally vital is the training and effective use of the generalists who must be responsible for the affairs of such enterprises.

---

[8] John H. McArthur and Bruce R. Scott, *Industrial Planning in France* (Boston: Division of Research, Harvard Business School, 1969), p. 525.

Appendixes
Bibliography
Index

APPENDIX A

Estimation Technique

MOST OF THE ANALYSES PRESENTED in Chapter 2 were based on estimates of the proportions of the largest 500 industrial firms that fell in various categories at some particular time. It is necessary, therefore, to explain how these estimates were obtained. To simplify the exposition, the problem of estimating the percentage of firms in the Dominant-Vertical category will be used as an example. By chance, the sampling errors associated with this category turned out to be the most serious, so that while similar procedures were applied to all categories, the Dominant-Vertical category most clearly illustrates their need.

The random samples taken from the largest 500 firms in 1949, 1959, and 1969 can be used to provide estimates of the percentage of Dominant-Vertical firms in each of these years. Of the 100 firms in the 1949 sample, for example, 17 were classified as Dominant-Vertical in 1949. Similarly, 18 of the 100 firms in the 1959 sample, and 9 of the 97 firms in the 1969 sample were classified as Dominant-Vertical in those years. Table A-1 displays these results. The percentages shown in the table are, of course, only estimates of the true percentage of firms in the Dominant-Vertical class in these years.[1] It is important to note that (1) some of the firms in one sample also appear in other samples, so that the total number of firms involved is 246 rather than 297; (2) although the strategic class of each firm was determined for all three years, the only information used in constructing Table A-1 was the firms' classifications in the years corresponding to the samples to which they belonged.

If the estimates are reasonably good, there is little incentive to develop more cumbersome procedures in order to use all of the data. In this case, however, a rather serious sampling error seems to have occurred. The apparently striking drop in the proportion of Dominant-Vertical firms between 1959 and 1969 is not consistent with other evidence. Investigation of the sources of this change revealed that of the 18 Dominant-Vertical firms in the 1959 sample, 17 were still in this category and still among the top 500 in 1969. Furthermore, of all firms in all samples, 32 were Dominant-Vertical in 1959 and 33 in 1969. Why then did the estimated percentage drop from 18.0 to 9.3?

---

[1] The 95 percent confidence intervals for the three percentages are 10.1–23.9 percent, 11.1–24.9 percent, and 4.0–14.6 percent respectively.

TABLE A-1. Dominant-Vertical Firms in Each Sample.

Sample	Sample Size	Number Dominant-Vertical	Percentage Dominant-Vertical
1949	100	17	17.0
1959	100	18	18.0
1969	97	9	9.3

The only reasonable explanation is that, *by chance,* the 1969 sample contained an unusually small number of Dominant-Vertical firms.

The very fact that this error was discovered suggests that a better estimate can be made, and such inconsistencies in the data can be resolved. One method that might be used to make fuller use of the available data would be to pool all the firms, counting the number that were Dominant-Vertical among all firms in the largest 500 in a given year without regard to their sample membership. This procedure, however, invites bias. Firms selected randomly from the 500 in 1949 and 1959, even though they may still be among the top 500 in 1969, are likely to be larger than the average firm of the 500 in 1969, and perhaps differ in other ways as well. To use all of the available data and avoid this type of bias we must take into account the fact that firms selected randomly from the top 500 in one year are not typical representatives of the top 500 in another year. This can be accomplished by defining seven mutually exclusive collectively exhaustive groups of firms, each group corresponding to a different pattern of membership in the top 500s of 1949, 1959, and 1969. One group consists of firms that were among the top 500 in 1959 but not in 1949 or 1969; another, of those firms that were among the top 500 in 1959 and 1969 but not 1949, and so on. These seven groups are described in Table A-2.

All the firms among the top 500 in any of the years of interest fall among some subset of these groups. For example, the top 500 in 1969 is composed of $G_{69} + G_{49, 69} + G_{59, 69} + G_{49, 59, 69}$. For our purposes, the most important characteristic of these groups is that, for instance, the chance that a firm randomly selected from the top 500 in 1959 will fall in group $G_{59, 69}$ is the same as the chance that a firm randomly selected from the

TABLE A-2. Defining the Groups.

Group	Symbol	Number of Sampled Firms in Group	Years in Which Group Members Were Among the Largest 500		
			1949	1959	1969
1	G_{49}	18	X		
2	G_{59}	14		X	
3	$G_{49,59}$	31	X	X	
4	G_{69}	18			X
5	$G_{49,69}$	3	X		X
6	$G_{59,69}$	25		X	X
7	$G_{49,59,69}$	137	X	X	X
	Total	246			

top 500 in 1969 will fall in that group. Therefore, those firms of the 246 that fall in each group, regardless of their original sample memberships, constitute valid random samples from each group and may be used to estimate the properties of these groups. Then, if the true values of the group sizes are known, the properties of the appropriate groups can be combined to give an estimate pertaining to the top 500 in any of the three years in question. Thus, all of the data can be employed without bias.

Clearly there is some true number of firms in each group which could be established by comparing lists of the largest 500 firms. The problems of name changes, the lack of such a list for 1949, and the fact that we wish to use this procedure for the top 100 and top 200 as well, greatly complicated the task of counting. Hence, estimates were used. The size of each group was estimated by combining the independent estimates obtained from each sample in a weighted linear regression. The results are shown in Table A-3.

Returning to the problem of estimating the percentage of Dominant-Vertical firms, we find the percentage of Dominant-Vertical in each group for each year to which it applies, weight these estimates by the fraction of the top 500 represented by each group, and then sum over the appropriate years. For the case of 1969 calculations are shown in Table A-4.

Similar calculations for 1949 and 1959 result in these estimates for the percentage of Dominant-Vertical firms:

TABLE A-3. ESTIMATED GROUP WEIGHTS.

Group	Estimated Number of Firms	Estimated Proportion of the Largest 500 in the Relevant Years
G_{49}	102.3	0.2046
G_{59}	48.1	0.0963
$G_{49,59}$	78.3	0.1565
G_{69}	108.7	0.2174
$G_{49,69}$	17.7	0.0354
$G_{59,69}$	71.9	0.1438
$G_{49,59,69}$	301.7	0.6035

TABLE A-4. SAMPLE CALCULATIONS.

Group	(a) Percentage Dominant-Vertical	(b) Fraction of 1969 500 in the Group	(a) × (b)
G_{69}	5.56	0.2174	1.21%
$G_{49,69}$	33.33	0.0354	1.18
$G_{59,69}$	0.0	0.1438	0.0
$G_{49,59,69}$	21.90	0.6035	13.22
		Weighted estimate =	15.61%

| | Percentage Dominant-Vertical Among |
Year	the Largest 500
1949	15.7
1959	14.8
1969	15.6

As can be seen, the sharp decrease of Table A-1 is no longer evident. In addition to providing better estimates, the procedure just described also insures that the estimates will be consistent with analyses of the sources of change. All of the estimates presented in Chapter 2 were obtained in this manner.

Statistical Procedures

T HIS APPENDIX CONTAINS DESCRIPTIONS of the algorithms that were used in computing the values of financial variables for firms, estimated category means, and associated statistics. In addition, precise financial definitions of the variables studied are provided.

GROWTH RATES

Given a sequence of annual observations of a variable, $X_1, X_2, X_3, \ldots X_n$, there are several interpretations of the "average growth rate" that best describes the sequence. The simplest growth rate measure is the annual compounded rate of growth which, applied to X_1, would produce X_n after $n - 1$ years. This summary value G_c, is defined as

$$G_c = \left[\frac{X_n}{X_1} \right]^{1/n-1} - 1$$

and, provided that X_1 and X_n are both positive, is unambiguous. The problem with this measure is that it depends only on values of X_1 and X_n. Thus, if the sequence of values of X_i is 5, 6, 7, 8, 9, 10, 5, the compound annual growth rate is zero. While this cannot be disputed, the measure clearly does not reflect the "typical" or "average" annual growth rate. Changing the period in question slightly can greatly alter the value of G_c when growth is not actually smooth.

Frequently the attempt is made to avoid this dilemma by using an arithmetic average. Defining $g_i = (X_i/X_{i-1}) - 1$, the average arithmetic growth rate is

$$G_A = \frac{1}{n - 1} \sum_{i=1}^{n-1} g_i$$

The problem with this measure is its consistent upward bias. Given the sequence: $1, 2, 1, 2, 1, 2, \ldots$, the value of G_A is 0.25 even though no net growth occurs. This is simply because we are averaging ratios whose bases differ.

The average growth rates used in this research were computed by a third method: regression fit to a uniform growth model. The time spans involved were nine or ten years and observations were annual. We assumed that the "true" growth during this period was uniform and exponential but that each observation was subject to multiplicative error:

$$\tilde{X}_t = A e^{gt} \tilde{\gamma} \tag{1}$$

where $\tilde{X}_t$ is the observed value of the variable, g is the "true" uniform growth rate, $\tilde{\gamma}$ is a random error term with a mean of one and A is a constant. Taking the logarithm of (1) we have

$$\text{Log } \tilde{X}_t = \text{Log } A + gt + \tilde{\epsilon} \tag{2}$$

where $\tilde{\epsilon}$ is the now additive error with zero mean.

When values of X_t are zero or negative, logarithms cannot be taken. This is to be expected as growth rates based on nonpositive terms are not meaningful in a financial context (earnings going from -1 to 1 produce a growth rate of -100%). Our procedure was to drop observations that were nonpositive, treating them like missing values.

Using equation (2) as the basis for a linear regression gives estimates of the value of g and the standard deviation of the error, σ.

Values of X_t close to zero can produce absurd estimates of g. If, for instance, earnings per share drops to $0.01 for one year and then returns to the usual level of about $3.00, a one-year growth rate of 30,000% is included in the regression. This is easy to detect when computations are done by hand, but processing close to one thousand growth rates with a computer requires an automatic procedure for detecting such problems. What was done was to use the estimated value of the standard deviation to screen out observations that were more than three standard deviations below regression estimates. The regression was then recomputed with the outliers omitted and the screen reapplied until all observations passed. If, after the final regression was obtained, more than four observations were missing or had to be dropped, the estimates of g and σ were discarded and special missing value codes returned to the main program.

FINANCIAL VARIABLES

The financial variables used in this research were obtained from financial data in the *Compustat* data bank. Wherever possible, these figures represent the consolidated financial position of the firm with some adjustments of account definitions to insure maximum comparability among firms. Data were available on an annual basis for 1951–1970 for most of the firms in the sample that remained in existence through 1970. The data consisted of reported values rather than pro forma accounts prepared after acquisitions, and adjustment factors were available to correct price and per-share statistics for stock splits and stock dividends. The definitions of the variables and the symbols used to represent them are given below:

(1) *GSALES:* The annual mean uniform growth rate in net sales. Net sales is defined as gross revenues less returns and discounts. The mean annual growth rate was computed by the regression technique.

(2) *GERN:* The annual mean uniform growth rate in earnings available for distribution to common stockholders. Earnings net for common is defined as net after-tax income less preferred dividends and after-tax extraordinary income or expenses. Since preferred dividends represent a fixed claim on income, they are more like interest than a return to owners from a managerial point of view, so earnings net for common is a

better measure of profit than net income and is the only valid numerator for return on equity and earnings per share. The mean annual growth was computed by the regression technique.

(3) *GEPS:* The annual mean uniform growth rate in earnings per share. Earnings per share is defined as the ratio of earnings net for common to outstanding common shares adjusted for splits and dividends. The mean annual growth rate was computed by the regression technique.

(4) *SDEPS:* The relative standard deviation in earnings per share about the uniform growth trend. *SDEPS* is obtained from the regression used to compute *GEPS*. It is *not* the standard deviation of earnings per share but a ratio quantity that can be thought of as the standard deviation of annual growth rates.

(5) *PE:* The price-earnings ratio. Annual average share price is approximated as the mean of the high and low for the year and adjusted for subsequent stock splits and dividends. Annual values of *PE* are the ratios of average share prices to earnings per share. After each annual value of *PE* was determined, nonmeaningful values of annual *PE* were screened out. The rules used were (1) drop any negative values of annual *PE*, (2) drop values of *PE* for years in which corporate return on capital was less than 2%, and (3) drop values of *PE* for years in which earnings per share had dropped to less than 75% of the previous year's level. Since earnings per share can be zero or negative while price is always positive, negative earnings or unusually low levels of earnings do not create proportional changes in price. Hence, the above rules served to screen out those values of *PE* that bore little relation to the concept of a market capitalization rate applied to earnings. The rules were derived by trial and error with the researcher and several other individuals supplying judgments as to what constituted a meaningful price-earnings ratio. After screening, the arithmetic average of the remaining values was obtained. If more than four annual values had been dropped or were missing, the average was discarded and a missing value code returned.

(6) *ROC:* The average return on invested capital. Invested capital was defined as total assets less current liabilities. The numerator of this annual ratio was after-tax net income plus interest on long-term debt (i.e., returns to all contributors of capital). *ROC* was computed as the arithmetic average of annual values.

(7) *ROE:* The average return on equity. Annual return on equity was taken to be the ratio of earnings net for common to book equity. *ROE* was computed as the arithmetic average of annual values.

(8) *E/C:* The average ratio of equity to capital. Annual values of this ratio were taken to be book equity divided by invested capital (defined above). *E/C* was computed as the arithmetic average of the annual ratios.

(9) *IFR:* Internal financing ratio. This measure, suggested by Lynch, is defined as the ratio of increases in equity valued at market rates to earnings.[1] More precisely, *IFR*, for the period in question, was taken to be the market value of new shares issued during the period plus earnings retained during the period all divided by *total* earnings net for common during the period. It is helpful in understanding the meaning of *IFR* to know that under conditions of uniform growth,

$$IFR = RTN + PE \times GSHR$$

where *RTN* is the rate of earnings retention, *PE* is the price-earnings ratio and *GSHR* is the rate of growth in common shares outstanding. Normally, high values of *IFR* (values larger than 1.0) are associated with heavy issuance of shares to finance mergers and acquisitions.

---

[1] Lynch, "Conglomerate Performance," p. 69.

TABLE B-1. Initial Tableau.

	F	F/S	PD	Combined
1951–1959	10.57	11.78	13.65	11.64
	(51)	(15)	(26)	(92)
1960–1969	13.80	16.87	18.87	17.98
	(15)	(13)	(87)	(115)
Combined	11.30	14.14	17.67	15.16
	(66)	(28)	(113)	(207)

Total sum of squared observations = 58,092

(10) *RPR:* The average risk premium ratio. *RPR* is defined as

$$RPR = (GEPS - 0.015)/SDEPS$$

and is the risk associated growth per unit of variability in growth. Its interpretation is discussed in Chapter 3.

CATEGORY ESTIMATES

The estimated mean values of the financial variables for each category were obtained by analysis of variance. The procedure is theoretically and computationally equivalent to dummy variable regression but the development and meaning of the test statistics is easier to follow in an analysis of variance context. We will not present a rigorous symbolic description as many standard references are available.[2] Instead, we will demonstrate how the procedure applies in a particular case. The example we shall use is the derivation of category means of *PE* for the categories of organizational structure.

Table B-1 shows a summary tableau of the data pertaining to *PE* and organizational structure. Decade average *PE*s for each firm that did not move between categories during that decade have been averaged by categories within decades, across decades and overall data points. The data show a pronounced time trend. In addition, the product-division (*PD*) structure appears to be associated with larger *PE*s. The problem of separating the effects of structure and time is complicated by the unequal number of data points in different cells. To what degree is the higher 1960–1969 average *PE* due to a time trend versus the existence of relatively more *PD* structures in the second decade? To separate these two effects we construct a linear model:

$$PE = m + a_1 F + a_2 FS + a_3 PD + b_1 T_1 + b_2 T_2 + \tilde{\epsilon} \tag{1}$$

where m is some overall mean, $a_1, a_2,$ and a_3 are the differential effects of functional, functional-with-subsidiaries and product-division structure on *PE*; b_1 and b_2 are the differential effects of the first and second decades, and $\tilde{\epsilon}$ is a random error term. The important assumption implicit in this model is that time affects all categories equally and that category effects do not change over time. The validity of this assumption will be tested later.

Equation 1 is not usable as it stands because it is overdetermined. For example, we could set m to any value at all and still find *a*s and *b*s that produce the same predicted

---

[2] See, for example, S. R. Searle, *Linear Models* (New York: John Wiley & Sons, 1971).

category and decade *PE*s. It is not hard to show that two coefficients of equation 1 are redundant and we shall elect to omit m and b_2 giving

$$PE = a_1F + a_2FS + a_3PD + b_1T_1 + \tilde{\epsilon} \tag{2}$$

Here, a_1, a_2 and a_3 will be the estimated 1960–1969 category means and b is the amount that must be added to obtain 1951–1959 estimated category means. We assume that $\tilde{\epsilon}$ is normally distributed.

Determining these coefficients is essentially a regression problem and involves the solution of a set of linear equations. However, for the simple case at hand, it can be shown that

$$b_1 = \frac{(92)(11.64) - (51)(11.3) - (15)(14.14) - (26)(17.67)}{92 - \dfrac{51^2}{66} - \dfrac{15^2}{28} - \dfrac{26^2}{113}} = 4.6$$

and that a_1, a_2 and a_3 can be obtained by subtracting b_1 from each 1951–1959 category average and then recomputing the total pooled category averages:

$$F: a_1 = 14.86$$
$$FS: a_2 = 16.60$$
$$PD: a_3 = 18.73$$

which are the estimated category means shown in Table B-2. The estimated means for 1951–1959 are 4.6 less in each case.

To see how well this linear model has fit the averages of Table B-1, we can compute the predicted cell values and the deviations of actual from predicted. This is shown in Table B-2.

As can be seen from the table, the linear model provides a fairly good fit to the averaged data. The analysis of variance procedure provides a precise measure of the quality of the fit and also indicates which portions of the model are most important.

The sum of the squared values of all 207 observations, *SST*, is 58,092 in this example. If there were no variability in the data, so that each observation were equal to the observed average, the sum of squared observations would be $207(15.16)^2 = 47,586$, which is defined as *SSM*. The difference between *SST* and *SSM* represents the variability about the mean in the raw data. We call this SST_m:

$$SST_m = SST - SSM = 10,506.$$

The basic idea behind analysis of variance is to partition the variability into components that can be associated with different sources of variability. The completed analysis is shown in Table B-3.

Here SST_m has been partitioned into portions due to time trend effects, category effects and residual error. The final column of the table shows the proportions allocated to each source.

TABLE B-2. ACTUAL MINUS PREDICTED.

	F	*FS*	*PD*	*AVG*
1951–1959	0.31	−0.23	−0.48	0.0
1960–1969	−1.05	0.26	0.14	0.0
AVG	0.0	0.0	0.0	0.0

TABLE B-3. ANALYSIS OF VARIANCE.

Source of Variation	Sum of Squares Corrected for the Mean	Degrees of Freedom	Mean Square	F-Ratio	Level of Significance	R^2
Time	2,055	1	2,055.0	52.30	0.001	0.196
Categories	478	2	238.5	6.08	0.05	0.045
Error	7,973	203	39.3			0.759
Total	10,506	206				1.000
		Testing for Interaction				
Linear Model	2,533	3	844.0	21.40	0.001	0.241
Interaction	34	2	17.0	0.43	not sig.	0.003
Error	7,939	201	39.5			0.756
Total	10,506	206				1.000

The residual error portion, when divided by the appropriate degrees of freedom, gives an estimate of the variance of the error term, $\bar{\varepsilon}$, in the model.[3] The square root of this variance, σ, is shown in Table 3-3 in Chapter 3.

The first line of Table B-3 tells us that the portion of sum-squares due to *introducing* the time-trend term in the model is 2,055, or 19.6 percent of the total. In addition, since there are only two time periods in question, the estimated variance due to the time trend is 2,055. The F-ratio is the ratio of this variance to the residual variance. The F-ratio of 52.3 is quite large, indicating that the time trend effect is much larger than random variability can account for. More precisely, the F-ratio tests the hypothesis "$b_i = 0$," or more generally, "all time coefficients are equal." Standard tables of the F distribution are widely available and show that an F-ratio of 52.3 with 1 degree of freedom in the numerator and 203 in the denominator is significant at at least the 0.001 level. This means that there is less than one chance in one thousand that random error effects could have produced this large an F-ratio if time effects were actually absent. We thus reject the hypothesis "$b_i = 0$" and proceed on the assumption that time correction is necessary. In many other cases time effects were not significant, particularly when growth rate variables were being analyzed. We took the critical level to be 0.1 and assumed time corrections were necessary if it was equaled or exceeded. When the time-trend terms were not significant, the linear model was discarded and the simple pooled averages for each category were taken as the estimated category means. Analysis of variance was then carried out on just the category effects.

The second line of Table B-3 indicates that category effects (differences among the categories) created 4.5 percent of the variability and that the variance among categories is estimated to be 238.5. The F-ratio is 6.08 which is significant at the 0.05 level. It is very important to note that these figures refer to the explanatory power of the categories *after* the effects of time have been taken into account. It is this F-ratio and R^2 that appear on Table 3-3 in Chapter 3.

The next step is to check the validity of the linear model. That is, we wish to check

---

[3] Two hundred and seven data points less 4 coefficients in the model leaves 203 degrees of freedom for estimating residual variance.

the original assumption that time trends affect all categories equally and category differences are stable over time. When these assumptions are not true, it is said that interaction effects are present. We test for interaction effects by comparing the linear model to the actual category averages in each decade. More precisely, we assume a new model which has a term for each cell in Table B-1 and test the degree to which it is a significant improvement over the simple linear model. As can be seen from the lower portion of Table B-3, interaction effects had an F-ratio of only 0.43 and were not significant. We took the critical level of significance to be 0.05 on interaction effects and it was not equaled or exceeded for any of the variables analyzed.

If interaction effects had been significant, the concept of a single category effect could not have been used since category effects would have been changing relative to one another over time.

APPENDIX C

List of Firms in the Sample

THIS APPENDIX consists of Table C-1, which lists all of the firms in the sample. The firms are listed in alphabetical order and, unless the firm came into being after 1949 or was merged or acquired before 1969, information on product lines, rank in the *Fortune 500,* and the strategic and structural classifications that were assigned to them are given for 1949, 1959, and 1969.

Whenever it was possible to determine which of a firm's activities was its *largest single business,* that business is listed in italics. In many cases it was not possible to identify the largest single business even though it was obvious that it accounted for less than 70 percent of total revenues. Businesses that were judged to be unrelated to the firm's largest group of somehow related businesses are contained in square brackets. Lists of businesses after the first do not repeat businesses in which the firm was still active. Instead, they show businesses that were *added* or *eliminated* since the time of the last list.

Ranks among the top 500 firms refer to assets in 1949 and sales in 1959 and 1969. In addition, only ranks among the top 100 are given exactly for 1949; others are given as 101–200 or 200–500.

The strategic and structural categories assigned to each firm are indicated by symbols. Their meaning is as follows:

Strategy Symbol	*Strategic Class*
S	Single Business
DV	Dominant-Vertical
DC	Dominant-Constrained
DL	Dominant-Linked
DU	Dominant-Unrelated
RC	Related-Constrained
RL	Related-Linked
UP	Unrelated-Passive
AC	Acquisitive Conglomerate

Structure Symbol	*Structure Class*
F	Functional
FS	Functional-with-subsidiaries
PD	Product-division
G	Geographic-division
H	Holding company

TABLE C-1. THE SAMPLE: COMPANIES, PRODUCTS, AND CLASSIFICATIONS.

	Rank	Strategy	Structure
ABBOTT LABORATORIES			
1949 *Antibiotics,* hormones, bulk medicinal chemicals, proprietary drugs, animal health products.	201–500	RC	F
1959 *Antibiotics,* + as above. Added: artificial sweeteners, hospital solutions and diagnostic agents.	328	RC	F
1969 *Hospital supplies:* solutions and diagnostics; + as above. Added: *rubber and plastic hospital supplies,* eye-care products, diet and infant foods, medical electronics instruments.	248	RC	PD
ABEX Prior to 1966, American Brake Shoe.			
1949 *Railroad brake shoes and related forgings,* other forged and cast parts for general industry, machined parts for industrial and farm equipment and automobiles, air compressors.	201–500	DC	H
1959 *Railroad brake shoes and related forgings,* as above. Exited: air compressors. Added: heavy hydraulic equipment, aerospace hydro-servo valves.	265	RC	PD
1968 Acquired by Illinois Central Industries.			
ACF INDUSTRIES Prior to 1954, American Car and Foundry.			
1949 *Railroad cars,* mine hauling cars, storage tanks, wheels, other forgings and castings [automobile fuel pumps and carburetors].	201–500	DL	FS
1959 *Railroad cars,* + as above. Added: heavy valves, pressure vessels [aerospace electronics systems, airframe and missile components].	252	DU	PD
1969 *Railroad cars,* + as above. Exited: electronics, aircraft, and missile components. Added: hydraulic controls [nylon hose and parts, nylon resins].	343	RL	PD
ADDRESSOGRAPH-MULTIGRAPH			
1949 *Addressograph machines, parts and accessories;* offset office reproduction equipment.	—	DC	F
1959 *Addressograph machines, parts and accessories,* + as above. Added: type composition machine, office supplies.	306	DC	F
1969 As above. Added: *Office copiers,* microfilm printer, precision-printed plastics.	244	RC	PD
AIR REDUCTION			
1949 *Gases:* medical, scientific, and industrial; acetylene welding equipment.	201–500	DC	FS
1959 *Gases,* + as above. Added: specialty chemicals and plastic intermediates.	225	DC	PD
1969 As above. Added: Ferro-alloys, electron beam metallurgy, vacuum metals, special metals [carbon and			

TABLE C-1 (continued)

	Rank	Strategy	Structure
Air Reduction (continued)			
graphite products, electronic components, vinyl molded parts and hose].	221	*UP*	*PD*
ALLIS-CHALMERS MANUFACTURING			
1949 *Farm equipment,* earthmoving equipment, electric power machinery, hydraulic machinery, marine engines, industrial process machinery of wide variety.	65	*RL*	*PD*
1959 *Farm equipment,* + as above. Added: materials handling equipment, diesel engines, atomic power plant equipment.	80	*RL*	*PD*
1969 *Farm equipment,* + as above. Added: electronic control systems, garden tractors, all terrain vehicles, fuel cells, household appliances, water pollution control equipment [educational materials].	140	*RL*	*PD*
ALUMINUM COMPANY OF AMERICA			
1949 Integrated aluminum: *mill products,* primary aluminum, building products, cookware, cans, wire, architectural shapes, by-products and joint products: magnesium, bauxite, chemicals.	28	*DV*	*FS*
1959 Integrated aluminum: *architectural shapes and structures,* + as above. Added: real estate development.	48	*DV*	*FS*
1969 Integrated aluminum: *architectural shapes and structures,* + as above.	67	*DV*	*FS*
AMERICAN BILTRITE RUBBER Prior to 1951, Panco Rubber.			
1949 *Rubber shoe heels and soles,* rubber floor tiles.	—	*RC*	*F*
1959 *Rubber shoe heels and soles,* + as above. Added: carpets, rubber chemicals, rubber industrial products.	—	*RC*	*PD*
1969 *Rubber shoe heels and soles,* + as above. Added: synthetic rubber.	481	*RC*	*PD*
AMERICAN CHAIN AND CABLE			
1949 *Chain, cable, wire and wire products,* springs, machine tools, automobile brakes and steering mechanisms, materials handling equipment, pressure and hardness instruments, lawnmowers.	201–500	*RC*	*FS*
1959 *Chain, cable, wire and wire products,* + as above. Added: electronic instruments.	352	*RC*	*FS*
1969 *Chain, cable, wire and wire products,* + as above. Added: industrial tools, electro-mechanical relays [blades and saws, pollution control systems, computer data loggers, gyros].	424	*RL*	*PD*

TABLE C-1 (continued)

	Rank	Strategy	Structure
AMERICAN ENKA			
1949 *Rayon tire yarn.*	201–500	S	F
1959 *Rayon and nylon yarn and fiber.* Added: cable, wire, insulating materials.	366	DL	FS
1969 *Synthetic yarns and fibers,* + as above.	355	DL	PD
AMERICAN METAL CLIMAX Prior to 1957, American Metal.			
1949 Mining, smelting, refining: *copper,* lead, zinc; silver, gold.	201–500	DV	F
1959 Mining, smelting, refining: *copper,* lead, zinc, + as above. Added: Potash, molybdenum, vanadium, oil and gas production.	66	RC	PD
1969 As above. Exited: oil and gas. Added: *aluminum:* primary and fabricated; iron ore, coal [pre-cast concrete].	147	RC	PD
AMERICAN MOTORS Prior to 1954, Nash-Kelvinator.			
1949 *Automobiles* [electrical appliances].	101–200	DU	F
1959 *Automobiles* [electrical appliances].	47	DU	PD
1969 *Automobiles.* Exited: electrical appliances.	152	S	F
AMERICAN OPTICAL			
1949 *Eyeglasses and ophthalmic equipment,* microscopes, slide projectors, industrial safety equipment.	201–500	DC	F
1959 *Eyeglasses and ophthalmic equipment,* + as above. Added: astronomical instruments, medical office furniture, aerospace optics, dentists' equipment.	418	RC	PD
1967 Acquired by Warner-Lambert Pharmaceutical.			
AMERICAN STANDARD Prior to 1967, American Radiator and Standard Sanitary.			
1949 *Plumbing equipment,* fans and heat exchangers, bathroom accessories, heating equipment.	91	RC	F
1959 *Plumbing equipment,* + as above. Added: heating and cooling systems [aerospace guidance and industrial instruments].	85	RC	PD
1969 *Plumbing equipment,* + as above. Added: water treatment and waste disposal equipment [safes, business information systems, land development, air brakes].	82	UP	PD
ARMCO STEEL			
1949 Integrated steel: steel ingots, *mill products,* building products, fabricated products.	101–200	DV	F
1959 Integrated steel: *mill products,* + as above. Added: oil field equipment.	48	DV	PD

TABLE C-1 (continued)

	Rank	Strategy	Structure
Armco Steel (continued)			
1969 Integrated steel: *mill products,* + as above. Added: nonmetallic composites [mobile homes, snowmobiles, equipment leasing].	63	*DV*	*PD*
Armour			
1949 Integrated meat packer: *meat,* leather, soap, chemicals; dairy, poultry, vegetable oil.	30	*DV*	*F*
1959 Integrated meat packer: *meat,* + as above.	16	*DV*	*PD*
1969 Acquired by General Host.			
Armstrong Cork			
1949 *Floor tiles,* insulation, corks and caps, bottles, rubber medical and shoe products; bricks, cement and tile building products, rugs.	101–200	*DL*	*F*
1959 *Floor tiles,* + as above.	157	*DL*	*PD*
1969 *Floor tiles,* + as above.	196	*DL*	*PD*
Ashland Oil Prior to 1970, Ashland Oil and Refining.			
1949 *Oil refining.*	201–500	*S*	*F*
1959 *Oil refining.* Added: petrochemicals, ammonia, detergent, plasticizer.	150	*S*	*F*
1969 *Oil refining,* + as above. Added: synthetic rubber [construction work, fiberglass boats, crushed stone].	101	*RC*	*PD*
Atlantic Richfield Prior to 1966, Atlantic Refining.			
1949 *Integrated oil.*	34	*S*	*F*
1959 *Integrated oil.* Added: petrochemicals, ammonia, plasticizers.	79	*S*	*F*
1969 *Integrated oil,* + as above. Added: nuclear fuel.	29	*DV*	*F*
Avco Prior to 1959, Avco Manufacturing; prior to 1947, Aviation Corp.			
1949 *Refrigerators, freezers,* TV and radio sets, kitchen ranges and sinks, radar and fire control systems [aircraft engines, boilers, buses, farm equipment, broadcasting].	101–200	*UP*	*H*
1959 As above. Exited: almost all consumer appliances, buses, shipyards. Added: *aerospace R & D,* electronic control and guidance systems, aerospace structures.	148	*UP*	*PD*
1969 *Helicopter engines,* + as above. Added: [steel wire, abrasives, motion pictures, insurance, consumer finance, savings and loan companies, credit card finance].	129	*AC*	*PD*

TABLE C-1 (continued)

	Rank	Strategy	Structure
BANGOR PUNTA Prior to 1967, Bangor Punta Alegre Sugar; prior to 1964, Punte Alegre Sugar.			
1949 *Sugar.*	—	*S*	*H*
1959 *Sugar.*	—	*S*	*H*
1969 Exited: Sugar. Added: *light aircraft* [grain elevator, metals distribution, textile converting, railroad, foundry equipment, boats, jewelry, finance company, handguns, refrigeration equipment, tear gas, materials handling equipment, cottonseed oil, local power systems, recreational vehicles, knit fabrics].	288	*AC*	*H*
BECTON, DICKINSON			
1949 *Thermometers,* syringes, bandages and other medical supplies.	—	*RC*	*F*
1959 *Thermometers,* + as above. Added: rubber gloves, surgical instruments, reagents, electronic components, laboratory equipment.	—	*RC*	*FS*
1969 As above. Added: laboratory animals, science education aids, biochemicals, medical electronic devices, laboratory environmental control, hospital computer systems, Sportade, navigational instruments, aircraft fabrics, packaging machinery.	417	*RL*	*PD*
BELL INTERCONTINENTAL Prior to 1960, Bell Aircraft.			
1949 *Helicopters,* rockets and missiles, aircraft subassemblies, R & D on advanced aircraft [stove parts].	201–500	*DC*	*F*
1959 As above. Added: aviation electronic systems [abrasive cleaning equipment, molded fiberglass, hydraulic and extrusion presses].	314	*RC*	*PD*
1969 *Abrasive cleaning equipment,* + as above. Exited: helicopters, rockets, missiles, electronics, R & D, fiberglass, hydraulic presses. Added: [service station accessories, carbon paper, ink, air conditioning equipment, galvanized metal products].	552	*UP*	*PD*
BOISE CASCADE Prior to 1957, Boise Fayette Lumber.			
1949 Integrated forest products: timber, *lumber,* building materials; non-wood building materials.	—	*DV*	*F*
1959 Integrated forest products: timber, *lumber,* building materials; + as above. Added: pulp, paper, paperbags and boxes [all extension of vertical chain].	321	*DV*	*PD*
1969 *Lumber and wood building products,* + as above. Added: prefab buildings and parts, plastic containers [real estate development, recreational equipment, mobile homes, computer software].	55	*UP*	*PD*

TABLE C-1 (continued)

		Rank	Strategy	Structure
BORDEN				
1949	*Dairy products,* chemical by-products, coffee.	67	*DC*	*PD*
1959	*Dairy products,* + as above. Added: other grocery products [hose and tubing, cosmetics].	44	*RC*	*PD*
1969	*Dairy products,* + as above. Added: convenience and snack foods, pet foods [perfumes and toiletries, adhesives, protective coatings, packaging films, ink, varnish, plastic housewares, diapers].	54	*RL*	*PD*
BORG-WARNER				
1949	*Auto parts,* household appliances, special steels and structural steel parts, electric motors, power-transmission devices, airplane engines.	101–200	*RL*	*H*
1959	*Auto parts,* + as above. Added: air-conditioning and heating systems, pumps, electronic components and instruments, rubber industrial products, materials handling equipment [thermoplastic resins, synthetic latex].	68	*RL*	*PD*
1969	*Auto parts,* + as above. Exited: appliances. Added: electronics: aerospace, industrial controls, communications and data handling systems [coin-op dry cleaners, plasticizers].	108	*RL*	*PD*
BRISTOL-MYERS				
1949	*Proprietary drugs,* toiletries, ethical drugs [brushes and rollers, metal containers].	201–500	*RC*	*PD*
1959	*Proprietary drugs,* + as above. Exited: brushes and rollers, metal containers.	307	*RC*	*PD*
1969	*Proprietary drugs,* + as above. Added: diet and infant foods, medical testing products, electric hair-setters [household cleaners].	123	*RC*	*PD*
BROWN SHOE				
1949	*Shoes.*	201–500	*S*	*F*
1959	*Shoes.*	172	*S*	*F*
1969	*Shoes.* Added: handbags, luggage.	253	*DC*	*PD*
BRUNSWICK Prior to 1960, Brunswick-Balke-Collender.				
1949	*Bowling and billiards products.*	—	*S*	*F*
1959	*Bowling and billiards products.* Added: sports equipment [gym equipment, defense supplies and aircraft parts, plastic filament radomes].	175	*DL*	*PD*
1969	As above. Exited: gym equipment, defense supplies. Added: [yachts, outboard motors, medical supplies and instruments, bulk chemicals].	230	*AC*	*PD*

TABLE C-1 (continued)

	Rank	Strategy	Structure
BUCYRUS-ERIE			
1949 *Power cranes and excavators,* drilling machines and tools, tractor equipment.	201–500	RC	F
1959 *Power cranes and excavators,* + as above.	481	RC	PD
1969 *Power cranes and excavators,* + as above. Added: conveyors and conveyor systems, industrial packaging machinery.	588	RC	PD
BULOVA WATCH			
1949 *Watches.*	201–500	S	F
1959 *Watches.* Added: clock radios, radios, electronic timers, defense electronics, servo-control, electric razors, phonographs.	—	RL	FS
1969 *Watches,* + as above. Exited: Razors, phonographs.	527	RC	FS
BUNKER-RAMO Prior to 1968, Amphenol; prior to 1965, Amphenol-Borg Electronics.			
1958 Formed by merger of Amphenol Electronics and Borg (Geo. W.) Co.			
1959 *Electronic components: cables and wire, connectors, switches, relays;* electronic instruments [auto clocks, pile fabrics].	—	RC	PD
1969 *Electronic components;* + as above. Added: electronic systems: information, guidance, communication; numerical controls [electric advertising signs].	357	RL	PD
BUTLER MANUFACTURING			
1949 *Prefab building components,* farm equipment, storage and transport tanks [dry-cleaning equipment, electric meter boxes].	—	RC	FS
1959 *Prefab building components,* + as above. Exited: storage tanks, dry-cleaning equipment, electric meter boxes.	439	RC	FS
1969 *Prefab building components,* + as above. Added: *construction from prefab parts,* materials handling systems and electronic controls.	—	RL	PD
CALUMET AND HECLA Prior to 1952, Calumet and Hecla Consolidated Copper.			
1949 Integrated copper: *tubing,* refined, by-products [zinc].	201–500	S	F
1959 Integrated copper: *tubing,* + as above. Added: noncopper tubing, magnesium, uranium mining, heat exchangers for power generators [vulcanizing equipment, lumber].	455	DV	PD
1968 Acquired by Universal Oil Products.			

TABLE C-1 (continued)

	Rank	Strategy	Structure
CAMPBELL SOUP			
1949 *Canned soup*, other canned foods.	101–200	DC	F
1959 *Canned soup*, + as above. Added: frozen food.	88	DC	FS
1969 *Canned soup*, + as above. Added: baked goods, candy.	131	DC	FS
CAMPBELL TAGGERT ASSOCIATED BAKERIES			
1949 Baked goods.	—	S	G
1959 Baked goods.	257	S	G
1969 Baked goods.	320	S	G
CANADA DRY			
1949 *Soft drinks and syrups*, alcoholic beverages.	—	DC	PD
1959 *Soft drinks and syrups*, + as above.	440	DC	PD
1968 Merged with Hunt Foods to form Norton Simon.			
CARBORUNDUM			
1949 *Abrasives*, refractories, heating elements, resistors.	201–500	RC	F
1959 *Abrasives*, + as above. Added: refractory metals, ceramic electric products, abrasive machinery.	349	RC	PD
1969 *Abrasives*, + as above. Exited: refractory metals. Added: industrial machinery, carbon and graphite products, china, liquid-metal pumps, waste incineration, filters.	323	RL	PD
CARRIER			
1949 *Air conditioners and refrigeration equipment.*	201–500	S	F
1959 *Air conditioners and refrigeration equipment.* Added: heating, steam-turbines, compressors and blowers, precision potentiometers, heavy motors and generators, electronic mechanisms.	181	DL	PD
1969 *Air conditioners,* + as above. Exited: heavy motors and generators, refrigeration equipment, electronic mechanisms.	208	DL	PD
CATERPILLAR TRACTOR			
1949 *Tractors and earthmoving equipment*, diesel-generator sets.	101–200	DC	F
1959 *Tractors and earthmoving equipment*, + as above.	53	DC	F
1969 *Tractors and earthmoving equipment*, + as above. Added: turbine engines.	42	DC	GW
CENTRAL SOYA			
1949 *Soybean processing: oil, feed, meal, flour.*	201–500	S	F
1959 *Soybean processing:* + as above. Added: *chemical products of soy.*	162	S	F
1969 *Soybean processing*, + as above. Added: [part of vertical chain] poultry, agricultural chemicals.	194	S	FS

TABLE C-1 (continued)

	Rank	Strategy	Structure
CHAMPION SPARK PLUG			
1949 *Spark plugs.*	201–500	S	F
1959 *Spark plugs.*	375	S	F
1969 *Spark plugs.* Added: steel bars, aircraft safety equipment [nondestructive testing equipment, medical diagnostic instruments, spraying and finishing equipment, x-ray tubes, magnetic tape player].	334	UP	FS
CHRYSLER			
1949 *Cars,* trucks, air conditioners, powder metals, engines.	25	S	F
1959 *Cars,* trucks, + as above. Added: [ordnance, missiles].	9	DU	PD
1969 *Cars,* trucks, + as above. Added: [rockets].	6	DL	PD
CINCINNATI MILACRON Prior to 1970, Cincinnati Milling Machine.			
1949 *Machine tools,* cutting fluid, industrial chemicals.	—	DC	FS
1959 *Machine tools,* + as above. Added: grinding wheels, metal treating machines, plastic moldings.	370	DC	PD
1969 *Machine tools,* + as above. Added: numerical controls for machine tools, computers.	322	DL	PD
CLARK EQUIPMENT			
1949 *Fork trucks and towing tractors,* RR car parts, auto parts.	201–500	RC	PD
1959 *Fork trucks and tractors,* + as above. Added: shovels, cranes, trailers and vans.	218	RC	PD
1969 *Trucks and tractors,* + as above. Added: motor homes [refrigeration equipment, food service equipment].	175	RC	PD
CLEVITE Prior to 1952, Cleveland Graphite Bronze.			
1949 *Auto parts:* precision engine parts.	—	S	F
1959 *Precision engine parts.* Added: [electronic components, microphones, instruments, phonograph needles, piezo-electric materials].	443	UP	PD
1969 Merged with Gould-National Batteries to form Gould.			
CLINTON FOODS			
1949 *Corn refining: starch, sugar, syrup, oils, pudding, preserves;* frozen and canned foods.	201–500	DC	PD
1956 Acquired by Standard Brands.			
CLUETT, PEABODY			
1949 *Men's clothing.*	201–501	S	F
1959 *Men's clothing.*	359	S	F

TABLE C-1 (continued)

	Rank	Strategy	Structure
Cluett, Peabody (continued)			
1969 *Men's clothing.* Added: *women's clothing,* retail clothing stores, knit mill [luggage].	223	RC	PD
COCA-COLA			
1949 *Coke syrup.*	78	S	F
1959 *Coke syrup.*	132	S	F
1969 *Soft drinks.* Added: orange juice, coffee.	79	RC	PD
COLLINS AND AIKMAN			
1949 *Upholstery fabrics,* other fabrics, yarn.	201–500	DC	F
1959 *Upholstery fabrics,* + as above. Added: car rugs, synthetic fur.	—	RC	PD
1969 *Apparel fabrics,* + as above. Added: knit fabrics, carpets, hosiery.	419	RC	PD
COLORADO MILLING AND ELEVATOR			
1949 *Flour milling:* flour, animal feed; merchants of grain, seed and coal.	201–500	S	F
1959 *Flour milling,* + as above.	318	S	F
1967 Merged with Great Western Sugar to form Great Western United.			
COLT INDUSTRIES Prior to 1964, Fairbanks Whitney; prior to 1959, Penn-Texas; prior to 1954, Pennsylvania Coal and Coke.			
1949 *Coal.*	—	S	F
1959 Coal. Added: *Machine tools,* materials handling equipment, power shovels, pumps and compressors, engines, valves and controls [oil and gas properties, firearms, caps and closures, electronic systems, home water systems, wire and cable].	284	AC	PD
1969 As above. Exited: wire and cable, shovels, oil and gas. Added: carburetors, special steels, transformers.	155	AC	PD
COMMONWEALTH OIL REFINING			
1953 Incorporated.			
1959 *Oil refining.*	—	S	F
1969 *Oil refining.* Added: petrochemicals, retail gas stations [both part of vertical chain].	452	DV	F
CONSOLIDATED CIGAR			
1949 *Cigars.*	201–500	S	F
1959 *Cigars.*	468	S	F
1968 Acquired by Gulf and Western.			

TABLE C-1 (continued)

	Rank	Strategy	Structure
CONTAINER CORPORATION OF AMERICA			
1949 *Paperboard, containers and fiber cans.*	101–200	*S*	*PD*
1959 *Paperboard, containers and fiber cans.* Added: lumber, plastic packaging.	139	*DC*	*PD*
1968 Merged with Montgomery Ward to form Marco.			
CONTINENTAL OIL			
1949 *Integrated oil company.*	61	*S*	*F*
1959 *Integrated oil company.* Added: petrochemicals, detergent, fertilizer, ammonia.	61	*DV*	*G*
1969 *Integrated oil company,* + as above. Added: plastics, resin, coal, fiberglass.	35	*DV*	*PD*
CORNING GLASS WORKS			
1949 *Electrical glass products,* glass housewares, fireglass, lab ware and optical glass, electronics glass.	101–200	*RC*	*F*
1959 *Electrical glass products,* + as above. Added: refractories [nuclear fuel].	221	*RC*	*PD*
1969 *Electrical glass products,* + as above. Exited: nuclear fuel. Added: integrated circuits, medical equipment, home appliances, food service equipment, computer logic [plastic packaging].	210	*RC*	*PD*
CPC INTERNATIONAL Prior to 1959, Corn Products; prior to 1958, Corn Products Refining.			
1949 Corn processing: *oil,* starch, syrup, sugar, feed, in bulk and for consumers.	201–500	*DV*	*F*
1959 Corn processing: *bulk corn mill products,* + as above. Added: grocery products, household products: dyes, rinses, wax.	65	*RC*	*PD*
1969 *Bulk corn mill products,* + as above. Added: seeds, industrial and agricultural chemicals, plastics and resins, food service.	92	*RL*	*PD*
CROWELL-COLLIER & MACMILLAN Prior to 1965, Crowell-Collier Publishing.			
1949 Publishing: *magazines,* books.	201–500	*DC*	*FS*
1959 *Book publishing.* Exited: magazines. Added: radio station, record club.	—	*DL*	*FS*
1969 *Book publishing,* + as above. Added: bookstores, educational supplies, adult education, laboratory equipment, information data banks, academic robes, school janitor services, magazines, film distribution [musical instruments].	255	*RL*	*PD*
CROWN CORK AND SEAL			
1949 *Caps, cans, containers,* cork, bottling and dairy machines.	201–500	*S*	*F*

TABLE C-1 (continued)

	Rank	Strategy	Structure
Crown Cork and Seal (continued)			
1959 *Caps, cans, containers,* + as above.	135	S	F
1969 *Caps, cans, containers,* + as above.	264	S	F
CRUCIBLE STEEL			
1949 Integrated specialty steel producer: *alloys,* high grade, specialty carbon steel; in semi-finished, mill and finished forms.	201–500	DV	F
1959 Integrated specialty steel producer: *alloy steels,* + as above. Added: titanium and titanium alloys.	209	DV	F
1968 Acquired by Colt Industries.			
CUDAHY Prior to 1966, Cudahy Packing.			
1949 Meat packing: *meat,* skins, soap. chemical by-products; poultry, dairy products.	201–500	DV	FS
1959 Meat packing: *meat,* + as above.	128	DV	FS
1969 Meat packing: *meat,* + as above.	274	DV	FS
CURTISS-WRIGHT			
1949 *Aircraft engines, frame parts and rockets,* metal parts for automobiles and industry [motion picture equipment].	100	DC	PD
1959 *Aircraft engines, frame parts and rockets,* + as above. Exited: motion picture equipment. Added: electronic instruments, military vehicles, rocket motors, missile R & D, hovercraft, nuclear reactor and instruments [plastic textiles, plastic industrial parts, heavy earthmoving equipment].	135	UP	PD
1969 *Aircraft engines, frame parts and rockets, and aerospace electronics,* + as above. Exited: plastic products, missiles, military vehicles, hovercraft. Added: [water management and pollution control, process equipment, shot peening, real estate development].	318	UP	PD
DANA			
1949 *Auto parts.*	101–200	S	F
1959 *Auto parts.* Added: industrial parts.	200	DC	F
1969 *Auto parts,* + as above. Added: boat trailers, car transporters.	173	DC	PD
DEERE			
1949 *Farm equipment.*	63	S	F
1959 *Farm equipment.* Added: fertilizer, industrial and construction machinery: tractors, bulldozers.	78	DC	F
1969 *Farm equipment,* + as above. Added: materials handling equipment.	112	DC	F

TABLE C-1 (continued)

	Rank	Strategy	Structure
DI GIORGIO Prior to 1964, Di Giorgio Fruit.			
1949 Vertically integrated produce company: *growing and selling fresh produce* and wine, selling lumber and wooden boxes.	—	*DV*	*FS*
1959 As above. Added: *canned and packaged fruits, vegetables, some grocery specialties.*	393	*RC*	*PD*
1969 *Lumber,* + as above. Exited: canned and packaged fruits and vegetables. Added: *house frames* [retail and wholesale sale of food and drugs, soft drinks, snack food, furniture, campers, trailers, plastic cutlery, proprietary drugs, food accounting machinery].	268	*UP*	*PD*
DIAMOND INTERNATIONAL Prior to 1964, Diamond National; prior to 1959, Diamond Gardner; prior to 1957, Diamond Match			
1949 Vertically integrated forest products: *lumber,* sanitary paper products, pulp products, matches, and small woodenware.	201–500	*DV*	*FS*
1959 As above. Exited: sanitary paper products, pulp products. Added: *paper packaging,* advertising materials, charcoal briquets [all part of the vertical chain], packaging and papermaking machinery.	201	*DV*	*PD*
1969 Vertically integrated forest products: *lumber,* + as above. Added: commercial printing, cans and plastic packaging, fine paper [poultry-raising equipment].	216	*DV*	*PD*
DOEHLER-JARVIS			
1949 *Die castings.*	201–500	*S*	*F*
1953 Acquired by National Lead.			
DONNELLEY (R. R.) AND SONS			
1949 *Commercial printing and binding.*	201–500	*S*	*F*
1959 *Commercial printing and binding.*	312	*S*	*F*
1969 *Commercial printing and binding.*	304	*S*	*PD*
DOW CHEMICAL			
1949 *Industrial chemicals,* agricultural chemicals, plastic chemicals and film, pharmaceutical intermediaries.	52	*RC*	*FS*
1959 *Industrial chemicals,* + as above. Added: styrofoam, acrylic fiber, coated paper [wrapping paper and ribbons].	58	*RC*	*FS*
1969 *Industrial chemicals,* + as above. Added: ethical drugs, animal health products, packaging machin-			

TABLE C-1 (continued)

	Rank	Strategy	Structure
Dow Chemical (continued)			
ery, medical diagnostic instruments and services, plastic building products [aluminum extruded parts].	49	*RL*	*GW*
Dresser Industries			
1949 Equipment for oil and gas industries: *drills, rigs and bits,* pumps, engines, meters, etc.	201–500	*RC*	*H*
1959 *Drills, rigs and bits,* + as above. Added: electronic seismographs.	199	*RC*	*PD*
1969 *Equipment for oil and gas industry,* + as above. Added: cranes, hoists, refractories, lead mine, pneumatic tools, vacuum technology, glass, sand and clay, recording instruments, valves and fittings.	163	*RL*	*PD*
Dumont (Allen B.) Laboratories			
1949 *TV sets,* cathode ray tubes, TV broadcasting and broadcasting equipment and oscilloscopes.	201–500	*DC*	*PD*
1959 *Cathode ray tubes, and oscilloscopes.* Exited: TV sets, broadcasting and broadcasting equipment, TV tubes. Added: mobile radio, automobile testing equipment, military electronics: TV, radar, telemetry.	—	*DC*	*PD*
1960 Acquired by Fairchild Camera.			
Du Pont (E. I.) de Nemours			
1949 *Nylon and rayon fibers, yarn and fabrics,* explosives, dyestuffs, finishes, pigments, heavy industrial chemicals, tetraethyl lead, plastics, insecticides and other agricultural chemicals, refrigerants, firearms (Remington), photographic film.	8	*RL*	*PD*
1959 *Synthetic fibers, yarns and fabrics,* + as above. Added: vinyl plastics, teflon, dacron, orlon, mylar polyester film, special rubber synthetics.	12	*RL*	*PD*
1969 *Synthetic fibers, yarns and fabrics,* + as above. Added: corfam shoe upper material, magnetic tape, synthetic elastomeric yarns, photo instruments, antifreeze, wide variety of new plastics.	15	*RL*	*PD*
Eastman Kodak			
1949 *Photographic supplies:* films, cameras, projectors, plates and paper; motion picture films, chemicals, cellulose acetate products: yarn, plastic molding compounds; organic and commercial chemicals, military optical and other precision equipment, vacuum equipment, microfilm and equipment, and vitamins.	33	*RC*	*F*

TABLE C-1 (continued)

		Rank	Strategy	Structure
1959	*Photographic supplies,* + as above. Added: light chemicals, office copiers, plastic parts and tubing, microfilm EDP.	45	*RC*	*PD*
1969	*Photographic supplies,* + as above.	27	*RC*	*PD*

EATON YALE AND TOWNE Prior to 1963, Eaton Manufacturing.

		Rank	Strategy	Structure
1949	*Auto parts.*	101–200	*S*	*F*
1950	*Auto parts.* Added: industrial parts, heaters and air conditioners and dynamometers	160	*RC*	*F*
1969	*Auto parts,* + as above. Added: boat engines, valves and controls for autos and industry, fork lift trucks, materials handling and construction equipment [locks and builders hardware].	110	*RL*	*PD*

ELECTRIC AUTO-LITE

		Rank	Strategy	Structure
1949	Auto parts; *electrical parts and batteries,* castings and forgings, plastic parts, meters; industrial motors and generators, pressure and temperature gauges.	101–200	*RC*	*F*
1959	*Auto parts,* + as above.	223	*RC*	*PD*
1963	Merged with Mergenthaler Linotype to form Eltra.			

ELTRA

		Rank	Strategy	Structure
1963	Formed by merger of Electric Auto-Lite and Mergenthaler Linotype.			
1969	Auto parts: *electrical parts and batteries,* die castings, speedometers and tachometers; industrial batteries, die castings and measuring instruments [refractories, plumbers' fittings, typesetting equipment, flour, and flour mixes].	238	*AC*	*PD*

ENDICOTT JOHNSON

		Rank	Strategy	Structure
1949	*Shoes.*	101–200	*S*	*F*
1959	*Shoes.*	287	*S*	*F*
1969	*Shoes.*	524	*S*	*F*

ENGELHARD INDUSTRIES Prior to 1958, Baker and Co.

		Rank	Strategy	Structure
1949	*Precious metals: smelting, mining and fabricating;* quartz products, electrical wire and contacts.	101–200	*DC*	*H*
1959	*Precious metals: smelting, mining and fabricating,* + as above. Added: metal-based catalysts and chemicals.	320	*DC*	*H*
1967	Merged with Minerals and Chemicals Phillip to form Engelhard Minerals and Chemicals.			

TABLE C-1 (continued)

	Rank	Strategy	Structure
Ex-Cell-O			
1949 *Precision parts and assemblies for aircraft,* machine tools, cutting tools [dairy and packaging machinery].	—	RC	F
1959 *Precision parts and assemblies for aircraft,* + as above.	355	RC	F
1969 As above. Added: electronic products: computer memory systems, numerical controls for machine tools, tape readers, etc.	270	RC	PD
Fairmont Foods			
1949 *Dairy products,* poultry and eggs, animal feed, oils and fats, frozen food, store equipment and produce distribution.	201–500	RC	F
1959 *Dairy products,* + as above. Exited: oils and fats, animal feed, store equipment, produce distribution. Added: snack foods.	389	RC	F
1969 *Dairy products,* + as above. Added: soft drink syrups, retail convenience stores.	327	RC	PD
Falstaff Brewing			
1949 *Beer.*	—	S	F
1959 *Beer.*	360	S	F
1969 *Beer.*	516	S	F
Fibreboard Prior to 1966, Fibreboard Paper Products; prior to 1956, Pabco.			
1949 *Paperboard containers,* glass bottles and jars [electrotype, paint, roofing, flooring and insulating products].	101–200	DU	FS
1959 *Paperboard containers,* + as above. Exited: glass containers. Added: *paperboard.*	334	DU	PD
1969 *Paperboard and paperboard containers.* Exited: flooring, paint, and roofing products. Added: lumber, plywood, inks, real estate development.	450	DL	PD
Firestone Tire and Rubber			
1949 Vertically integrated rubber company: *tires and tubes,* latex, flooring, insulation, etc.; steel auto parts, plastic auto parts, and tire cord.	39	DV	FS
1959 Vertically integrated rubber company: *tires and tubes,* + as above. Added: synthetic fibers for tires [part of vertical chain]; plastics.	30	DV	FS
1969 Vertically integrated rubber company: *tires and tubes,* + as above. Added: seat belts.	37	DV	PD

TABLE C-1 (continued)

	Rank	Strategy	Structure
FLINTKOTE			
1949 *Building materials of asphalt, asbestos and paper:* roofing, insulation, wallboard, siding, building papers, floor coatings, tiles; industrial products from same materials: adhesives and cements, coatings; paperboard containers.	201–500	*RC*	*FS*
1959 *Building materials,* + as above. Added: lime and limestone products, building slabs, cement; gypsum building products, pipes.	131	*RC*	*FS*
1969 *Building products,* + as above. Added: spray machine for roofing.	77	*RC*	*PD*
FMC Prior to 1961, Food Machinery and Chemical.			
1949 *Agricultural chemicals,* industrial chemicals, phosphates, chlorides; food preparation and processing equipment; agricultural equipment: tractors, sprayers; industrial equipment: fire fighters.	201–500	*RL*	*PD*
1959 *Agricultural chemicals,* + as above. Added: plasticizers, packaging machinery, oil field equipment, pumps and water systems [automotive service, waste disposal systems, industrial castings, prestressed concrete, defense materiel, rocket motors, electronic components].	131	*RL*	*PD*
1969 As above. Exited: Rocket motors. Added: *Synthetic fibers and films;* fibers, tire cord, packaging film [recreational vehicles, power transmission equipment, materials handling systems, railroad cars, construction machinery, auto parts, power tools].	77	*AC*	*PD*
FORD MOTOR			
1949 *Cars and trucks,* tractors, aircraft engines.	10	*S*	*PD*
1959 *Cars and trucks,* + as above. Added: [defense electronic systems].	3	*DC*	*PD*
1969 *Cars and trucks,* + as above. Exited: aircraft engines. Added: [home electronic machines, and home appliances].	3	*DU*	*PD*
FOREMOST DAIRIES			
1949 *Dairy products;* jams and jellies, frozen foods.	—	*S*	*F*
1959 *Dairy products,* + as above. Exited: frozen foods. Added: light chemicals (fatty acids), canned fruits, vegetables and juices.	97	*DC*	*G*
1967 Merged with McKesson and Robbins to form Foremost-McKesson.			

TABLE C-1 (continued)

	Rank	Strategy	Structure
FOSTER WHEELER			
1949 Power plant equipment, oil refinery equipment, chemical process equipment, and the design and construction of entire plants in the above fields or other industries.	—	RC	F
1959 As above. Added: nuclear plant equipment.	268	RC	F
1969 As above. Added: pressure vessels, furnaces.	265	RC	PD
GAF Prior to 1968, General Aniline and Film.			
1949 *Photographic equipment:* cameras, film, paper, darkroom equipment; dyes and pigments, heavy and special chemicals, textile chemicals.	201–500	RL	PD
1959 *Photographic equipment,* + as above. Added: microfilm, data handling equipment.	273	RL	PD
1969 [As above]. Added: *asphalt, asbestos and gypsum building products: roofing, siding, flooring, insulation, coatings;* industrial products from same materials: acoustical coverings, filters, etc. [business forms, office copiers, micrographics, pharmaceutical, agricultural and polymer chemicals].	184	UP	PD
GENERAL CABLE			
1949 *Wire and cable.*	201–500	S	F
1959 *Wire and cable.* Added: poles and crossarms, insulated cord.	260	DC	F
1969 *Wire and cable,* + as above. Added: electrical switches and panels, pole line hardware, aerial lift vehicles, dryers for cables, cable pressure systems.	265	DC	PD
GENERAL ELECTRIC			
1949 *Electric power generation equipment,* motors, motor controls, lighting equipment, electric appliances, TV and radio, jet engines, electronic parts and systems.	9	RL	PD
1959 As above. Added: plastics, computers, semi-conductors, aerospace contracting.	4	RL	PD
1969 As above. Added: cable TV, TV-radio broadcasting, time-share computers [rapid-transit cars, urban systems study].	4	RL	PD
GENERAL FOODS			
1949 *Coffee,* wide variety of grocery products.	73	RC	PD
1959 *Coffee,* + as above.	37	RC	PD
1969 *Coffee,* + as above.	46	RC	PD
GENERAL HOST Prior to 1967, General Baking.			
1949 *Baked goods.*	201–500	S	G
1959 *Baked goods.* Added: [restaurants, candy].	261	DU	G

TABLE C-1 (continued)

	Rank	Strategy	Structure
1969 *Baked goods, +* as above. Added: frozen dinners [tourist concessions, recreational area development, general retail stores].	425	*AC*	*PD*

GENERAL INSTRUMENT

	Rank	Strategy	Structure
1949 *Components for electronic entertainment equipment:* tuners, other components; phonograph record changers, defense electronic components.	—	*DC*	*F*
1959 *Entertainment electronic components, +* as above. Added: semi-conductors, military electronic equipment and systems.		*RC*	*PD*
1969 As above. Added: data collecting, processing and display systems, registers and ticket issuers, cable TV, magnetic recording heads, thermo-electric products, electro-optical products.	369	*RL*	*PD*

GENERAL MILLS

	Rank	Strategy	Structure
1949 Flour miller: *flour, feeds,* cereals, packaged grain-based foods, chemical and pharmaceutical milling by-products; contract machining for defense, small appliances, distribution of feeds and other farm supplies.	101–200	*DV*	*PD*
1959 Flour miller: *flour, +* as above. Exited: contract machining. Added: ready-to-bake foods, pet food, defense electronics, steroids [sponges, plastic consumer products].	77	*RC*	*PD*
1969 Flour miller: flour, *cereals,* grain-based packaged foods, chemical and pharmaceutical by-products, + as above. Exited: feed, home appliances, defense electronics, ready-to-bake foods. Added: *snack foods,* other grocery products, chemicals and resins [restaurants, jewelry, clothes, mail-order merchandising, toys and games].	130	*RC*	*PD*

GENESCO   Prior to 1959, General Shoe.

	Rank	Strategy	Structure
1949 *Shoes, shoe stores.*	201–500	*S*	*H*
1959 *Shoes, shoe stores.* Added: clothing stores, jewelry stores, silverware, women's apparel.	173	*DL*	*H*
1969 *Shoes, shoe stores, +* as above. Exited: jewelry stores, silverware. Added: men's apparel.	95	*RL*	*PD*

GILLETTE   Prior to 1953, Gillette Safety Razor.

	Rank	Strategy	Structure
1949 *Razors, blades, and shaving cream;* hair care products.	201–500	*DC*	*FS*
1959 *Razors, blades, and shaving cream, +* as above. Added: cosmetics, proprietary drugs, contract R & D [ball-point pens].	216	*RC*	*PD*

TABLE C-1 (continued)

	Rank	Strategy	Structure
Gillette (continued)			
1969 *Razors, blades, and shaving cream.* Exited: proprietary drugs. Added: men's toiletries [disposable hospital supplies, electric appliances, photographic equipment, audio systems].	182	*RC*	*PD*
GLEN ALDEN Prior to 1959, Glen Alden Coal.			
1949 *Coal mining.*	—	*S*	*F*
1959 *Coal mining.* Added: air conditioners, fire trucks and equipment, movie theatres, textile finishing, auto parts warehouses, gas and oil properties.	364	*UP*	*PD*
1969 [As above]. Exited: coal, fire equipment, textile finishing, auto parts, gas and oil. Added: *alcoholic beverages* [appliances, textiles, family consumer products: toothbrushes, sanitary products, etc.; men's and women's apparel, wholesale and retail; building materials, medical electronics, Apollo space suits, air-supported structures].	—	*AC*	*PD*
1969 Acquired by Rapid-American.			
GLIDDEN			
1949 *Vegetable oils processor:* margarine, dressings and other foods, feed, chemical by-products; spices, paint and pigments, pine gum processing: resin, turpentine.	101–200	*RL*	*PD*
1959 *Paint and pigments,* + as above. Exited: pine tar processing, animal feed, chemical by-products of soy processing. Added: titanium powder, organic chemicals.	230	*RL*	*PD*
1967 Acquired by SCM.			
GOODRICH (B. F.)			
1949 Rubber: *tires and tubes,* industrial goods, synthetic rubber, druggists' goods, shoes, latex, rubber chemicals; other chemicals; tire fabrics, organic colors, wheels and brakes for aircraft, vinyl plastic.	62	*DV*	*FS*
1959 Rubber: *tires and tubes,* + as above. Added: auto wheels and brakes, imitation leather, floor and wall coverings; petrochemicals, synthetic fiber [aerospace and defense: fuel cells, rocket cases, fuel, motors, nose cones].	50	*DV*	*PD*
1969 Rubber: *tires and tubes,* + as above. Added: [materials handling system].	90	*DV*	*PD*
GOODYEAR TIRE AND RUBBER			
1949 Rubber: *tires and tubes,* consumer products, industrial products, aviation products, latex; chemicals, resins; synthetic rubber; vinyl goods, wheel rims.	32	*DV*	*FS*

TABLE C-1 (continued)

	Rank	Strategy	Structure
1959 Rubber: *tires and tubes,* + as above. Added: packaging film, plastics [rockets and missiles, radar and military electronics].	21	*DV*	*PD*
1969 Rubber: *tires and tubes,* + as above. Added: auto parts [heaters and air conditioners, railroad equipment, real estate development].	20	*DV*	*PD*

GRACE (W. R.)

	Rank	Strategy	Structure
1949 *Import-export;* airlines and shipping, agriculture, mining: tungsten and tin; banking and insurance; manufacturing: fertilizer, textiles, paints and varnishes, paper, vegetable oil, etc.	—	*UP*	*H*
1959 [As above]. Added: *chemicals:* industrial, agricultural, plasticizers, acids, petrochemicals, chemical products such as packaging film, sealing compounds; atomic fuel.	93	*AC*	*PD*
1969 *Chemicals,* + as above. Exited: airlines and shipping; textiles, vegetable oil, agriculture, paint, banking and insurance, atomic fuel. Added: *detergents and germicides, plastic products:* vinyl fabrics, imitation leather footwear, lubricants [frozen foods, snack foods, mail-order gifts, medical diagnostic laboratory, restaurants, women's clothing, shoe stores, leather goods].	50	*AC*	*PD*

GREAT NORTHERN NEKOSSA   Prior to 1970, Great Northern Paper.

	Rank	Strategy	Structure
1949 Integrated *paper:* pulp.	201–500	*S*	*F*
1959 Integrated *paper,* + as above. Added: kraft container board.	—	*S*	*F*
1969 Integrated forest products: *newsprint,* specialty and coated paper, container board. Added: plywood.	461	*DV*	*F*

GULF OIL

	Rank	Strategy	Structure
1949 *Integrated oil producer.*	7	*S*	*F*
1959 *Integrated oil producer.* Added: petrochemicals, synthetic rubber.	7	*S*	*F*
1969 *Integrated oil producer,* + as above. Added: fertilizers, plastics, coal, atomic energy [real estate development].	10	*DV*	*FS*

HANDY AND HARMON

	Rank	Strategy	Structure
1949 *Refined precious metals,* for jewelry, dentistry, industry.	201–500	*S*	*F*
1959 *Refined precious metals.* Added: steel and nickel tubing.	437	*DL*	*FS*

TABLE C-1 (continued)

	Rank	Strategy	Structure
Handy and Harmon (continued)			
1969 *Refined precious metals,* + as above. Added: steel bearings, belts and miscellaneous parts, heat treatment of metals.	416	*RL*	*FS*
HARSCO Prior to 1956, Harrisburg Steel.			
1949 *Steel forgings and castings.*	—	*S*	*F*
1959 *Steel forgings and castings.* Added: nonferrous castings, steel trackwork, auto tools, dies and frame parts [drilling machines, plastic parts].	396	*DC*	*PD*
1969 *Steel forgings and castings,* + as above. Exited: nonferrous castings, auto tools, dies and parts, drilling machines, plastic parts. Added: steel structures, building materials: bricks, pipes; sewage treatment equipment, hoist towers [farm, stone-crushing and materials handling machinery, defense vehicles, missile support equipment, power tools].	341	*RL*	*PD*
HART SCHAFFNER AND MARX			
1949 *Men's clothing and clothing stores.*	—	*S*	*F*
1959 *Men's clothing and clothing stores.*	451	*S*	*F*
1965 Dropped because greater than 50% nonmanufacturing.			
HERSHEY FOODS Prior to 1968, Hershey Chocolate.			
1949 *Chocolate and cocoa products.*	101–200	*S*	*F*
1959 *Chocolate and cocoa products.*	266	*S*	*F*
1969 *Chocolate and cocoa products.* Added: grocery products, prepared foods for food service [appliances, cookware, vending services, business aids].	298	*DL*	*PD*
HOBART MANUFACTURING			
1949 Commercial food machinery, kitchen appliances, scales.	—	*RC*	*F*
1959 As above.	—	*RC*	*FS*
1969 As above. Added: furniture for food service.	427	*RC*	*FS*
HOOKER CHEMICAL Prior to 1958, Hooker Electrochemical.			
1949 *Industrial chemicals,* mainly chlorine-based, agricultural chemicals, pharmaceutical intermediates, dyestuffs, electrolytic cells.	—	*RC*	*F*
1959 *Industrial chemicals,* + as above. Added: plastic chemicals, plastic compounds and foam, detergents, feed, solid rocket fuel.	283	*RC*	*PD*
1968 Acquired by Occidental Petroleum.			

TABLE C-1 (continued)

		Rank	Strategy	Structure
Hormel (Geo. A.)				
1949	Meat packing: *meat,* gelatine, by-products; canned soup.	101–200	*DV*	*F*
1959	Meat packing: *meat,* + as above. Added: frozen food, baby food.	117	*DV*	*F*
1969	Meat packing: *meat,* + as above. Added: prepared foods for mass feeding.	178	*DV*	*PD*
Hygrade Food Products				
1949	Meat packer: *meat,* by-products—dog food, soap, fertilizer; dairy foods, coffee, grocery products.	101–200	*DV*	*F*
1959	Meat packer: *meat,* + as above.	111	*DV*	*F*
1969	Meat packer: *meat,* + as above.	269	*DV*	*F*
Ingersoll-Rand				
1949	Heavy pumps and compressors, condensers, internal combustion engines, hand pneumatic tools, air conditioners and refrigeration equipment, mining machinery.	201–500	*RC*	*F*
1959	As above.	269	*RC*	*F*
1969	As above. Added: consumer tools, plastic molding machinery, bearings [industrial and surgical needles, precision parts].	160	*RC*	*PD*
Inland Container				
1949	*Kraft paper containers and kraft paper.*	201–500	*S*	*F*
1959	*Kraft paper containers and kraft paper.*	400	*S*	*F*
1969	*Kraft paper containers and kraft paper.* Added: printing inks, retailing of packaging machinery [real estate development].	444	*S*	*PD*
Inmont Prior to 1969, Interchemical.				
1949	*Printing inks,* pigments and dyes, finishes: paint, varnish; coated fabrics, carbon paper and ribbon.	201–500	*RC*	*PD*
1959	*Printing inks,* + as above. Exited: coated fabrics, paint and varnish. Added: clay, adhesives.	329	*RC*	*PD*
1969	*Printing inks,* + as above. Added: fine chemicals and pharmaceutical intermediates, foam rubber insulators, copier paper, auto finishes [oyster farm, candy].	289	*RC*	*PD*
International Business Machines				
1949	*Tabulating machines,* radio and audio equipment, clocks, typewriters, timers and meters.	68	*RC*	*F*
1959	As above. Exited: radio and audio equipment. Added: *electronic data processing systems.*	27	*RC*	*PD*
1969	*EDP systems,* + as above. Added: dictating machines.	5	*DC*	*PD*

TABLE C-1 (continued)

	Rank	Strategy	Structure
INTERSTATE BRANDS Prior to 1969, Interstate Bakeries.			
1949 *Bakery products.*	201–500	S	F
1959 *Bakery products.*	324	S	F
1969 *Bakery products.* Added: frozen pies, institutional canned vegetables, dog food.	374	S	PD
IOWA BEEF PROCESSORS Prior to 1970, Iowa Beef Packers.			
1960 Incorporated.			
1969 *Beef packing.*	167	S	F
IPL Prior to 1968, International Packers Limited.			
1950 Incorporated.			
1959 *Meat packing;* vegetable oil milling, poultry and grocery products distribution.	113	DC	F
1969 Merged with Deltec Panamerica SA to form Deltec International.			
JOHNSON AND JOHNSON			
1949 *Bandages, bandaids* and surgical supplies, baby care products, sanitary paper products, tooth and hair brushes, nonprescription pharmaceuticals, adhesives.	101–200	RC	F
1959 As above. Added: textiles, molded plastic medical equipment, ethical drugs, chemicals for textile manufacture, glue.	151	RC	PD
1969 *Bandages* and bandaids and surgical supplies, + as above. Exited: textiles, glue. Added: *medical and surgical instruments,* elastic fabric.	170	RC	PD
JONES AND LAUGHLIN STEEL			
1949 Integrated steel producer: *steel mill products,* fabricated products, structures, coal chemicals; distribution of oil well supplies.	35	DV	F
1959 Integrated steel producer: *steel mill products,* + as above.	51	DV	F
1968 Acquired by Ling-Temco-Vought.			
JOSLYN MANUFACTURING AND SUPPLY			
1949 Construction materials for electric, telephone and telegraph lines: poles and cross arms, insulators and switches, wood preservatives, lightning rods; street lighting equipment, iron castings, steel bars, wires and shapes [kitchen ware].	201–500	RC	F
1959 As above. Exited: [kitchen ware].	405	RC	F
1969 As above. Added: surge arrestors, fiberglass insulators, wood floor blocks, marine and industrial hardware.	606	RC	F

TABLE C-1 (continued)

	Rank	Strategy	Structure
Kaiser Aluminum and Chemical Prior to 1949, Permanente Metals.			
1949 Integrated aluminum producer: *sheet,* ingot, chemical by-products.	101–200	*DV*	*F*
1959 Integrated aluminum producer: *sheet,* + as above. Added: foil and packaging, rod and bar, screening and roofing, cans, electrical conductors (all part of vertical chain).	101	*DV*	*PD*
1969 Integrated aluminum producer: *sheet,* + as above. Added: urethane foams; agricultural chemicals; nickel, iron and uranium mining; modular buildings and building parts [real estate development, cattle production].	125	*DV*	*PD*
Karagheusian			
1949 *Carpets and rugs.*	201–500	*S*	*F*
1959 *Carpets and rugs.*	—	*S*	*F*
1964 Acquired by Stevens (J. P.)			
Kelsey-Hayes Prior to 1956, Kelsey-Hayes Wheel			
1949 *Auto parts;* wheels, brakes, small parts.	201–500	*S*	*F*
1959 *Auto parts,* + as above. Added: airplane parts: engine parts, transmissions, gear-boxes; hand tools, [vacuum-melted metals].	224	*RL*	*F*
1969 *Auto parts,* + as above. Exited: hand tools, vacuum-melted metals. Added: heavy iron and steel castings, aluminum auto parts, contract making of missile parts.	259	*RL*	*F*
Keystone Consolidated Industries Prior to 1969, Keystone Steel and Wire.			
1949 Integrated steel company: *wire and wire products,* fencing, barbed, builders' products, industrial; semi-finished steel, nails; locks, hardware.	201–500	*DV*	*FS*
1959 Integrated steel: *wire and wire products,* + as above. Added: wire tying machines and related tools; agricultural equipment: gates, feeders [plastic extrusions].	331	*DV*	*FS*
1969 Integrated steel: *wire and wire products.* Added: precision metal parts.	449	*DV*	*PD*
Kimberly-Clark			
1949 Integrated paper producer: *cellulose wadding;* white paper.	101–200	*DV*	*F*
1959 Integrated paper producer: *cellulose wadding,* + as above. Added: sanitary paper products, special purpose papers, stationery.	125	*DV*	*F*
1969 Integrated paper producer: + as above.	134	*DV*	*PD*

TABLE C-1 (continued)

		Rank	Strategy	Structure

KOPPERS

1949	*Engineering and construction:* of coke ovens, gas and chemical plants, etc.; tar processor: creosote, tars, pitches, chemicals; gas and coke; wood preserving of treated wood products; plastics and plasticizers, industrial chemicals and resins; metal products: contract machining, shaft couplings and propellers, pistol rings; coke and gas plant equipment.	101–200	*RL*	*F*
1959	*Tar processor,* + as above. Added: plastic film, dyestuffs, paper box machinery; air and gas filters, noise abatement equipment.	193	*RL*	*PD*
1969	*Wood preserving and treated wood products,* + as above. Added: *laminated wood products;* modular homes; glass reinforced plastics, fiberglass extrusions, thermo-plastics, polyester floor tile; water and sewage treatment; metallurgy.	209	*RL*	*PD*

LEAR SIEGLER   Prior to 1962, Siegler; prior to 1954, Siegler Heater.

| 1959 | *Home electronics:* radio, TV, phonographs, tape recorders; cable, and closed circuit TV; aerospace: structures, large antennas, avionics, telemetry, hydraulic jacks [materials handling equipment, electronic testing equipment and industrial controls, tools; heaters, furnaces, air conditioning]. | — | *UP* | *PD* |
| 1969 | *Home electronics,* + as above. Exited: cable TV, aerospace structures. Added: aircraft electric power systems, flight control systems, pumps, actuators; lasers; computers; home lighting [metal-cutting tools, auto parts; food display equipment; mattresses, bed frames; business schools]. | 186 | *AC* | *PD* |

LEHIGH PORTLAND CEMENT

1949	*Cement.*	101–200	*S*	*F*
1959	*Cement.*	438	*S*	*F*
1969	*Cement.* Added: aggregate concrete [carpets, furniture].	—	*DU*	*PD*

LIBBEY-OWENS-FORD   Prior to 1968, Libbey-Owens-Ford Glass.

1949	*Plate and auto glass,* insulating glass, mirrors; plastics and resins.	101–200	*DC*	*F*
1959	*Plate and auto glass,* + as above. Exited: plastics and resins.	147	*DC*	*FS*
1969	*Plate and auto glass,* + as above. Added: ornamental bronze; auto seals [hose and fluid couplings, cargo tiedown equipment; industrial rubber products; custom plastic and cellulose products].	232	*RL*	*FS*

TABLE C-1 (continued)

		Rank	Strategy	Structure
LIEBMANN BREWERIES				
1949	*Beer and ale.*	201–500	*S*	*F*
1959	*Beer and ale.*	—	*S*	*F*
1964	Acquired by Pub United (Rheingold > 1964).			
LING-TEMCO-VOUGHT Prior to 1961, Ling-Temco Electronics; prior to 1960, Ling-Altec Electronics; prior to 1959, Ling Electronics; prior to 1956, L. M. Electronics.				
1953	Incorporated.			
1959	Electronic components, information display systems, super-power electronics, broadcasting and sound reproduction: TV, stereos, recording equipment; sonar and radar, measurement devices.	—	*RC*	*PD*
1969	[As above]. Exited: electronic components. Added: *meat packing:* meat, fats, by-products [athletic goods, pharmaceutical chemicals, industrial chemicals and resins; aircraft, missiles, weapon systems, aerospace electronic systems; rockets and launch vehicles; engineering and architecture, insulated wire; steel: mill products, structural products, modular housing; airline; banking and insurance, car rental; hotels; ski area; business colleges; floor coverings, industrial maintenance].	14	*AC*	*H*
LITTON INDUSTRIES Prior to 1954, Electro-Dynamics.				
1953	Incorporated.			
1959	*Business machines:* computers, calculators; guidance systems and aircraft instruments; x-ray equipment.	322	*RL*	*PD*
1969	*Guidance, navigational and control systems,* + as above. Added: tag punchers and readers, typewriters, business forms [office furniture; materials handling systems; motors, machine tools; optical and medical instruments; dental supplies; special printing; maps; textbooks; ship building, food display; prepared food; store fixtures].	39	*AC*	*PD*
LOCKHEED AIRCRAFT				
1949	*Aircraft and aircraft parts, ground equipment, air terminal and overhaul.*	101–200	*S*	*F*
1959	*Aircraft and aircraft parts,* + as above. Added: avionics, weapons systems, space satellites, missile work [ship building and repair; heavy construction].	28	*RC*	*PD*
1969	*Aircraft and aircraft parts,* + as above. Added: computers, electronic components, oceanography [plastic parts, steel fabricated products, materials handling equipment, meters and measuring devices].	41	*RC*	*PD*

TABLE C-1 (continued)

	Rank	Strategy	Structure
LONGVIEW FIBRE			
1949 *Containerboard and kraft paper.*	201–500	S	F
1959 *Containerboard and kraft paper.*	—	S	F
1969 *Containerboard and kraft paper.* Added: containers, bags.	—	S	FS
LONG-BELL LUMBER			
1949 Integrated lumber company: *lumber,* wood building materials, furniture; retail building materials outlets.	201–500	DV	F
1956 Acquired by International Paper.			
LORILLARD (P.)			
1949 *Cigarettes and tobacco.*	101–200	S	F
1959 *Cigarettes and tobacco.*	171	S	F
1968 Acquired by Loew's Theatres.			
LUKENS STEEL			
1949 Integrated steel company: *steel plate shapes;* steel plate, steel plate products, including machinery and steel machinery parts.	—	DV	F
1959 Integrated steel company: *steel plate shapes,* + as above. Added: alloys and clad materials, electrodes (both part of vertical chain).	453	DV	F
1969 Integrated steel company: *steel plate shapes,* + as above.	536	DV	F
MALLORY (P. R.)			
1949 *Batteries;* capacitors, rectifiers; resistors, tuners, switches; special metals, welding tips.	—	DC	PD
1959 *Batteries,* + as above. Added: non-ferrous forgings and castings, steel rolling mill [plastic molded household products].	435	RL	PD
1969 *Batteries,* + as above. Added: micro-modules.	—	RL	PD
MARATHON OIL Prior to 1962, Ohio Oil.			
1949 *Integrated oil company.*	201–500	S	F
1959 *Integrated oil company.*	130	S	F
1969 *Integrated oil company.* Added: petrochemicals.	126	DV	F
MARTIN MARIETTA Prior to 1961, Martin Company (The); prior to 1956, Glen L. Martin.			
1949 *Aircraft and parts,* military rockets and missiles, weapons systems.	201–500	DC	F
1959 *Rockets and missiles,* + as above. Added: *electronic aerospace systems.*	84	DC	F
1969 *Missiles and electronic aerospace systems.* Exited: aircraft, rockets. Added: [cement, lime, concrete			

TABLE C-1 (continued)

	Rank	Strategy	Structure
and tile; inks and dyes; aluminum; engineering off-shore oil installations; real estate development].	116	*UP*	*PD*

MAYTAG

1949	*Washing machines.*	201–500	*S*	*F*
1959	*Washing machines.* Added: dryers [missile products].	326	*S*	*FS*
1969	*Washing machines and dryers.* Exited: missile products.	486	*S*	*FS*

McCALL

1949	*Women's magazine publishing;* clothes pattern printing; contract printing; publication of fashion books.	—	*DC*	*PD*
1959	*Women's magazine publishing,* + as above.	485	*RC*	*PD*
1968	Merged with Hunt Foods to form Norton Simon.			

McGRAW EDISON Prior to 1957, McGraw Electric.

1949	*Electrical appliances:* kitchen appliances, fans, heaters; street lighting; pipe and conduit; fuses; pole-line hardware, transformers, capacitors, switches.	201–500	*RL*	*PD*
1959	*Electrical appliances,* + as above. Added: industrial furnaces and dryers, batteries, dictating machines, small motors, electrical tools [aircraft instruments, medical gases, juvenile furniture].	164	*RL*	*PD*
1969	*Electrical appliances,* + as above. Exited: industrial furnaces, medical gases, juvenile furniture. Added: coin laundries and dry cleaners, erection of utility poles, decorative lighting, timing devices [vacuum treatment of metal, textile machinery].	183	*RL*	*PD*

McLOUTH STEEL

1949	*Steel mill products.*	201–500	*S*	*F*
1959	*Steel mill products.*	254	*S*	*F*
1969	*Steel mill products.*	399	*S*	*F*

MEAD

1949	*Paper, paperboard.*	101–200	*S*	*F*
1959	*Paperboard,* + as above. Added: *paperboard containers.*	138	*RC*	*F*
1969	*Paper,* + as above. Added: school supplies, modeling clay, crayons [computer software, photographic testing and processing, iron, coke; cement, pipe, precision castings, effluent treatment, furniture, upholstery fabrics].	113	*RC*	*PD*

TABLE C-1 (continued)

	Rank	Strategy	Structure
MENGEL			
1949 Integrated forest products company: *finished wood products* (furniture, doors, cabinets), lumber, paperboard containers.	201–500	*DV*	*PD*
1954 Acquired by Container Corporation of America.			
MERCK AND COMPANY			
1949 *Bulk vitamins,* antibiotics, hormones, and medicinal chemicals, agricultural chemicals, industrial chemicals.	201–500	*RC*	*F*
1959 *Vitamins in bulk,* + as above. Added: *prescription vitamins, ethical drugs.*	210	*RC*	*PD*
1969 *Ethical drugs,* + as above. Added: chemicals for water purification and water purification systems, commercial cleaning products.	174	*RC*	*PD*
MIDLAND-ROSS Prior to 1957, Midland Steel Products.			
1949 *Heavy steel auto parts and frames,* pneumatic controls, steel tubing.	201–500	*DC*	*F*
1959 *Heavy steel auto parts and frames,* + as above. Added: door openers, aircraft coupling and controls [industrial dryers; plastic extruding machinery; furnaces, air conditioners; air purification equipment, glass plant; nonferrous die casting].	422	*UP*	*PD*
1969 *Heavy steel auto parts and frames,* + as above. Added: iron and steel castings [water and air pollution control equipment; winding and slitting machinery; electric plugs, connectors, fixtures and controls; grinding balls; jet engine and missile components; steel boxes; letter presses].	335	*UP*	*PD*
MILES LABORATORIES			
1949 *Proprietary medicines,* pharmaceutical chemicals.	—	*RC*	*F*
1959 *Proprietary medicines,* + as above. Added: prescription medicines, diagnostic tests, enzymes.	497	*RC*	*PD*
1969 *Proprietary medicines,* + as above. Added: medical electronic instruments, laboratory supplies, cyclamates, dairy cultures, refined corn products; household cleaning products.	331	*RL*	*PD*
MINNESOTA MINING AND MANUFACTURING			
1949 *Pressure sensitive electrical, magnetic tape,* adhesives, abrasives, gummed paper, heavy chemical by-products.	101–200	*RL*	*PD*
1959 *Tape,* + as above. Added: office copier, microfilm equipment, photo offset plates; electric ceramics; refractories; concrete, stone; coated paper, plastic			

TABLE C-1 (continued)

		Rank	Strategy	Structure
	insulator, ribbon, RFP sheet and pipe, varnish, resins, floor covering; synthetic rubber.	86	*RL*	*PD*
1969	*Tape,* + as above. Added: cameras, projectors, video-tape equipment; film processing, radio broadcasting; cable, EDP microfilm.	59	*RL*	*PD*

MOBIL OIL Prior to 1966, Socony Mobil Oil; prior to 1955, Socony-Vacuum Oil; prior to 1934, Socony-Vacuum; prior to 1931, Standard Oil (N.Y.).

		Rank	Strategy	Structure
1949	*Integrated oil company.*	5	*S*	*F*
1959	*Integrated oil company.*	6	*S*	*F*
1969	*Integrated oil company.* Added: petrochemicals, plastics (both part of vertical chain), phosphates, paint and chemical coatings.	7	*DV*	*FS*

MOHASCO INDUSTRIES Prior to 1955, Alexander Smith; prior to 1951, Alexander Smith and Sons, Carpet Co.

		Rank	Strategy	Structure
1949	*Carpets,* floor tile, plastic wall coverings, plastic household utensils.	201–500	*DC*	*FS*
1959	*Carpets.* Exited: floor tile, plastic wall coverings, plastic household utensils.	384	*S*	*F*
1969	*Carpets.* Added: furniture.	300	*DC*	*PD*

MONSANTO Prior to 1964, Monsanto Chemical.

		Rank	Strategy	Structure
1949	*Plastics, synthetic resins, coatings,* phosphates, detergents, plasticizers, resins; pharmaceutical chemicals, rubber, petrochemicals; heavy industrial chemicals, agricultural chemicals, wood preservatives, food additives.	86	*RC*	*PD*
1959	*Plastics, synthetic resins, coatings,* + as above. Added: integrated oil production; synthetic fibers; explosives.	70	*RC*	*PD*
1969	*Synthetic fibers,* + as above. Added: high protein food, water treatment processes, electronic testing instruments; automatic control valves.	43	*RL*	*PD*

NATIONAL BISCUIT

		Rank	Strategy	Structure
1949	*Baked goods,* snack foods, cereals, dog food.	97	*DC*	*F*
1959	*Baked goods,* + as above. Added: cake mixes, other grocery products.	104	*DC*	*F*
1969	*Baked goods,* + as above. Added: candy, frozen baked goods, institutional food service.	157	*DC*	*PD*

NATIONAL CASH REGISTER

		Rank	Strategy	Structure
1949	Business machines: *cash registers,* accounting and adding machines.	201–500	*DC*	*F*

TABLE C-1 (continued)

	Rank	Strategy	Structure
National Cash Register (continued)			
1959 *Accounting machines,* + as above. Added: electronic data processing computers, commercial and aircraft; typewriter paper.	108	*RC*	*F*
1969 *Accounting machines,* + as above. Added: defense communications electronics; paper capsules for drugs.	87	*RC*	*F*
NATIONAL CASTINGS Prior to 1961, National Malleable and Steel Castings.			
1949 *Iron and steel castings* (for railroad and automobiles).	201–500	*S*	*F*
1959 *Iron and steel castings.* Added: grinding balls.	—	*S*	*PD*
1965 Acquired by Midland-Ross.			
NATIONAL CONTAINER			
1949 Paperboard and paperboard containers.	201–500	*S*	*F*
1956 Acquired by Owens-Illinois.			
NATIONAL LEAD			
1949 *Paints and pigments;* lead chemicals, paint oils; lead products: pipes, sheets, washers, wires; lead alloy products: solders, type; other metal products: bearings, castings; acid handling equipment; titanium alloy manufacturing; lubricating devices [well drilling equipment].	84	*RL*	*FS*
1959 *Paints and pigments,* + as above. Added: refractories, nonferrous die casting; nickel processing; screws; nuclear metals, R & D, processing aluminum tooling.	82	*RL*	*FS*
1969 *Paints and pigments,* + as above. Added: [chemicals for petroleum industry; aluminum architectural structures; plastics for industry; hardwood veneer; bank; precision parts for electronics].	122	*RL*	*PD*
NATIONAL STEEL			
1949 Integrated steel producer: *steel strips and sheet,* bars, shapes, structural shapes, tin plate, pig iron and ores, chemical by-products.	43	*DV*	*F*
1959 Integrated steel: *strips and sheet,* + as above. Added: coated steel [part of vertical chain].	54	*DV*	*F*
1969 Integrated steel: *strips and sheet,* + as above. Added: aluminum building products.	91	*DV*	*F*
NATIONAL SUPPLY			
1949 Oil well drilling equipment: tubes, pumps, motors, etc., and distribution of these and other oil well supplies.	201–500	*RC*	*FS*
1958 Acquired by Armco Steel.			

TABLE C-1 (continued)

	Rank	Strategy	Structure
NEW YORK TIMES			
1949 *Newspaper publishing,* radio station, facsimile transmission.	—	*DC*	*FS*
1959 *Newspaper publishing,* + as above. Exited: facsimile transmission.	377	*DC*	*FS*
1969 *Newspaper publishing,* + as above. Added: book publishing, magazine publishing, teaching materials.	381	*DL*	*FS*
NEWPORT NEWS SHIPBUILDING			
1949 *Shipbuilding;* hydraulic turbines; heavy industrial machinery.	201–500	*S*	*F*
1959 *Shipbuilding,* + as above.	238	*S*	*F*
1968 Acquired by Tenneco.			
NORTH AMERICAN ROCKWELL Prior to 1967, North American Aviation.			
1949 *Airplanes and parts,* rocket engines, missiles; electronic and electro-mechanical equipment for aerospace; designing, building and operating nuclear reactors	101–200	*DC*	*F*
1959 *Airplanes and parts,* + as above. Added: electronic systems for aerospace.	38	*RC*	*PD*
1969 [As above]. Added: *auto parts;* industrial machine parts, textile machinery, graphic arts equipment.	30	*UP*	*PD*
NORTHERN PAPER MILLS			
1949 Sanitary paper products: toilet paper, paper towels, napkins.	201–500	*S*	*F*
1953 Acquired by Marathon.			
OLIN Prior to 1969, Olin-Mathieson Chemical; prior to 1954, Mathieson Chemical.			
1949 Industrial heavy chemicals: *bulk heavy alkalis,* chlorides, nitrogen products, etc.; agricultural chemicals.	101–200	*RC*	*F*
1959 [As above]. Added: *primary aluminum, nonferrous fabricated parts* [arms, ammunition, explosives; cellophane, cigarette filter and paper; lumber, kraft paper, outdoor furniture; nuclear fuel; pharmaceuticals: drugs, vitamins, proprietary products].	60	*UP*	*PD*
1969 *Primary aluminum, nonferrous parts,* + as above. Exited: pharmaceuticals; nuclear fuel. Added: *aluminum: consumer products, architectural products* [polyvinyl chloride and polyvinyl chloride pipe; outdoor recreation: equipment, area development, books; mobile homes; real estate development; wood furniture, floors].	99	*UP*	*PD*

TABLE C-1 (continued)

	Rank	Strategy	Structure
OTIS ELEVATOR			
1949 *Elevators and escalators.*	—	S	F
1959 *Elevators and escalators.* Added: fork-lift trucks [military electronics; shipping and maintaining automatic bowling pinsetters].	203	DL	FS
1969 *Elevators and escalators.* Exited: military electronics.	192	DL	FS
OUTBOARD MARINE Prior to 1956, Outboard Marine and Manufacturing.			
1949 *Outboard motors.*	—	S	F
1959 *Outboard motors.* Added: power lawnmowers, chain saws, utility vehicles.	259	DC	F
1969 *Outboard motors, +* as above. Added: snowmobiles; camping trailers, grass care equipment.	290	DC	PD
OWENS-ILLINOIS Prior to 1965, Owens-Illinois Glass.			
1949 *Glass containers, closures;* glass insulators, blocks, glass laboratory equipment, glass TV tubes, glass tableware, paper containers, plywood and veneer; plastic molding machines [brush-making machines; brushes].	85	DC	PD
1959 *Glass containers, closures, +* as above. Exited: plywood and veneer; brushes and brush machines. Added: *plastic containers,* paperboard, paper bags; plastic tableware; precision glass electronic components.	76	RC	PD
1969 *Glass and plastic containers, closures, +* as above. Added: fiber cans; plywood; glass resins; glass for fiber optics; optical systems; gyro test systems; engineering for aerospace; paper cups and plates.	85	RL	PD
PACIFIC CAR AND FOUNDRY			
1949 *Railroad cars;* logging and construction equipment; trucks and buses; shipbuilding and repair, structural steel plates and shapes.	—	RC	F
1959 *Trucks, +* as above. Added: *off-highway construction vehicles.*	374	RC	F
1969 *Trucks and construction vehicles, +* as above.	227	DC	F
PACIFIC MILLS			
1949 Textiles: *cotton,* rayon, worsted; for apparel, furnishings, industry and other uses.	101–200	RC	PD
1959 Acquired by Burlington Industries.			

TABLE C-1 (continued)

	Rank	Strategy	Structure
PENNWALT Prior to 1969, Pennsalt; prior to 1957, Pennsylvania Salt Manufacturing.			
1949 *Heavy industrial chemicals;* agricultural chemicals; household chemical products: cleansers, water softeners; chemical builders' products: paint, rust inhibitor.	—	RC	F
1959 As above. Added: fertilizer.	428	RC	PD
1969 As above. Added: specialized equipment: tabletting, freeze-drying, plastic molding, separating; health products: ethical and proprietary drugs, dentists' equipment and supplies	248	RL	PD
PET Prior to 1966, Pet Milk.			
1949 *Dairy products:* evaporated milk, milkpowder, ice cream mix, cottage cheese.	101–200	S	FS
1959 *Dairy products,* + as above. Added: frozen foods.	270	DC	FS
1969 *Dairy products,* + as above. Added: diet foods, candy, snacks, fruit products; food stores; restaurants, service stations; store equipment; institutional food service.	181	RC	PD
PFIZER (CHAS. A.)			
1949 *Pharmaceutical chemicals,* industrial chemicals, food supplements.	201–500	RC	F
1959 As above. Added: ethical drugs: *antibiotics,* and others; plasticizers, lubricating additives; proprietary drugs; syringes.	189	RC	F
1969 *Antibiotics,* + as above. Added: plastics; adhesives [lime, limestone, calcium, magnesium, powder metals, paint pigments, refractories].	139	RC	PD
PHILCO			
1949 *Radios, TVs, phonographs:* cathode ray tubes, air conditioners and refrigerators, electric ranges; government electronics; TV broadcasting.	101–200	RL	PD
1959 *Radios, TVs, phonographs,* + as above. Added: washing machines; transistors; special purpose computers.	122	RL	PD
1961 Acquired by Ford Motor.			
PHILIP MORRIS			
1949 *Cigarettes and tobacco.*	101–200	S	F
1959 *Cigarettes and tobacco.* Added: [adhesives, glassine paper; textile processing chemicals: printing].	156	DU	FS
1969 *Cigarettes and tobacco,* + as above. Added: [beer; gum, razor blades, toiletries; hospital and surgical supplies; labels, parts for power tools].	145	DU	PD

TABLE C-1 (continued)

	Rank	Strategy	Structure
PHILLIPS PETROLEUM			
1949 *Integrated oil;* fertilizer, carbon black (both part of vertical chain).	22	*DV*	*FS*
1959 *Integrated oil,* + as above. Added: synthetic rubber, polyethylene [both part of chain]; plastic containers.	31	*DV*	*FS*
1969 *Integrated oil,* + as above. Added: packaging film and machinery; polyethylene coated paper; plastic pipe, paper containers; synthetic fibers [jute, twine, carpet yarn].	38	*DV*	*FS*
PILLSBURY Prior to 1958, Pillsbury Mills.			
1949 *Bulk flour and flour-based mixes,* consumer flour and mixes, animal feed, soy and feed by-products.	101–200	*DC*	*F*
1959 *Bulk flour and flour-based mixes,* + as above. Added: frosting mix.	126	*RC*	*PD*
1969 *Bulk flour and flour mixes,* + as above. Added: snack foods, artificial sweetener, canned food, household cleaner [poultry processing; restaurants; time-shared computer].	189	*RC*	*PD*
PITTSBURGH STEEL			
1949 *Steel mill products:* wire, tubing, semi-finished products.	101–200	*S*	*FS*
1959 *Steel mill products,* + as above.	282	*S*	*FS*
1968 Merged with Wheeling Steel to form Wheeling-Pittsburgh Steel.			
PPG INDUSTRIES Prior to 1968, Pittsburgh Plate Glass.			
1949 *Flat glass,* mirrors, optical glass; related chemicals; paint, varnish.	70	*RL*	*PD*
1959 *Flat glass,* + as above. Added: fiberglass yarn, insulation; resins; titanium dioxide.	72	*RL*	*PD*
1969 *Flat glass,* + as above. Added: polyvinyl chloride; fertilizers.	102	*RL*	*PD*
PROCTER AND GAMBLE			
1949 *Soaps, detergents;* oils and fats; chemical dissolving cottonseed pulp.	48	*DC*	*F*
1959 *Soaps, detergents,* + as above. Added: *cleansers,* peanut butter, toiletries, baking mixes, sanitary paper goods; chemical dissolving pulp, bleach, disinfectant.	25	*DC*	*PD*
1969 *Soaps, detergents, cleansers,* + as above. Exited: bleach, disinfectant. Added: coffee.	28	*RC*	*PD*

TABLE C-1 (continued)

	Rank	Strategy	Structure
PULLMAN			
1949 *Railroad and street cars, forgings and parts* [design and construction of petroleum and chemical plants; also separate sale of equipment: pipes, heat exchangers, pressure vessels; R & D: metallurgy, atomic energy].	81	*UP*	*H*
1959 *Railroad and street cars, forgings and parts.* Exited: separate sale of process plant equipment; metallurgical R & D. Added: *truck trailers* [furnaces, kilns; construction of paper mills; engineering of power plants, water systems, highway construction].	114	*UP*	*H*
1969 *Railroad and street cars, truck trailers,* + as above.	151	*UP*	*PD*
QUESTOR Prior to 1968, Dunhill International.			
1949 *Cigarettes, tobacco, pipes* [toiletries, cosmetics; leather gifts, luggage].	—	*DU*	*H*
1959 *Cigarettes, tobacco, pipes,* + as above. Added: [freight terminals].	—	*DU*	*H*
1969 Exited: cigarettes, tobacco, pipes; toiletries, cosmetics; leather goods; freight terminals. Added: *auto parts;* [children's furniture, bottles, clothes, books, toys; recreational equipment; building products: ventilators, shutters, metal grid ceiling system].	378	*AC*	*PD*
RALSTON PURINA			
1949 *Animal feeds; soy products,* animal health products; cereal, Ry-Krisp.	101–200	*DC*	*F*
1959 *Animal feeds; soy products,* + as above. Added: dog food.	81	*DC*	*F*
1969 *Animal feed, soy products,* + as above. Added: grocery products, tuna and fish meal [restaurant food supplying; restaurants].	78	*DC*	*PD*
RATH PACKING			
1949 Meat packing: *meat,* by-products.	101–200	*DV*	*F*
1959 Meat packing: *meat,* + as above. Added: chemical by-products.	176	*DV*	*F*
1969 Meat packing: *meat,* + as above.	349	*DV*	*F*
RAYBESTOS-MANHATTAN			
1949 *Asbestos and rubber auto parts;* asbestos and rubber industrial products; packings and gaskets; bowling balls; powdered metal parts; auto brake service equipment; abrasive and diamond wheels.	201–500	*RC*	*F*

TABLE C-1 (continued)

		Rank	Strategy	Structure

Raybestos-Manhattan (continued)

		Rank	Strategy	Structure
1959	*Asbestos and rubber auto parts,* + as above. Added: hydraulic brake parts and fluid; teflon and nylon industrial products, resin-asbestos molding material and aerospace components.	423	*RC*	*F*
1969	*Asbestos and rubber auto parts,* + as above. Added: rivets, riveting machines.	525	*RC*	*FS*

RAYONIER

1949	Integrated forest products: *cellulose,* pulp, paper.	201–500	*S*	*F*
1959	Integrated forest products: *cellulose,* + as above. Added: lumber [tannin].	313	*S*	*F*
1968	Acquired by International Telephone and Telegraph.			

REMINGTON RAND

| 1949 | *Typewriters,* adding and accounting machines, supplies and forms; electric shavers. | 101–200 | *RC* | *PD* |
| 1955 | Merged with Sperry to form Sperry Rand. | | | |

REPUBLIC AVIATION

1949	*Highspeed aircraft.*	201–500	*S*	*F*
1959	*Highspeed aircraft.* Added: R & D missiles.	228	*S*	*F*
1965	Acquired by Fairchild Hiller.			

REPUBLIC STEEL

1949	Integrated steel producer: *mill products,* fabricated products.	29	*DV*	*F*
1959	Integrated steel producer: *mill products,* + as above.	36	*DV*	*F*
1969	Integrated steel producer: *mill products,* + as above.	69	*DV*	*F*

REVLON　　Prior to 1955, Revlon Products.

1949	*Cosmetics and toiletries,* hair care preparations, perfumes, manicure equipment.	—	*DC*	*F*
1959	*Cosmetics and toiletries,* + as above. Added: proprietary drugs [shoe polish].	323	*DC*	*FS*
1969	*Cosmetics and toiletries,* + as above. Exited: shoe polish. Added: beauty parlor fixtures, ethical drugs.	296	*DC*	*PD*

REYNOLDS METALS

1949	Integrated aluminum: *mill products,* fabricated products, primary aluminum, pigments.	101–200	*DV*	*F*
1959	Integrated aluminum: *mill products,* + as above. Added: plastic wrap.	91	*DV*	*F*
1969	Integrated aluminum: *mill products,* + as above.	114	*DV*	*PD*

TABLE C-1 (continued)

	Rank	Strategy	Structure
RICHFIELD OIL			
1949 *Integrated oil.*	101–200	S	F
1959 *Integrated oil.* Added: petrochemicals.	178	DV	F
1966 Merged with Atlantic Refining to form Atlantic Richfield.			
ROCKWELL MANUFACTURING			
1949 *Gas, oil and water meters and regulators;* valves, pumps; hydraulic transmissions [parking and fare meters, power tools].	201–500	UP	H
1959 *Fluid meters, regulators,* + as above. Added: *pneumatic and electronic process control instruments* [gas and diesel engines; steel and iron foundry; automatic voting machines].	327	UP	PD
1969 *Power tools,* + as above. Exited: pneumatic and electronic process control instruments. Added: industrial machine tools [brass plumbing fittings].	344	UP	PD
ROCKWELL-STANDARD Prior to 1958, Rockwell Spring and Axle.			
1953 Formed by merger of Standard Steel Spring and Timken Detroit Axle.			
1959 Axles and transmissions for autos and other vehicles; vehicle springs, seats, brakes and other parts [lighting standards; filters; light aircraft].	163	RC	PD
1967 Merged with North American Aviation to form North American Rockwell.			
ROHM AND HASS			
1949 *Organic resins,* plastic powder and sheet; chemicals for leather and textile industries; agricultural chemicals.	201–500	RC	FS
1959 *Organic resins,* + as above. Added: detergent.	211	RC	PD
1969 *Organic resins,* + as above. Added: elastic fabric; silk and synthetic yarn; ethical drugs; animal health products; medical testing laboratory and instruments.	233	RC	PD
ROHR Prior to 1961, Rohr Aircraft.			
1949 Formed as spinoff of Newport Steel.			
1949 *Aircraft power packages,* air frame components.	—	DC	F
1959 *Aircraft power packages,* + as above.	237	DC	F
1969 *Aircraft power packages,* + as above. Added: rocket motor cases and nozzles, large antennas, power boats [computer software and systems].	348	DC	PD

TABLE C-1 (continued)

	Rank	Strategy	Structure
ROYAL MCBEE Prior to 1954, Royal Typewriter.			
1949 *Typewriters, supplies.*	201–500	S	F
1959 *Typewriters, supplies.* Added: keysort machines, business forms, office copying machines, general purpose computer.	376	DC	F
1965 Acquired by Litton Industries.			
RUBEROID			
1949 Asphalt and tar building and industrial materials: *roofing,* siding, felt, coatings; asbestos-cement building products: roofing, siding, building board; kraft building and packaging paper.	201–500	RC	F
1959 *Asphalt and tar roofing,* + as above. Added: gypsum building materials; roofing granules; asbestos auto parts; floor tiles.	317	RC	F
1967 Acquired by GAF.			
RYAN AERONAUTICAL			
1949 *Airplanes and airplane parts;* missiles.	—	S	F
1959 *Airplanes and airplane parts,* + as above. Added: aerospace and military electronic systems.	442	RC	F
1967 Acquired by Teledyne.			
SANDERS ASSOCIATES			
1951 Incorporated.			
1959 *Defense electronic systems,* R & D for defense electronic systems; electronic aerospace instruments, microwave equipment; servo-valves, gyroscopes, blowers; oceanographic equipment.	—	RC	FS
1969 *R & D for defense electronic systems,* + as above. Added: lasers, long-range communication systems, commercial computer systems, information handling and display systems.	440	RC	PD
SCHERING			
1949 Ethical drugs: *hormones,* antihistamines, sulfas, etc.; proprietary drugs; cosmetics; bulk pharmaceutical chemicals.	—	RC	F
1959 Ethical drugs: *hormones,* + as above. Added: animal health products.	463	RC	F
1969 Ethical drugs: *hormones,* + as above.	408	RC	PD
SCHLITZ (JOS. P.) BREWING			
1949 *Beer.*	101–200	S	F
1959 *Beer.*	274	S	F
1969 *Beer.*	243	S	F

TABLE C-1 (continued)

	Rank	Strategy	Structure
Scott Paper			
1949 Integrated paper company: *sanitary paper products,* wax paper, industrial paper wipers.	101–200	*DV*	*F*
1959 Integrated paper: *sanitary paper products,* + as above. Added: sulphite papers; urethane foam, plastic cups.	153	*DV*	*F*
1969 Integrated paper: *sanitary paper products,* + as above. Added: plastic wrap, plastic coating, printing paper; nonwoven textiles [projectors, copiers, film and microfilm, educational films and slides].	154	*DV*	*PD*
Servel			
1949 *Refrigerators,* central air conditioners, heaters, ice makers.	201–500	*DC*	*F*
1959 [Icemakers.] Exited: refrigerators, air conditioners, heaters. Added: *batteries.*	—	*S*	*F*
1967 Acquired by Clevite.			
Sperry			
1949 *Instruments and controls:* electronic instruments and controls, gyroscopes, navigational equipment, computing systems, precision instruments; motors and generators; photocells [farm and quarry equipment; hydraulic equipment: variable speed transmissions; packaging equipment, winches, aluminum roofing and siding].	101–200	*UP*	*PD*
1955 Merged with Remington Rand to form Sperry Rand.			
St. Regis Paper			
1949 Integrated paper company: *paper bags,* ground wood paper, kraft pulp, paper and paperboard, plastic/paper laminates; bag-making and filling machines.	99	*DV*	*F*
1959 Integrated paper company: + as above. Added: *paper containers,* waxed paper, printing paper, lumber, plywood (all part of integrated chain), polyethylene film and bags, injection molded plastics.	92	*DV*	*F*
1969 Integrated paper: *kraft pulp, paper and paperboard,* + as above. Added: stationery, school supplies [both part of chain]; [dairy products processing and handling equipment; special industrial equipment].	133	*DV*	*PD*
Staley (A. E.) Manufacturing			
1949 *Soy bean products:* oil, meal, sauce; corn products: starch, syrup, oil; refining crude soy and corn oil; chemical by-products.	101–200	*RC*	*F*

TABLE C-1 (continued)

	Rank	Strategy	Structure
Staley (A. E.) Manufacturing (continued)			
1959 As above. Added: industrial chemical products; polymers; marshmallows.	203	RC	PD
1969 *Soy: oil, meal, corn: starch, syrup, oil.* Added: *spices, flavorings,* household cleaner, grocery products; adhesives.	315	RL	PD
STANDARD BRANDS			
1949 *Coffee,* tea, grocery products; bakers' ingredients; liquor.	101–200	RC	F
1959 *Coffee,* + as above. Added: dog food; refined corn products.	102	RC	FS
1969 *Coffee,* + as above. Added: candy [industrial chemicals; latex, resin, adhesives].	120	RC	FS
STANDARD KOLLSMAN INDUSTRIES Prior to 1960, Standard Coil Products.			
1949 *TV and radio-tuners.*	—	S	F
1959 *Tuners.* Added: air navigation instruments, air guidance systems; precision motors.	489	RL	PD
1969 As above. Added: automobile cigarette lighters; electric blankets; semi-conductors, rectifiers; aerospace electronic systems; switches; fire extinguishers; rear view mirrors.	—	RL	PD
STANDARD OIL (OHIO)			
1949 *Integrated oil company.*	69	S	F
1959 *Integrated oil company.* Added: ammonia, urea, nitric acid; plastic intermediates.	118	S	F
1969 *Integrated oil company,* + as above. Added: molded plastics, plastic housewares; plastic powder, plastic pipe, building materials; coal; water heaters; motels, restaurants; vending machines [low density glass foam; mass food service].	97	DV	FS
STANLEY WORKS			
1949 Power tools, hand tools; full line of hardware; coatings and finishes; steel stripping.	201–500	RC	PD
1959 As above. Added: aluminum windows; automatic door opener; drapery hardware.	373	RC	PD
1969 Building materials: hardware, windows, door openers, + as above. Added: doors, curtain walls [electronic stampings].	354	RC	PD
STAUFFER CHEMICAL			
1949 Basic industrial chemicals; agricultural chemicals; battery cases.	201–500	RC	FS

TABLE C-1 (continued)

	Rank	Strategy	Structure
1959 As above. Exited: battery cases. Added: petrochemicals; ethical drugs; organo-metals; plastic foam; plastic pipes and tubes.	202	*RC*	*PD*
1969 As above. Added: refractory metal alloys, plasticizers; sanitary chemicals; coated fabrics; vinyl wall covering.	215	*RC*	*PD*

STERLING DRUG

1949 *Proprietary drugs;* ethical drugs; pharmaceutical chemicals; soaps and cleansers; shoe polish; ammonia, bleach; toiletries, dye, industrial chemicals.	201–500	*RC*	*PD*
1959 *Proprietary drugs,* + as above. Exited: ammonia, bleach. Added: animal health products; industrial waste treatment; insecticides [pet accessories].	217	*RC*	*PD*
1969 *Ethical drugs,* + as above. Exited: pet accessories. Added: cosmetics and perfumes; wax; starch.	200	*RC*	*PD*

STEVENS (J. P.)

1949 Textiles: *rayon and cotton "grey goods";* wide variety of woolen and worsted finished textile products.	96	*DC*	*F*
1959 *"Grey goods,"* + as above. Added: nonwoven fabrics, plastics.	94	*DC*	*F*
1969 As above. Exited: plastics. Added: hosiery, carpets.	115	*RC*	*F*

STEWART-WARNER

1949 Auto parts: fuel pumps, gears, instruments; auto servicing equipment; die castings; hardware [TV, radio receivers; phonographs; military electronic devices; heaters, furnaces].	201–500	*UP*	*PD*
1959 As above. Exited: TV, radio. Added: automobile lights [heat exchangers, air conditioners; industrial electronics: automatic controls for machines, facsimile transmission; meters; switches].	347	*UP*	*PD*
1969 As above. Added: lubricating equipment, vehicle servicing [data display systems; integrated circuits; pneumatic and hydraulic equipment for aircraft and missiles; fluid materials handling equipment].	441	*UP*	*PD*

STOKELY-VAN CAMP

1949 *Canned fruits, vegetables and cooked food,* frozen fruits and vegetables.	201–500	*DC*	*FS*
1959 *Canned food,* + as above. Added: frozen main dishes, grocery products.	275	*DC*	*FS*

TABLE C-1 (continued)

	Rank	Strategy	Structure
Stokely-Van Camp (continued)			
1969 *Canned food,* + as above. Added: oils, margarine; Gatorade.	307	*RC*	*FS*
STUDEBAKER-WORTHINGTON			
1967 Formed by merger of Studebaker and Worthington.			
1969 *Electrical industrial products and electronic components:* power plants, motors and generators, transformers, silicon rectifiers, electron tubes, read-out devices; turbines, pumps, compressors; air conditioners, heaters, refrigerators [springs, forgings; construction equipment: water meters; utility vehicles, automotive products: oil and gas treatments, brakes, brake-fluid, lamps, flashers; locomotives].	141	*RL*	*PD*
SUNDSTRAND Prior to 1959, Sundstrand Machine Tool.			
1949 *Machine tools,* aircraft hydraulic machinery, industrial hydraulic machinery, sanding and rubbing equipment, castings.	—	*RC*	*F*
1959 *Aircraft: hydraulic machinery,* + as above. Added: *aircraft hydraulic drives and motors;* power supplies for missiles.	457	*RL*	*PD*
1969 *Aircraft hydraulic machinery, drives and motors,* + as above. Added: aviation: electronic controls and instruments, music and announcement systems, mechanical actuators, light-weight castings; numerical and computer controls for machine tools; materials handling equipment.	310	*RL*	*PD*
SUNSHINE BISCUIT			
1949 *Bakery products,* cereal, dog food.	201–500	*DC*	*F*
1959 *Bakery products,* + as above. Added: snack foods.	242	*DC*	*F*
1965 Acquired by American Tobacco.			
SYBRON Prior to 1968, Ritter Pfaudler.			
1965 Formed by merger of Ritter and Pfaudler Permutit.			
1949 *Steel processing tanks.*	—	*S*	*F*
1959 *Steel processing tanks.* Added: water and waste treatment equipment; sanitation chemicals [brewers' equipment].	—	*DC*	*PD*
1969 Steel processing tanks, + as above. Added: *electronic and pneumatic process control instruments* [dental and hospital and laboratory equipment; textile chemicals; government R & D].	311	*UP*	*PD*

TABLE C-1 (continued)

	Rank	Strategy	Structure
SYLVANIA ELECTRIC PRODUCTS			
1949 *Radio and TV tubes, special military tubes,* radio sets, TV chassis; light bulbs and light fixtures; electronic components; radar components.	101–200	*RL*	*F*
1959 Acquired by General Telephone and Electronics.			
TEXACO Prior to 1959, Texas Co. (The).			
1949 *Integrated oil company;* petrochemicals.	6	*DV*	*F*
1959 *Integrated oil,* + as above. Added: synthetic rubber [uranium mining and processing].	8	*DV*	*FS*
1969 *Integrated oil,* + as above. Added: fertilizer.	8	*DV*	*FS*
TEXAS INSTRUMENTS Prior to 1951, Geophysical Service.			
1949 *Seismic exploration;* military electronics; military electromechanical equipment.	—	*DC*	*F*
1959 As above. Added: *electronic components:* semiconductors, transistors, etc.; gravity meters; optical components; special clad metals, motor controls; nuclear fuel.	234	*RL*	*PD*
1969 *Electronic components,* + as above.	135	*RL*	*PD*
TIMES MIRROR			
1949 *Newspaper publishing;* paper; job printing.	201–500	*DC*	*F*
1959 *Newspaper publishing,* + as above. Added: paper bags; TV station; TV programs.	394	*DL*	*PD*
1969 *Newspaper publishing,* + as above. Exited: TV station, programs. Added: lumber, plywood; book publishing, binding; chart and map printing: magazine publishing: globes and teaching aids [CATV].	256	*RL*	*PD*
TIME			
1949 *Magazine publishing,* news films.	101–200	*DC*	*FS*
1959 *Magazine publishing.* Exited: news films. Added: book publishing; printing supplies and equipment; pulp, paper; radio, TV broadcasting.	177	*DC*	*FS*
1969 *Magazine publishing.* Added: textbooks; educational materials and supplies; CATV [business information service].	180	*RL*	*PD*
TRANS UNION Prior to 1968, Union Tank Car.			
1949 *Building and leasing railroad tank cars.*	—	*S*	*F*
1959 *Building and leasing railroad tank cars.* Added: tanks for cars, storage tanks; castings and forgings; oil and water treatment equipment [atomic reactor].	342	*RL*	*PD*

TABLE C-1 (continued)

	Rank	Strategy	Structure
Trans Union (continued)			
1969 *Building and leasing railroad tank cars,* + as above. Added: [import-export; credit bureau; real estate development; fasteners].	459	*RL*	*PD*
TRW Prior to 1965, Thompson Ramo Wooldridge; prior to 1958, Thompson Products.			
1949 *Aircraft engine parts,* aircraft fluid and fuel control parts; auto engines and parts; electronic switches [pumps, valves, couplings].	201–500	*RC*	*PD*
1959 *Aircraft engine parts,* + as above. Added: radar; rocket nozzles; space systems, missile power; avionics; parts for entertainment electronics; TV cameras and related equipment; transformers, capacitors, semi-conductors; electronic systems R & D [industrial electronic control systems; process control and general computers; records, tapes; nuclear power unit; special chemicals].	109	*UP*	*PD*
1969 *Electronic components,* + as above. Added: RFP components, electronic educational systems; automated industrial plants; high-speed camera [coatings, plastic chemicals, small arms, ball and roller bearings; oil and gas exploration and service].	61	*UP*	*PD*
Uniroyal Prior to 1967, United States Rubber.			
1949 Rubber: *tires and tubes,* manufactured industrial and consumer, medical items, footwear, textile, latex, etc.; adhesives, coatings, seals; insulated wire and cable, bulk plastics, plastic film, tire yarn and textile, agricultural chemicals.	37	*DV*	*PD*
1959 Rubber: *tires and tubes,* + as above. Exited: wire, cable. Added: rubber flooring, orlon textiles, plastic pipe; synthetic rubber; plastic consumer products [fuel cells].	43	*DV*	*PD*
1969 Rubber: *tires and tubes,* + as above.	66	*DV*	*PD*
United Aircraft			
1949 *Airplane engines,* propellers, helicopters, military aircraft.	101–200	*DC*	*PD*
1959 *Airplane engines,* + as above. Exited: military aircraft. Added: aircraft fuel systems, controls, gyros and other parts; military electronics systems; commercial and industrial control systems; meteorological system; aerospace R & D.	35	*DC*	*PD*
1969 *Airplane engines,* + as above. Added: turbines and compressors for industry and ships; fuel cells, rocket engines, nuclear power plant, electron beam			

TABLE C-1 (continued)

	Rank	Strategy	Structure
welding, electronic components, telemetry devices, medical electronic equipment, turbo-trains, industrial valves [glass fiber/plastic material].	36	*DC*	*PD*

UNITED STATES STEEL

1949 Integrated steel: *sheet, strip,* other mill products, wire, pipe, tube, building materials, prefabricated buildings; coke oven chemicals; construction of buildings, bridges, ships, barges; railroad cars; oil well equipment, cement.	3	*DV*	*FS*
1959 Integrated steel: *pipes, tubes,* + as above. Exited: ships, barges, railroad cars.	5	*DV*	*FS*
1969 Integrated steel: *pipes, tubes,* + as above. Added: titanium, titanium semi-fabricated products; aluminum building products; engineering consulting service; industrial, agricultural chemicals; plasticizers; chemical coatings; plastic parts [lumber; real estate development].	12	*DV*	*FS*

USM   Prior to 1968, United Shoe Machinery.

1949 *Shoe machinery,* boxes, cartons; adhesives, resins; shoe hardware.	201–500	*S*	*FS*
1959 *Shoe machinery,* + as above. Added: special industrial equipment [military electronics; aerospace electronics; nuclear R & D; equipment for electronics industry; data processing machinery; power transmission for aircraft].	411	*RC*	*FS*
1969 *Shoe machinery,* + as above. Added: [fasteners; bolts, motors; molds for plastics industry, and plastic parts; precision parts; stampings; electronic components].	271	*UP*	*PD*

WARD FOODS   Prior to 1964, Ward Baking.

1949 *Bread and cake.*	201–500	*S*	*F*
1959 *Bread and cake.* Added: *frozen pies.*	381	*S*	*F*
1969 *Bakery products.* Added: meat packing; coffee, tea; grocery products; dairy products; candy; seafood; institutional foods; restaurants [food machinery].	252	*RL*	*PD*

WARNER AND SWASEY

1949 *Machine tools;* textile machinery; earthmoving equipment; foundry [astronomical instruments and observatories].	—	*DC*	*F*
1959 *Machine tools,* + as above.	—	*RL*	*F*

TABLE C-1 (continued)

	Rank	Strategy	Structure
Warner and Swasey (continued)			
1969 *Machine tools,* + as above. Exited: astronomical instruments and observatories. Added: numerical controls for machine tools, diagnostic computers; spectrometers, circuit boards.	482	*RL*	*PD*
WARNER-LAMBERT PHARMACEUTICAL Prior to 1955, Warner-Hudnut; prior to 1950, Warner (Wm. R.) and Co.			
1949 *Proprietary medicines:* cosmetics and toiletries.	—	*RC*	*PD*
1959 *Proprietary medicines,* + as above. Added: ethical drugs; toothbrushes [molded plastics, glass containers].	248	*RC*	*PD*
1969 As above. Exited: glass containers, toothbrushes. Added: eyeglasses and ophthalmic goods; optical instruments; medical instruments; medical electronics; gum, candies.	138	*RL*	*PD*
WESTINGHOUSE ELECTRIC			
1949 *Motors and controls,* turbines, condensers, generators; transformers; switchgear; appliances; radio and TV sets and stations; military electronics, missiles; elevators, escalators; air and marine engines [industrial education; housing construction].	17	*RL*	*PD*
1959 *Electric power machinery,* + as above. Added: avionics, radar, industrial electronics systems; integrated circuits.	15	*RL*	*PD*
1969 *Electrical power machinery,* + as above. Added: rocket engines; computer controlled industrial systems [learning systems].	17	*RL*	*PD*
WESTVACO Prior to 1969, West Virginia Pulp and Paper.			
1949 Integrated forest products: *paper,* paperboard, chemical by-products.	101–200	*DV*	*F*
1959 Forest products, + as above. Added: *paper containers.*	198	*DV*	*PD*
1969 Forest products, + as above. Added: [land development].	242	*DV*	*PD*
WEYERHAEUSER Prior to 1959, Weyerhaeuser Lumber.			
1949 Forest products: *lumber,* pulp, plywood, miscellaneous wood products.	101–200	*DV*	*F*
1959 Forest products: *lumber,* + as above. Added: paperboard, particle board; cartons; coated paper.	95	*DV*	*PD*
1969 Forest products: *lumber,* + as above. Added: wood building products, chemical by-products, fine paper [ski area; banking, home building].	89	*DV*	*PD*

TABLE C-1 (continued)

	Rank	Strategy	Structure
WHITE MOTOR			
1949 *Trucks and buses.*	201–500	*S*	*F*
1959 *Trucks.* Exited: buses. Added: diesel engines.	133	*DC*	*F*
1969 *Trucks,* + as above. Added: farm equipment, industrial tractors, rebuilt auto parts [design, building, installation of heating and cooling systems].	118	*RC*	*PD*
WHITTAKER Prior to 1964, Telecomputing.			
1949 *Digital electronics.*	—	*S*	*F*
1959 Digital electronics. Added: *valves, controls for aircraft and missiles;* gyros; warhead test equipment; high energy batteries; precision electronic components, electronic and electro-mechanical parts for aircraft and missiles; aircraft and missile subassemblies; radar and communications systems; air traffic control systems.	—	*RC*	*PD*
1969 As above. Added: *industrial and commercial metals:* ferro-alloys, other alloys, pipes, casing, tubing, valves, fittings, architectural products; aluminum siding and trim, pipes, fittings; pipelines, fasteners [railroad rolling stock, materials handling vehicles, fiberglass boats, sailboats; custom-made industrial polymers, also polymer coatings and pastes; resins; aerospace exotic materials].	148	*AC*	*PD*
WORTHINGTON Prior to 1952, Worthington Pump and Machinery.			
1949 Pumps; electric power generation and distribution equipment; compressors; engines, heat transfer equipment; heavy construction equipment; air conditioners, refrigerators; turbines; water and sewage treatment equipment.	201–500	*RL*	*F*
1959 As above. Added: home heaters and incinerators; electric control devices and relays; valves and controls for ships, missiles, industry; precision valves and actuators.	251	*RL*	*PD*
1967 Merged with Studebaker to form Studebaker-Worthington.			
WRIGLEY (WM. JR.)			
1949 *Chewing gum.*	201–500	*S*	*F*
1959 *Chewing gum.*	401	*S*	*F*
1969 *Chewing gum.*	480	*S*	*F*
XEROX Prior to 1961, Haloid Xerox; prior to 1958, Haloid.			
1949 *Photocopying machines;* microfilm projectors.	—	*S*	*F*
1959 As above. Added: *xerographic equipment and supplies.*	—	*DC*	*PD*

TABLE C-1 (continued)

	Rank	Strategy	Structure
Xerox (continued)			
1969 *Xerographic equipment and supplies,* + as above. Added: military and aerospace optical products [digital computers and software, educational materials; book publishing].	71	DL	PD
YALE AND TOWNE MANUFACTURING			
1949 *Materials handling equipment* [locks; builders hardware].	201–500	UP	PD
1959 *Materials handling equipment,* + as above.	289	UP	PD
1963 Merged with Eaton Manufacturing to form Eaton Yale and Towne.			

Bibliography

Ackerman, Robert W. "The Impact of Integration and Diversity on the Investment Process." Unpublished paper, Harvard Business School, 1969.

Alberts, William W., and Joel E. Segall (eds.). *The Corporate Merger*. Chicago: University of Chicago Press, 1966.

Andrews, Kenneth R. *The Concept of Corporate Strategy*. Homewood, Ill.: Dow Jones-Irwin, 1971.

Ansoff, H. Igor. *Corporate Strategy*. New York: McGraw-Hill Book Company, 1965.

Ansoff, H. Igor, *et al.* "Planning for Diversification Through Merger," in H. Igor Ansoff (ed.), *Business Strategy: Selected Readings*. Baltimore: Penguin Books, 1970.

Arditti, Fred D. "Risk and the Required Return on Equity," *Journal of Finance*, March 1967.

Bain, Joe S. *Industrial Organization*. 2d ed. New York: John Wiley & Sons, 1968.

Baumol, William J. *Business Behavior, Value and Growth*. New York: Harcourt, Brace & World, 1967.

Berg, Norman A. "Corporate Organization in Diversified Companies." Unpublished paper, Harvard Business School, 1970.

———— "What's Different About Conglomerate Management?" *Harvard Business Review*, November–December 1969.

———— "Strategic Planning in Conglomerate Companies," *Harvard Business Review*, May–June 1965.

Bower, Joseph L. *Managing the Resource Allocation Process: A Study of Corporate Planning and Investment*. Boston: Division of Research, Harvard Business School, 1970.

———— "Planning Within the Firm," *American Economic Review*, May 1970.

Burck, Gilbert. "The Perils of the Multi-Market Corporation," *Fortune*, February 1967.

Burns, Tom, and G. M. Stalker. *The Management of Innovation*. London: Social Science Paperbacks, 1961.

Carleton, Willard T., and Eugene M. Lerner. "Measuring Corporate Profit Opportunities," *Journal of Financial and Quantitative Analysis*, September 1967.

Chandler, Alfred D., Jr. *Strategy and Structure*. Garden City, N.Y.: Doubleday & Company 1966.

———— "The Structure of American Industry in the Twentieth Century, a Historical Overview," *Business History Review*, Autumn 1969.

Federal Trade Commission. *Industrial Concentration and Product Diversification in the 1,000 Largest Manufacturing Companies: 1950*. Washington: Government Printing Office, 1957.

Fisher, M. R. "Towards a Theory of Diversification" *Oxford Economic Papers,* October 1961, pp. 293–311.

Fouraker, Lawrence E., and J. M. Stopford. "Organizational Structure and the Multinational Strategy," *Administrative Science Quarterly,* June 1968.

Galbraith, John Kenneth. *The New Industrial State.* Boston: Houghton Mifflin Company, 1970.

Gort, Michael. *Diversification and Integration in American Industry.* Princeton, N.J.: Princeton University Press, 1962.

Hanna, Richard. "The Concept of Corporate Strategy in Multi-Industry Companies." Unpublished doctoral dissertation, Harvard Business School, 1968.

Kaplan, A. D. H. *Big Enterprise in a Competitive System.* Washington, D.C.: The Brookings Institution, 1954.

Kern, Kenneth R. (ed.). *Corporate Diagrams and Administrative Personnel of the Chemical Industry.* Princeton: Chemical Economic Services, 1964.

Laffer, Arthur B. "Vertical Integration by Corporations, 1929–1965," *Review of Economics and Statistics,* February 1969.

Lawrence, Paul R., and Jay W. Lorsch. *Organization and Environment: Managing Differentiation and Integration.* Boston: Division of Research, Harvard Business School, 1967.

Lynch, Harry H. *Financial Performance of Conglomerates.* Boston: Division of Research, Harvard Business School, 1971.

Marris, Robin. *The Economic Theory of "Managerial" Capitalism.* London: Macmillan & Co., 1964.

Marris, Robin, and Adrian Wood (eds.). *The Corporate Economy: Growth Competition, and Innovative Potential.* Cambridge: Harvard University Press, 1971.

McArthur, John H., and Bruce R. Scott. *Industrial Planning in France.* Boston: Division of Research, Harvard Business School, 1969.

Miller, Richard A. "Market Structure and Industrial Performance: Relation of Profit Rates to Concentration, Advertising Intensity, and Diversity," *Journal of Industrial Economics,* April 1969.

Miller, Stanley S. *The Management Problems of Diversification: A Pilot Study of the Corporation Diversifying from an Established Base.* New York: John Wiley & Sons, 1963.

Nelson, Richard R., Merton J. Peck, and Edward D. Kalachek. *Technology, Economic Growth and Public Policy.* Washington, D.C.: The Brookings Institution, 1967.

O'Hanlon, Thomas. "The Odd News About Conglomerates," *Fortune,* June 15, 1967.

Penrose, Edith. *The Theory of the Growth of the Firm.* Oxford: Basil Blackwell, 1959.

Reid, Samuel Richardson. *Mergers, Managers and the Economy.* New York: McGraw-Hill Book Company, 1968.

Salter, Malcolm S. "Stages of Corporate Development," *Journal of Business Policy,* 1970.

Scherer, F. M. *Industrial Market Structure and Economic Performance.* Chicago: Rand McNally, 1970.

Scott, Bruce R. "Stages of Corporate Development." Unpublished paper, Harvard Business School, 1970.

Servan-Schreiber, J.-J. *The American Challenge.* New York: Atheneum, 1968.

Sloan, Alfred P., Jr. *My Years With General Motors.* New York: Doubleday & Company, 1964.

Stieglitz, Harold, and C. Daniel Wilkerson. *Corporate Organization Structure.* New York: National Industrial Conference Board, Studies in Personnel Policy No. 210, 1968.

Stopford, John M. "Growth and Change in the Multinational Firm." Unpublished doctoral dissertation, Harvard Business School, 1968.

Thompson, James D. *Organizations in Action*. New York: McGraw-Hill Book Company, 1967.

U.S. Congress, Senate Committee on the Judiciary, Hearings before the Subcommittee on Antitrust and Monopoly:

Economic Concentration, Part 1, *Overall and Conglomerate Aspects,* Statement of Dr. Irwin Stelzer, pp. 181–202. 88th Cong., 2d sess. Washington: Government Printing Office, 1964.

———— Part 2, *Mergers and Other Factors Affecting Industry Concentration,* Statement of Dr. Michael Gort, pp. 683–686. 89th Cong., 1st sess., 1965.

———— Part 2, *Mergers and Other Factors Affecting Industry Concentration,* pp. 745–777. 89th Cong., 1st sess., 1965.

———— Part 3, *Concentration, Invention, and Innovation,* Statement of Dr. Jesse Markham, pp. 1269–1281. 89th Cong., 1st sess., 1965.

———— Part 8, *The Conglomerate Merger Problem,* Statement of Prof. Donald F. Eslick, pp. 4996–5026. 91st Cong., 2d sess., 1970.

Vernon, Raymond. "Organization as a Scale Factor in the Growth of Firms," in J. W. Markham and G. F. Papanek (eds.), *Industrial Organization & Economic Development: Essays in Honor of E. S. Mason.* Boston: Houghton Mifflin Company, 1970.

Weston, J. Fred, and Surenda K. Mansinghka. "Tests of the Efficiency Performance of Conglomerate Firms." *Journal of Finance,* September 1971.

White, K. K. *Understanding the Company Organization Chart.* New York: American Management Association, Research Study No. 56, 1963.

Williamson, Oliver E. *Corporate Control and Business Behavior: An Inquiry into the Effects of Organizational Form on Enterprise Behavior.* Englewood Cliffs, N.J.: Prentice Hall, 1970.

Woodward, Joan (ed.). *Industrial Organization: Behavior and Control.* Oxford: Oxford University Press, 1970.

Wrigley, Leonard. "Divisional Autonomy and Diversification." Unpublished doctoral dissertation, Harvard Business School, 1970.

Index